MAKING CONNECTIONS

HIGH INTERMEDIATE

A Strategic Approach to Academic Reading

Kenneth J. Pakenham

Second Edition

CAMBRIDGE
UNIVERSITY PRESS

CAMBRIDGE UNIVERSITY PRESS
Cambridge, New York, Melbourne, Madrid, Cape Town, Singapore, São Paulo, Delhi

Cambridge University Press
32 Avenue of the Americas, New York, NY 10013-2473, USA

www.cambridge.org
Information on this title: www.cambridge.org/9780521542845

First published 1998
12th printing 2008

Printed in Hong Kong, China, by Golden Cup Printing Company Limited

A catalog record for this publication is available from the British Library

ISBN 978-0-521-54284-5 student's book

Art direction and book design: Adventure House, NYC
Layout services: Page Designs International

To my mother Kathleen,
and the memory of my father John

TABLE OF CONTENTS

INTRODUCTION
TO THE INSTRUCTOR

LEVEL

Making Connections High Intermediate is an academic reading skills book. It carefully prepares students to read college-level texts. Students who successfully complete this book should typically be ready to study in an English-speaking university.

APPROACH

Making Connections High Intermediate incorporates the following insights from second language reading theory and practice:

- Reading is an interactive process, in which readers use their knowledge of language, rhetorical organization, and the world to understand a text.
- Reading is goal-oriented and strategic; good academic readers are metacognitively aware readers.
- While reading, good readers engage in a search for coherence – i.e., they look for the propositional and rhetorical connectedness of shorter and longer stretches of text.
- Readers are ultimately judged by the product of their reading – i.e., the accuracy of the picture they are able to produce of a text.

CONTENT AND ORGANIZATION

Each of the four units of *Making Connections High Intermediate* focuses on one general topic, with each of the five readings in a unit dealing with a specific aspect of the topic. This gives students the opportunity to develop background knowledge that will facilitate their reading of later articles in the unit, especially the longer, final article.

Each of the four units of the book is organized into a number of sections:

- Three Skills and Strategies sections, interwoven with the readings, introduce and practice specific skills and strategies for reading. For easier orientation and reference, all Skills and Strategies pages are lightly colored.
- Four shorter readings (average length: 8 paragraphs) are accompanied by associated activities in pre-reading, reading, vocabulary-building and review, research, discussion, and writing.

- One main reading (average length: 30 paragraphs) is accompanied by associated activities in pre-reading, reading, research, discussion, and writing. These longer articles offer students a reading experience closer to the challenges of the reading assignments they will meet in their future academic studies.
- A final section provides coherence-building tasks and a review of the vocabulary, skills, and strategies introduced in the unit.

The structural, lexical, and organizational forms targeted in a given section recur in subsequent readings and activities throughout the remainder of the book. Similarly, after certain text-processing strategies are introduced and practiced in a Skills and Strategies section, students are cued to use these strategies while reading the articles in the rest of the book.

READING ACTIVITIES

The articles in **Making Connections High Intermediate** are accompanied by the following activities:

Getting into the Topic

This pre-reading activity gives students the opportunity to activate their knowledge of the general topic of the article.

Getting a First Idea about the Article

This previewing activity enables students to develop expectations about the content and organization of the article before they begin to read it.

While You Read

This activity consists of a set of tasks that students complete while reading the article. Each task sets a short-term goal and activates an appropriate text-processing strategy introduced in an earlier Skills and Strategies section. The tasks are cued by boldface text and appear in colored boxes in the margin of the page. Students signal their completion of a task by highlighting or underlining text or by writing margin notes.

Main Idea Check

An activity that requires students to read for the main idea of the article in Readings 1–3 of Unit 1, and of each paragraph in all readings thereafter. It is recommended that reading for main ideas be the goal of the first read-through of each article. It is also recommended that students pause after each paragraph and choose its main idea before reading the next paragraph.

A Closer Look

This activity requires students to look for specific information in each article. Typically, students respond to True/False and multiple-choice questions. Other tasks include identifying the elements in cause and effect connections, linking specific solutions to problems, and locating technical terms and definitions.

Vocabulary Study and Review

This set of activities begins with *Vocabulary Study: Synonyms*, which uses contexts provided by the accompanying article to focus student attention on fifteen of the 24–26 vocabulary items selected as target vocabulary for the article. *Vocabulary Study: Words in Context* gives students practice in using the remaining target vocabulary while *Vocabulary Review: Same or Different* offers opportunities to review the vocabulary of the two preceding readings. *Vocabulary Study and Review* activities do not accompany the main readings.

Beyond the Reading

These activities give students an opportunity to do some research on the topic, to engage in discussion, and to complete a short writing assignment.

VOCABULARY

The target vocabulary items introduced in the sixteen shorter articles of **Making Connections High Intermediate** have been selected for their usefulness in general academic English. After its introduction, each vocabulary item is reused as often as possible in readings and activities within the same unit and in subsequent units. These words and phrases are listed alphabetically and by article in Appendix 3 (pages 245–269). Each entry contains a simple definition and an example, making this section of the book a useful resource for students expanding their academic vocabulary.

Also at the back of the book in Appendix 1 is a skills and strategies section, "Dealing with Unknown Vocabulary" (pages 239–242). This section provides strategies for, and practice in, dealing with unknown vocabulary while reading. The skill practice exercises (see pages 240–242) contain vocabulary from Unit 1, Readings 1–4 and are intended to be completed in class before students begin these readings.

Following the section on dealing with unknown vocabulary is Appendix 2, "Strategies for Vocabulary Learning" (pages 243–244). This section gives students useful advice on how best to study new vocabulary and gives them strategies to help them retain it.

FIELD TESTING

Like the first edition, this edition has been extensively field tested with students in the English Language Institute at The University of Akron.

COURSE LENGTH

Making Connections High Intermediate has enough material for a reading course of 50–70 class hours, assuming a corresponding number of hours available for homework assignments. Completing all the *Beyond the Reading* tasks that accompany each reading might make the course longer.

GUIDELINES FOR USING *MAKING CONNECTIONS HIGH INTERMEDIATE*

Through its sequencing of materials, ***Making Connections High Intermediate*** helps students gradually integrate knowledge, skills, and strategies into an effective approach to academic reading.

- To enable students to derive the greatest benefit from the sequenced materials, we recommend that you use each unit and each section within that unit in the order of their appearance in the book.
- Before beginning the shorter readings in Unit 1, we recommend that students work through "Dealing with Unknown Vocabulary" and complete the appropriate accompanying *Skill Practice* exercises.
- Most of the activities are suitable for both in-class work and homework assignments. However, it is best if they are introduced, modeled and practiced in class – in some cases repeatedly – before they are assigned for completion as homework.
- As you approach a reading, imagine yourself as a reader grappling with the text for the first time. The insights gained from such self-observation can be used in class to supplement the *While You Read* activities.
- Many more suggestions for the use of specific materials are included in the *Teacher's Manual,* which also includes a complete set of answers.

Finally, an invitation: I know that you will use this book in new and original ways that I have not imagined. When you do, and if you have the time for professional exchange, I would greatly enjoy hearing from you.

TO THE STUDENT

WHAT YOU WILL LEARN IN *MAKING CONNECTIONS HIGH INTERMEDIATE*

Welcome to ***Making Connections High Intermediate***. We have developed this book to help you do the following: build your academic vocabulary, understand how academic texts are written, and develop effective reading strategies.

1. Build your academic vocabulary

Like most students of English, you probably believe that a better knowledge of vocabulary will make you a better reader. You are right. In this book, you have the opportunity to expand your vocabulary by more than four hundred non-technical words that are common in academic English. To help you remember and learn these words after they have been introduced, they appear frequently in later readings and activities.

2. Understand how academic texts are written

A larger vocabulary, however, is not enough to make you the best reader you can be. You will also improve as a reader by developing your knowledge of English academic writing, especially the way texts are organized and the way sentences are structured. In the Skills and Strategies sections in this book, you will have many opportunities to learn about the sentence structure and organization of academic English.

3. Develop effective reading strategies

In addition, research has shown that while they read, good readers consciously use a number of effective reading strategies. These are techniques that they use to improve their understanding of what they are reading.

In the Skills and Strategies sections, you will be introduced to many helpful reading strategies. You will also have a large number of opportunities to consciously apply these new strategies in practice exercises and while you are reading the articles in the book.

HOW *MAKING CONNECTIONS HIGH INTERMEDIATE* IS ORGANIZED

Making Connections High Intermediate contains four units. Each unit deals with one general topic of interest and has the same internal organization.

- Three Skills and Strategies sections
- Two sections each with two shorter articles and related activities in reading, vocabulary study, research, discussion, and writing
- One section with a longer article and related activities in reading, research, discussion, and writing
- A final Making Connections section that helps you review what you have learned in the unit

At the end of the book, you will find a number of useful sections. The first one, Appendix 1, shows you how to deal with unknown vocabulary in a reading without stopping to use a dictionary. Appendix 2 gives you some strategies to help you study and learn vocabulary. Appendix 3 is similar to a dictionary. It explains and gives examples of the 24–26 academic vocabulary items that you will study from each reading. Finally, Appendix 4 is an index that allows you to find the entry for any of the more than 400 words in Appendix 3.

HOW TO GET THE MOST OUT OF *MAKING CONNECTIONS HIGH INTERMEDIATE*

What can you do to get the greatest benefit from using **Making Connections High Intermediate**? Here are a few suggestions.

- Whenever you read, consciously use the reading strategies introduced in the Skills and Strategies sections of the book.
- Use the strategies for vocabulary learning on pages 243–244.
- Successful academic reading is hard work! Study hard and expect to be tired after class work or homework.
- Outside of class, read as much English as you can. Balance the hard work of academic reading with other reading just for your own personal interest and enjoyment.

ACKNOWLEDGEMENTS

Completion of **Making Connections High Intermediate** would not have been possible without the help and support of a large number of people.

At Cambridge University Press, thanks are especially due to Bernard Seal, commissioning editor, for his commitment to this project and for the care with which he approached the task of working with me to prepare it for the press. The results of his dedication and of his discerning eye are visible on every page. Also at Cambridge, I want to thank project editors Anne Garrett and Helen Lee, the former for getting the production process off the ground and the latter for bringing it to completion. For their invaluable work in improving the manuscript's consistency and clarity, I also want to thank copyeditor, Susan Joseph; freelance development editor, Margo Gramer; and freelance lexicographer, Carol-June Cassidy.

Thanks are also due to Don Williams, the compositor, for his fast and meticulous work in producing the typeset copies of the manuscript and to the designers at Adventure House.

I would also like to acknowledge the careful and helpful comments provided by the following reviewers:

Kathryn Brady, University of Missouri-Columbia
Maria Dantas-Whitney, English Language Institute at Oregon State University
Linda Huff-Brinkman, International Center at University of Michigan
Irene Menegas, Diablo Valley College, California
Dantao Su, University of Hawaii at Manoa
Margo Trevino, Intensive English Institute at Houston Baptist University
Lorry Wilhelm, Mount Royal College, Calgary, Canada
Lois I. Wilson, English Language Institute at University of Pittsburgh

At the English Language Institute, University of Akron, I enjoyed, as always, the support of my long-time colleagues and friends Martha McNamara and Debra Deane. Thanks are also due to the students, unfortunately too many to name here, whose work with the emerging text both gave me much food for thought and helped determine the final version.

And finally I owe more thanks than I can possibly express to Pamela, Bethany, Michael, and Kate, my wife and children, whose forbearance has been severely tested, but never found wanting, during this lengthy project. Ultimately, it is they who sustain and inspire me.

CREDITS

TEXT CREDITS

All the readings in *Making Connections High Intermediate* have been written by the author; however, in two readings in Unit 4, the author has made extensive use of two sources, which he here acknowledges. (For a complete list of works consulted by the author in writing this second edition, please turn to the References section on page 273.)

UNIT 4, Reading 1

Totlyakov, V.M. 1991. The Aral Sea basin: a critical environmental zone. *Environment*, 33.1, pp. 4–38. Reprinted with permission of the Helen Dwight Reid Educational Foundation. Published by Heldref Publications, 1319 Eighteenth St., N.W., Washington, D.C. 20036-1802. Copyright ©1991.

UNIT 4, Reading 3

Ponting, C. 1990. Historical perspectives on sustainable development. *Environment*, 32.9, pp. 4–33. Reprinted with permission of the Helen Dwight Reid Educational Foundation. Published by Heldref Publications, 1319 Eighteenth St., N.W., Washington, D.C. 20036-1802. Copyright ©1990.

PICTURE CREDITS

All efforts have been made to trace rights holders and correctly attribute third-party material appearing in this book. We welcome information from anyone who feels that a piece has not been properly attributed so that we can put this right in any future printings.

page 1: ©Getty Images; page 23: ©Whiskey Tango/Corbis; page 46: ©Pinwell, George John; Death's Dispensary/Phildelphia Museum of Art, The William H. Helfand Collection, 1985; page 57: ©Bettmann/Corbis; page 65: ©Edwin Levick/The Library of Congress; page 95: ©Bettmann/Corbis; page 99: ©The Warshaw Collection of Business Americana, Archives Center, National Museum of History, Smithsonian Institution; page 111: ©Corbis; page 116: ©Dallas and John Heaton/SC Photo/Alamy; page 123: ©Timothy Shonnard/Getty Images; page 131: ©Adventure House; page 141: ©Adventure House; page 155: ©Glenn Bernhardt; page 156: ©Ken Packenham; page 171: ©Ben Osborne/Getty Images; page 186: ©AP/Wide World Photo; page 198: ©Jan Butchofsky-Houser/Corbis; page 206: ©Collar Herve/Corbis Sygma; page 218: ©Adventure House; page 222: ©AP/Wide World Photo; page 224: ©Scott Willis, The San Jose Mercury News, 1989

World Health in the Twenty-first Century

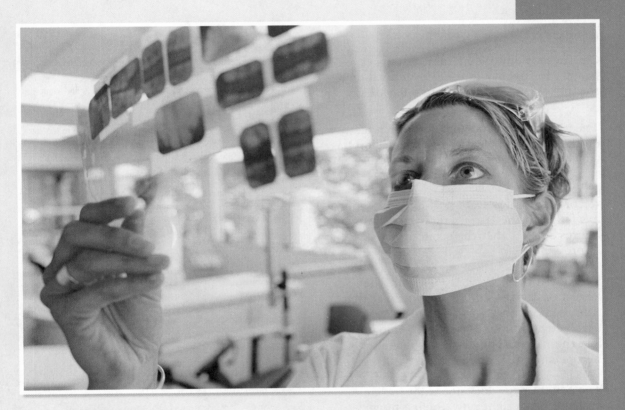

SKILLS AND STRATEGIES 1-3

- Continuing Ideas
- Cause and Effect
- Passive Sentences

READINGS

- Heart Disease and Changing Attitudes
- Cardiovascular Disease: A Good News – Bad News Story
- Medicine and Genetic Research: Promise and Problems
- AIDS – Not Someone Else's Problem
- Better Health for Everyone: Health Care in Two Worlds

SKILLS AND STRATEGIES 1
CONTINUING IDEAS

Continuing ideas are ideas that a writer has introduced in an earlier sentence and then repeats in a later sentence. Paying attention to continuing ideas will help you understand the connections between sentences and improve your academic reading.

EXAMPLES & EXPLANATIONS

Examples

On Tuesday and Wednesday, it snowed heavily for twenty-four hours. **This** forced the university to close for two days.

The company has decided to build a factory on the west side of town. **This decision** has angered a lot of people who live there.

According to new statistics, unemployment has fallen in the last six months. **These figures** suggest that the economy is improving.

On April 14–15, 1912, the *Titanic*, the largest passenger ship in the world at that time, sank in the North Atlantic. More than fifteen hundred passengers and crew lost their lives. **The disaster** shocked Europe and the United States.

The government does not want to increase taxes right now. **Such a move** would be dangerous with an election in only six months.

Explanations

Writers often use the word *this* to repeat an idea from the sentence before.

This = the heavy snow that fell for twenty-four hours on Tuesday and Wednesday.

Here the writer uses *this* + noun. *Decision* is a noun from the same word family as the main verb (*decide*) in the earlier sentence.

This decision = the company's decision to build a factory on the west side of town.

Here the writer uses *these* + noun. The noun *figures* is a synonym for the noun *statistics* in the earlier sentence.

These figures = the statistics about unemployment in the last six months.

The + noun does not always show a repeated idea, but here it does. In this sentence, the noun *disaster* is a general word that describes something in the two earlier sentences. If you know the meaning of *disaster*, the connection between the sentences is clear.

The disaster = the sinking of the *Titanic* and the deaths of more than fifteen hundred people.

Such + noun shows a repeated idea (*Such* = *like this* or *like these*).

Such a move = increasing taxes right now.

THE LANGUAGE OF CONTINUING IDEAS

Very often, certain words show that you are reading about ideas the writer has already introduced: *the, this, these, such.* These words are Continuing Idea Markers. In addition, writers often follow these markers with a noun, either a synonym for the idea in the earlier sentence or a general word. Here is a list of general words that may follow Continuing Idea Markers.

GENERAL WORDS FOR CONTINUING IDEAS			
FOR THINGS THAT HAPPEN	FOR THINGS THAT PEOPLE DO	FOR THINGS THAT PEOPLE SAY OR WRITE	FOR THINGS THAT PEOPLE THINK
circumstances	achievement	claim	attitude
crisis	action	complaint	belief
development	behavior	criticism	idea
disaster	conduct	objection	opinion
event	habit	offer	reaction
incident	move	request	view
occurrence	practice	statement	
problem	response	warning	
situation	task		
	tendency		

STRATEGIES

These strategies will help you identify and understand continuing ideas while you read.

- Look for Continuing Idea Markers: *this, this* or *these* + noun, *such* + noun, *the* + noun.
- Ask yourself what the Continuing Idea Marker refers to. If you are not sure, search for its meaning in the sentences before the marker.
- Use your knowledge of vocabulary: general words, synonyms, and word families.

SKILL PRACTICE 1

From the list below, find the noun that best continues an idea from the first sentence of each item. The first one has been done for you as an example.

| change | progress | discovery | risk | link |
| lack | increase | requirement | prediction | assistance |

1 The condition of the patient has improved in the last twenty-four hours. This ___progress___ . . .

2 The public's opinion of the president is more negative than it was six months ago. This ___change___ . . .

3 In 1960, researchers found the remains of tenth-century Norwegian houses in Canada. This ___discovery___ . . .

4 Some medical experts believe that there may be a connection between heart disease and bacteria. This ___link___ . . .

5 The chance of catching malaria is especially high in some tropical countries. This ___risk___ . . .

6 To graduate from that university, you need to take at least three computer classes. This ___requirement___ . . .

7 In the 1970s, researchers said that people today would work only four days a week. This ___prediction___ . . .

8 In many poorer countries, there are not enough doctors or other health workers. This ___lack___ . . .

9 Wealthier nations need to help poorer countries develop their health care systems. This ___assistance___ . . .

10 The cost of health care rose by 14 percent last year. This ___increase___ . . .

SKILL PRACTICE 2

For each pair of sentences, circle the Continuing Idea Marker in the second sentence. Then answer the question that follows. The first one has been done for you as an example.

1 The traffic was very slow on the Interstate this morning. (This) made me thirty minutes late for my class.

Question: What caused the speaker to be late for class?

Answer: There was slow traffic on the Interstate this morning.

2 In high school, students who have no interest in the subject often disturb the class. This makes it harder for students who really want to learn.

Question: What may stop good high school students from learning?

→ Make passive → The class is often disturbed by those students who really —

3 A lot of people realize that exercise is important for health. This realization is one reason for the increasing numbers of North Americans who are members of health clubs.
Question: What realization is causing more Americans to join health clubs?

4 The ancient Greeks and Egyptians knew a great deal about the movements of the Earth and the positions of the stars. Some people believe that this knowledge helped sailors from ancient Greece or Egypt to reach America over three thousand years ago.
Question: According to some people, what made it possible for the ancient Greeks or Egyptians to sail to America?

5 The workers are asking for a 20 percent wage increase, longer vacations, and better medical insurance. These demands may be too expensive for the company to agree to.
Question: What demands will the company probably not accept?

6 Tom's father did not get angry with him when Tom had an accident and wrecked the family car. This surprised Tom.
Question: What surprised Tom?

7 In the southern United States, black children were not allowed to go to the same schools as white children, so they were sent to all-black schools. This practice continued until the 1960s.
Question: What practice continued until the 1960s?

8 A number of developing countries have tried to introduce birth-control programs. These attempts have often failed because the family planning experts did not know enough about the lives and traditions of the people.
Question: What attempts have frequently failed?

9 To improve health care, the government would need to raise taxes by more than 10 percent. Such an increase now, six months before the next election, would be unpopular with most politicians.
Question: What would most politicians not want to do at this time?

10 The year 1968 was very bad for the United States. Both Martin Luther King, Jr., leader of the civil rights movement, and Robert Kennedy, who wanted to run for president, were murdered. These events shocked the country.
Question: What events shocked the United States in 1968?

SKILL PRACTICE 3

From the list below, find the noun that best continues an idea from the first sentence of each item. The boldface words will help you.

tendency	move	failures	attempts	views
incident	attitude	statements	circumstances	achievement

1 The first three tests of the new plane have been **unsuccessful.** These _____ failures _____ will slow development of the aircraft.

2 The government **believes** that the education system is weak but that testing students every year will improve it. These _____ views _____ are not shared by many teachers and parents.

3 Parents **tend to avoid talking** about AIDS with their children. This _____ tendency _____ is a problem all over the world for programs meant to fight AIDS.

4 For many years, different teams **tried to climb** to the top of Mount Everest. None of these _____ attempts _____ was successful until Edmund Hillary and Tenzing Norgay reached the summit in 1953.

5 Some people want **the government to limit cigarette advertising.** Others think that such a/an _____ move _____ would be difficult because many politicians receive support from the tobacco industry.

6 John has just lost his job, but he **is eager** to try something new. With this _____ attitude _____, I'm sure he'll be successful.

7 Medical technology **can keep a patient alive** even when his or her brain has stopped working. In such _____ circumstances _____, many people believe, the life support equipment should be switched off and the patient allowed to die.

8 Last night **a fight broke out downtown** outside City Hall. One person was seriously injured. If you know anything about the _____ incident _____, please contact the police.

9 In 1954, a British doctor and athlete **was the first to run a mile in under four minutes.** It's easy to forget this _____ achievement _____ today, when many runners have broken this record.

10 The striking workers **have said** that the company has no interest in improving job safety. The employers **have complained** that the workers want to destroy the company. These _____ statements _____ have not helped the two sides reach an agreement.

READING 1
HEART DISEASE AND CHANGING ATTITUDES

GETTING INTO THE TOPIC

Before you read an article, think of what you already know about the subject. Discuss the following questions with a partner.

1 What do we know today about the causes of heart disease that people fifty years ago did not know?
2 What ways do we have to prevent heart disease and to treat it?

GETTING A FIRST IDEA ABOUT THE ARTICLE

You will understand an article more easily if you can get an idea of its organization and content before you start reading. A quick way to do this is to read the first sentence of each paragraph. First sentences can help you because they often introduce the ideas that the writer will develop and explain in that paragraph.

For each paragraph, read the first sentence and think of a question that you expect this paragraph to answer. Then choose the question below that is most like your question. The first paragraph has been done for you as an example.

_____ A How has the change in attitude affected people's behavior?

_____ B How are attitude and behavior changes affecting people's health?

_____ C How are people's attitudes changing?

__1__ D What are the effects of these discoveries about heart disease?

WHILE YOU READ

As you read the article, stop at the end of each sentence that contains boldface text and follow the instructions in the box in the margin.

Heart Disease and Changing Attitudes

In the last decades of the twentieth century, medical researchers 1 showed that heart disease is associated with certain factors in our daily lives: stress, smoking, poor nutrition, and lack of exercise. Doctors and other health experts began to emphasize the fact that we can reduce the risk of heart disease by paying attention to **these factors**. As a result, many people realize that there is a connection between heart disease and lifestyle.

This new awareness is changing public attitudes about health. In 2 the past, people tended to think that it was sufficient to have access to doctors on whose expertise they could rely. Now people understand that merely receiving the best treatment for illness or injury is not enough. They have learned to take more responsibility for maintaining and improving their own health.

The shift in attitude can be seen in some behavioral changes that 3 have occurred since the 1970s. In the United States today, many smokers have broken the habit and fewer people take it up. The percentage of smokers is far below the level of the 1960s and 1970s. People are becoming more serious about reducing stress. Many have changed their diets and are eating food with less fat and cholesterol. More people are aware of the benefits of regular and frequent exercise like walking, running, and swimming; some even walk or bicycle to work instead of driving or using public transportation.

The health effects of these changes in attitude and behavior are 4 clear. Since the 1950s, the number of deaths from heart disease per 100,000 has fallen. (See Figure 1.1.) A partial explanation for this is that better diagnosis and treatment is helping people avoid or survive heart attacks. However, health experts have no doubt that much of **the improvement** has occurred because a better-educated public has become aware of the benefits of prevention.

FIGURE 1.1 U.S. Deaths from Heart Disease 1950–2000

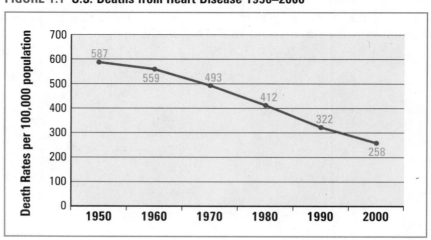

Side notes:

This is a continuing idea. Check back and highlight the words that show its meaning.

This also is a continuing idea. Check back for the meaning of *The shift in attitude*. Highlight it.

Check back for the meaning of the phrase *the improvement*. Highlight it.

MAIN IDEA CHECK

Identify the sentence that best expresses the main idea of the article.

a Better methods of diagnosis and treatment have reduced the number of deaths from heart disease in the United States.

b Medical research has shown that people should reduce the amount of fat they eat.

✓c As a result of information about the causes of heart disease, people are changing the way they think about health care and are leading healthier lives.

d The percentage of Americans who smoke today is much lower than it was in the 1970s.

A CLOSER LOOK

Look back at the article to answer the following questions.

1 What factor does the writer *not* associate with heart disease?

a Unhealthy food

b Cigarettes

✓c Poverty

d Lack of regular exercise

2 The article suggests that doctors in the past did not always inform their patients about the importance of exercise and good nutrition for health.
✓True or False?

3 According to the article, what happens to your risk of getting heart disease if you don't smoke, if you exercise regularly, and if you reduce the fat in your food?

a The risk increases.

✓b The risk decreases.

c The risk remains the same.

d The article does not discuss this question.

4 What change in attitude does the writer describe?

a More and more people are realizing that medical science can cure heart disease.

✓b Many people are realizing that they should take better care of their health.

c More and more people are realizing that they need a good doctor.

d A decreasing number of people are dying from heart disease.

5 It is still too early to see results from the change in attitude that the article describes. True or False?

VOCABULARY STUDY: SYNONYMS

Find words in the article that are similar in meaning to the following.

1 a period of ten years *(n)* Par. 1
2 to be connected with something or someone *(v)* Par. 1
3 pressure *(n)* Par. 1
4 the food the body needs *(n)* Par. 1
5 to give special importance to something *(v)* Par. 1
6 realization *(n)* Par. 2
7 enough *(adj)* Par. 2
8 to depend on someone or something *(v)* Par. 2
9 only *(adv)* Par. 2
10 to keep something in good condition *(v)* Par. 2
11 the food a person eats *(n)* Par. 3
12 happening often *(adj)* Par. 3
13 the way people think and feel about something *(n)* Par. 4
14 a feeling of not being sure *(n)* Par. 4
15 helpful effect *(n)* Par. 4

VOCABULARY STUDY: WORDS IN CONTEXT

Complete the sentences with words from the list below. If necessary, review the words in the Key Vocabulary from the Readings on page 245.

tend	regular	sufficient	factors	diagnose
expertise	access to	treatments	prevent	survive

1 A vitamin deficiency occurs when a person's diet does not have _____ vitamins to maintain good health.

2 We need to _____ heart disease as early as possible if we want to increase our chances of treating it successfully.

3 Because early diagnosis is important, you should have _____ examinations by your doctor.

4 Some people _____ not to think about their health until they become ill. Clearly they still don't understand the importance of prevention.

5 Stress and smoking are _____ that increase the risk of heart disease. Two others are diabetes and high blood pressure.

6 Medical scientists are researching new ways to fight cancer. Some of these _____ have been successful in studies on human patients.

7 Because of modern medicine, many people _____ diseases and injuries that would have killed them several decades ago.

8 It is possible to get excellent medical care in the United States. However, many other people don't have _____ such care because they have no health insurance.

9 It takes many years of study, training, and hard work to develop the _____ that is needed to become a world-class heart surgeon.

10 Health education teaches people to help _____ disease, for example, by following a healthy diet and exercising regularly.

BEYOND THE READING

Research
Do Internet or library research to find additional, up-to-date information on heart disease.

Discussion
Discuss the following question with a partner.
- What connection might there be between heart disease and poverty?

Writing
Write a short report on the results of your research or your discussion.

READING 2

CARDIOVASCULAR DISEASE: A GOOD NEWS — BAD NEWS STORY

GETTING INTO THE TOPIC

Thinking about the title of an article can help you get an idea of the content. Read the title of this article and discuss the following questions with a partner.

1 What do you think the good news about cardiovascular disease might be?
2 What do you think the bad news about cardiovascular disease might be?

GETTING A FIRST IDEA ABOUT THE ARTICLE

Sometimes you will want to get specific information from an article without reading the complete article. Scanning is a skill that will help you get an idea of the content and organization of an article or part of an article before you read it. Successful scanning has the following steps.

- Decide what information you want to find.
- Think of key words (and synonyms) that might help you find that information.
- Quickly look through the text for your key words.
- When you find a key word, stop scanning and start reading carefully to find the information you want.

Scan only the first sentence of each paragraph to find which paragraphs contain the good news and which contain the bad news about cardiovascular disease. Then complete the chart. Write *GN* for good news or *BN* for bad news. List the key words that help you. Paragraph 1 has been done for you as an example.

PARAGRAPH	TYPE OF INFORMATION	KEY WORDS
1	GN	Deaths . . . decrease
2		
3		
4		
5		
6		

WHILE YOU READ

As you read the article, stop at the end of each sentence that contains boldface text and follow the instructions in the box in the margin.

Cardiovascular Disease: A Good News—Bad News Story

Deaths from cardiovascular disease (CVD), which includes heart disease, high blood pressure, and strokes, first began to decrease in the 1960s in Western countries and have continued to do so since then. In the United States, the death rate from heart disease fell by over 35 percent between 1980 and 1997. Similar decreases have occurred in other Western countries.

How can we explain **this encouraging development**? One factor is that well-informed people are willing to change to a healthier lifestyle in order to reduce their risk of CVD. Another important factor is that the diagnosis and treatment of the disease have improved. Advances in technology have made possible the early diagnosis of conditions that may cause serious problems later. As a result, doctors can treat these conditions either by prescribing drugs to lower blood pressure or cholesterol or by performing surgery to repair damage to the heart. For patients who have already suffered a heart attack, the news is also good. Thanks to high-tech equipment, drugs, and experienced surgeons, many people recover and lead active lives after operations that were impossible four or five decades ago.

The news about cardiovascular disease, however, is not all good. **First**, in spite of the fall in death rates, CVD is still the most common cause of death in most Western countries. The 2000 statistics for the United States, for example, show that heart disease was responsible for more than 30 percent of deaths in that year and was the greatest single cause of death. The numbers, of course, would be even worse if we included deaths that are associated with high blood pressure and strokes. (See Figure 1.2.)

This encouraging development is a continuing idea. Check back for its meaning. Highlight it.

Scan forward to find out how many problems there are. Highlight the words that help you. Then come back and continue reading.

FIGURE 1.2 Cardiovascular Disease as a Cause of Death in the United States and India: 1990 and 2000

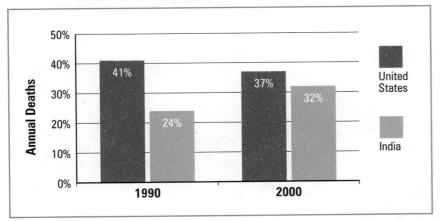

At the same time as CVD deaths are falling in developed countries, they are increasing in developing countries.

The second piece of bad news is that CVD, which was once consid- 4
ered a problem exclusively in wealthier countries, is becoming a
major health problem in developing countries. (See Figure 1.2.) Here,
rapid social change is introducing the risk factors that we usually
associate with CVD – a decrease in physical activity, an increase in
smoking, and a change to a less healthy diet. In 2001, the World
Health Organization predicted that CVD would be the leading cause
of death in the developing world within ten years. Clearly, CVD is a
health risk that needs urgent attention worldwide.

What can be done to fight this killer disease? The surgical treatment 5
of heart disease will continue to benefit patients in countries where
the expertise, equipment, and other resources are available. By itself,
however, **such treatment** is not an adequate response to the CVD
problem – for the following reasons. It is so expensive that it is an
enormous burden even for the wealthy nations that can afford to offer
it at present. For developing countries, which often do not have the
necessary financial, technological, and human resources, large treatment
programs are simply not possible.

For these reasons, health experts have concluded that a global 6
strategy to fight CVD must emphasize prevention of the disease
through community and government programs. Community programs
can attempt to reduce the major risk factors of CVD by educating
people about the connection between lifestyle and CVD. Governments
can discourage smoking and encourage healthier eating – for example,
by not allowing tobacco and food industries to advertise unhealthy
products. There are, however, considerable obstacles to the success of
such programs. In the next section of this article, we will turn our
attention to these obstacles.

Check back for the meaning of *such treatment*. Highlight it.

Check back to identify the reasons. Number them.

MAIN IDEA CHECK

Identify the sentence that best expresses the main idea of the article.

    a Cardiovascular disease is still the most common cause of death in the Western world.

 ✓ b In spite of progress in fighting it, cardiovascular disease is still a major problem in the developed world and is becoming one in the developing world.

    c Modern medicine is helping people recover from heart disease and live active lives afterward.

    d Because of advances in medicine, cardiovascular disease is no longer the problem it used to be in the industrial countries.

A CLOSER LOOK

Look back at the article to answer the following questions.

1 Cardiovascular disease and heart disease are the same. True or False?

2 According to the article, what could explain the fall in the CVD death rate in the wealthier countries?

    a Better drugs, earlier diagnosis, high-tech equipment, and expert surgeons

    b The public's readiness to make changes in lifestyle

    c A public that understands more about the causes of CVD

 ✓ d All of the above

3 According to health experts, where should we place the greatest emphasis when we develop a strategy to reduce CVD worldwide?

 ✓ a On preventing CVD

    b On treating CVD

    c On buying high-technology equipment for heart operations

    d All of the above

4 According to the writer, why can heart surgery not be the main response to CVD in the countries of the developing world?

    a They do not have enough trained specialists.

    b They cannot afford to offer large treatment programs for people with CVD.

    c The high-tech equipment that is necessary for such surgery is not available.

 ✓ d All of the above

5 According to the article, fighting CVD through community and government programs will be easy. True or False?

VOCABULARY STUDY: SYNONYMS

Find words in the article that are similar in meaning to the following.

1 causing feelings of hopefulness *(adj)* Par. 2

2 ready or eager *(adj)* Par. 2

3 improvements; progress *(n)* Par. 2

4 a medical operation *(n)* Par. 2

5 tools that are necessary for a task or activity *(n)* Par. 2

6 to get better after an illness *(v)* Par. 2

7 frequent *(adj)* Par. 3

8 only; not including anyone or anything else *(adv)* Par. 4

9 needing to be done immediately *(adj)* Par. 4

10 able to be found and used *(adj)* Par. 5

11 very large *(adj)* Par. 5

12 a difficult responsibility *(n)* Par. 5

13 to have sufficient money *(v)* Par. 5

14 big enough to be important *(adj)* Par. 6

15 things that prevent progress *(n)* Par. 6

VOCABULARY REVIEW: SAME OR DIFFERENT

The following pairs of sentences contain vocabulary from Readings 1 and 2. Write *S* in the blank if the two sentences have the same meaning. Write *D* if the meanings are different.

__S__ 1 The patient is recovering after suffering a heart attack last Monday.

The patient's condition is improving after her heart attack last Monday.

__S__ 2 Experts are sure that we can lower the death rate from heart disease if we emphasize the fact that exercise is important for maintaining health.

Experts have no doubt that we can reduce the number of deaths from heart disease by stressing the importance of exercise for health.

__D__ 3 John is going to perform major surgery tomorrow.

John is going to have a major operation tomorrow.

__D__ 4 A recent study concluded that, for millions of Americans, lack of health insurance is a major obstacle to getting access to good health care.

According to a recent study, good health care is readily available to millions of Americans who lack health insurance.

__D__ 5 We can decrease health care costs if we stress disease prevention and early diagnosis.

By emphasizing the prevention and early diagnosis of disease, we can reduce the financial resources we need to spend on health care.

_____ 6 According to medical research, there is a clear association between heart disease and stress, poor diet, and insufficient exercise.

Medical research shows that stress, poor nutrition, and lack of physical exercise are all factors that increase the risk of heart disease.

_____ 7 Instead of merely increasing resources to correct deficiencies in hospital care, the government is also financing programs to make people aware of the benefits of good nutrition.

The government is not spending more money on hospital care; instead, it is paying for programs that educate people about the importance of a healthy diet.

_____ 8 Early diagnosis may explain why survivors of cancer or heart disease are more common among Americans who have health insurance than among uninsured Americans.

Access to early diagnosis is the probably the reason why the death rate from heart disease is lower among Americans who have health insurance than among Americans without insurance.

BEYOND THE READING

Research
Do Internet or library research to find additional, up-to-date information on CVD in the developing world. The Web site of the World Health Organization (WHO) would be a good place to start.

Discussion
Discuss the following situation with a small group.

■ You belong to a government committee on health care. You have $20 million to finance a project that is intended to lower the death rate from heart disease. As a committee, decide which of the following two projects should receive the $20 million.

Project 1. Develop an artificial human heart.
Project 2. Inform the public about the link between heart disease and lifestyle.

Writing
Write a short report on the results of your research or your discussion.

SKILLS AND STRATEGIES 2
CAUSE AND EFFECT

Academic texts often examine cause and effect connections. Your reading will improve if you can recognize cause and effect organization and understand specific cause and effect connections.

EXAMPLES & EXPLANATIONS

Example

The talks between the workers and the company have failed.[1] The company is **attributing** the failure **to** the attitudes of the workers.[2] According to the company, the employees refuse to accept the idea that new technology is necessary and that the technology will need fewer workers to operate it.[3]

Explanation

Sentence 2 contains a possible cause for the event in Sentence 1. The verb *attributes* is a Cause and Effect Marker, a word or phrase that tells readers to expect a cause and effect connection. In the company's opinion, the connection is as follows:

The attitudes of the workers (cause)
↓
The talks have failed (effect)

Sentence 3 gives the details of the more general cause and effect connection that the writer introduced in Sentence 2.

THE LANGUAGE OF CAUSE AND EFFECT

Here's a list of Cause and Effect Markers. Review them and start learning those that are new to you.

CAUSE AND EFFECT MARKERS			
NOUNS		VERBS/VERB PHRASES	
cause	influence	to affect	to create
connection	origin	to attribute to	to force
consequence	outcome	to be associated with	to give rise to
effect	reason	to be responsible for	to lead to
factor	relationship	to blame	to play a part in
impact	result	to bring about	to produce
		to cause	to result from
		to contribute to	to result in

CAUSE AND EFFECT CONNECTING EXPRESSIONS

TO FORM A PHRASE	TO CONNECT CLAUSES	TO CONNECT SENTENCES
as a result of [+ Cause]	*as* [+ Cause]	*As a result* [+ Effect]
because of [+ Cause]	*because* [+ Cause]	*Consequently* [+ Effect]
due to [+ Cause]	*if* [+ Cause]	*For this reason* [+ Effect]
on account of [+ Cause]	*since* [+ Cause]	*Hence* [+ Effect]
thanks to [+ Cause]	*so* [+ Cause]	*Therefore* [+ Effect]
(in order) to [+ Cause]	*so* [+ Cause] . . . *that* [+ Effect]	*Thus* [+ Effect]

STRATEGIES

Here are three simple strategies that will help you identify and understand cause and effect while you read.

- Use Cause and Effect Markers to identify parts of a text that show cause and effect organization.
- Do not expect writers always to describe the cause first and the effect later.
- Make simple cause and effect diagrams with arrows to illustrate which specific causes lead to which specific effects.

SKILL PRACTICE 1

In the following sentences, circle the Cause and Effect Markers. Highlight each cause and mark it with a *C*. Underline each effect and mark it with an *E*. The first one has been done for you as an example.

        E   C

1 A great deal of pollution is caused by power plants that produce electricity by burning coal.

2 Because of a severe storm in the area, our plane was three hours late taking off.

3 The prices of new cars are forcing many people to keep their old cars longer than they used to.

4 On account of the bad weather, the baseball game has been canceled.

5 The police have identified a number of factors that contribute to traffic accidents, including alcohol, speeding, and mechanical failure.

6 A lack of rain is creating problems for farmers. Their crops are not growing well.

7 In the late twentieth century, there was an enormous increase in the percentage of female students in U.S. medical schools and law schools. This was partly due to a change in society's attitude towards women.

8 In the 1990s, world oil prices fell and stayed low. This brought about an improvement in the economies of countries that import oil.

9 Some human diseases have been associated with chemicals in the environment.

10 Two months ago, a large factory closed down. This resulted in fifteen hundred people losing their jobs.

SKILL PRACTICE 2

As you read the following texts, circle the Cause and Effect Markers and look for the specific causes and effects. Then complete the cause and effect diagrams. Write the correct letters in each box.

1　In the 1970s, there was an encouraging fall in the number of people who were killed in accidents on U.S. highways. According to some experts, the most important factor in the decrease was the 55 mph speed limit that was introduced in 1973. The original reason for lowering the speed limit was economic; the government was attempting to reduce gasoline use at a time when fuel prices were high.

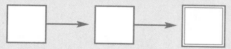

A There was a large decrease in traffic deaths on U.S. highways in the 1970s.
B The country needed to reduce the amount of gasoline people were using.
C The government introduced the 55 mph speed limit.

2　In 1912, the *Titanic*, the largest and best-equipped transatlantic liner of its time, hit an iceberg on its first crossing, from England to the United States, and sank. Of the more than two thousand passengers and crew, only 713 survived.
　　Research has shown that a number of factors contributed to the disaster. First, the *Titanic* carried only sixteen lifeboats, with room for about 1,100 people. This was clearly not enough for a ship of the *Titanic*'s size. In fact, the designer of the *Titanic* had originally planned to equip the ship with forty-eight lifeboats; however, to reduce the cost of building the ship, the owners decided to have only sixteen.
　　A second factor was that the *Titanic*'s crew was not given enough time to become familiar with the ship, especially with its emergency equipment. As a result, many lifeboats left the ship only half full and many more people died than needed to.
　　The third factor was the behavior of the *Titanic*'s officers on the night of the disaster. In the twenty-four hours before the tragedy, they received a number of warnings about icebergs in the area, but they took no precautions. They did not change direction or even reduce speed.

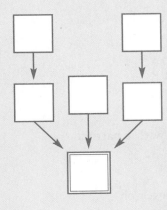

A Because of the crew's lack of experience, many lifeboats were only half full when they left the *Titanic*.

B The *Titanic* hit an iceberg in the North Atlantic and sank, with the loss of over 1,500 lives.

C The ship's officers paid no attention to warnings about icebergs near the *Titanic*.

D The ship's owners decided to save money by equipping the *Titanic* with sixteen lifeboats instead of the forty-eight the designer had planned.

E The crew had little time to get to know the ship and its emergency equipment.

F As a result of this decision, the Titanic did not have not enough lifeboats for all the passengers and crew.

SKILL PRACTICE 3

Use a word or phrase from the list to complete each item below.

attribute	factors	responsible for	bring about	blamed
contributed to	thanks to	consequences	lead to	link

1 Immediately after the *Titanic* sank, newspapers _____ the ship's owners for the disaster.

2 Most experts agree that a number of _____ played a part in the sinking of the *Titanic* in 1912.

3 In 1940, only 15 percent of married women in the United States had jobs outside the home. By 1980, the figure had risen to over 50 percent. To what can we _____ this major change in women's lives?

4 Some diseases – for example, AIDS – are often associated with people's behavior. Therefore, a basic question for preventive medicine is this: How can we _____ changes in behavior?

5 Research has shown that alcohol is _____ a large number of traffic deaths.

6 _____ advances in medical science, diseases that used to kill millions of children a year are no longer a danger in many countries.

7 The talks between the employees and the company are continuing. Both sides hope that the discussions will _____ a satisfactory agreement.

8 Improvements in diagnosis and treatment have _____ the falling death rate from cardiovascular disease.

9 Actions can have _____ we don't intend. For example, we used DDT to kill harmful insects, but then the pesticide entered the food chain and killed birds and animals.

10 Research has shown the _____ between smoking and an increased risk of heart disease.

READING 3
MEDICINE AND GENETIC RESEARCH: PROMISE AND PROBLEMS

GETTING INTO THE TOPIC

Study the title of the article. Then discuss the following questions with a partner.

1 What is genetic research?
2 What advances have genetic researchers achieved in recent years?
3 What is the possible connection between medicine and genetic research?

GETTING A FIRST IDEA ABOUT THE ARTICLE

Scan only the first sentence of each paragraph. If you expect the paragraph to be about positive developments, write *Promise* in the chart; if you think the paragraph will contain negative developments, write *Problems*. List the key words that help you. Paragraph 1 has been done for you as an example.

PARAGRAPH	TYPE OF INFORMATION	KEY WORDS
1	Promise	progress . . . benefitting
2		
3		
4		
5		
6		
7		

WHILE YOU READ

As you read the article, stop at the end of each sentence that contains boldface text and follow the instructions in the box in the margin.

Medicine and Genetic Research: Promise and Problems

Since the 1970s, medicine has been benefiting from progress in genetic research. Decades ago, for example, scientists succeeded in identifying the genes that are associated with some serious diseases and birth defects. **These advances** helped medical science to develop tests that, in turn, have enabled doctors to inform their patients about the potential risks of such genes for themselves and for their children. Some of the tests can determine if the patients themselves are carriers of a defective gene. Others, such as amniocentesis, can identify a variety of genetically inherited and often fatal abnormalities in unborn babies.

Check back for the meaning of *These advances*. Highlight it.

These early genetic tests offered the possibility of slowing the spread of, or even eliminating, a number of incurable genetic diseases. We can begin to do this, health experts argue, by informing people who carry defective genes about the health risks for any children they might have. This practice is already quite common in many countries. For example, after tests have shown that they have the faulty gene that causes Huntington's disease, a slow-developing but fatal neurological condition, some people have decided not to have children. They are unwilling to take the 1-in-2 risk that a child of theirs will inherit the gene and suffer from the same condition.

In the 1990s, genetic research advanced rapidly. Research institutions, biotechnology companies, and investors became more aware of the enormous potential of genetic medicine. This **led to** a rapid increase in financial support for the field, which, in turn, helped researchers

Cause and Effect Marker! Underline the cause and highlight two effects.

Thanks to advances in genetic research and medicine, we can look forward to a future in which babies are free of genetic disease.

to make rapid advances. By the year 2000, researchers had begun to develop and test treatments for life-threatening genetic illnesses. The early results of some of these tests were very promising. In 2000, for example, French doctors reported success with a procedure in which they treated three babies who suffered from a rare type of immune deficiency. They introduced into the infants' bone marrow a gene that functioned normally. Ten months later, the children's immune systems appeared completely normal.

However, in spite of the successes during this first decade, gene-therapy research experienced considerable problems and limitations. Some researchers overstated the progress that had been made and understated the many major problems that still remained. For example, they predicted that they would soon be able to cure diseases like cystic fibrosis and cancer. However, they ignored the fact that their successes had occurred in small numbers of patients with less complex genetic conditions.

There were also more serious problems. First, some researchers conducted clinical trials of new procedures before sufficient evidence was available that the procedures were capable of producing a scientific or medical benefit. As a result, the success rate in many trials was disappointing. Worse, clinical trials sometimes took place before researchers had adequately assessed the risks to the human participants. In one such case, an eighteen-year-old volunteer subject died after he developed an extreme immune system reaction to the procedure.

These problems, critics said, were **attributable to** the relationship between commercial biotechnology companies and researchers in clinics and universities, who are under pressure to find funding for their work. In this relationship, companies make funding available to researchers, who then test products and procedures that the companies are developing. The result was predictable. To make the profits that would satisfy their investors, biotech companies pressed researchers for early clinical trials. The researchers naturally wanted their funding to continue. In these circumstances, some researchers understated the risks to patients and test subjects and moved into clinical trials too soon.

For many researchers in genetic medicine, the criticism was justified. They accepted the need to return to the caution that is necessary in medical research. They became more careful both in deciding to proceed to clinical trials and in talking about any success they had achieved in very limited clinical trials. They did not lose their belief in the enormous potential of gene therapy to treat conditions like cancer, diabetes, and heart disease. However, they now warned that **such treatment** was still years, sometimes decades, in the future.

4

5

6

7

As you continue reading this paragraph, highlight the final outcome in each problem. Then mark the cause of each problem by writing *Cause* in the margin.

Cause and Effect Marker! Underline the cause of the problems. Use it to help you with the rest of the paragraph.

Check back for the meaning of *such treatment*. Highlight it.

MAIN IDEA CHECK

Identify the sentence that best expresses the main idea of the article.

x a Genetic researchers made progress toward treating or eliminating a small number of fatal diseases, but they also made some serious mistakes.

→ b Thanks to progress in genetic research, doctors can now identify people whose children will be born with certain genetic abnormalities.

c Medicine has benefited a great deal from the advances that have been made in genetic research since the 1980s.

x d In the 1990s, there was an enormous increase in funding for genetic research and for research into gene therapy.

A CLOSER LOOK

Look back at the article to answer the following questions.

1 What are the names of some diseases with a genetic component?

2 How did the early genetic tests offer the chance to fight some genetic diseases?

  a They helped people make informed decisions about having children.
  b They used new technology to cure the diseases.
  c They enabled doctors to perform surgery on children with genetic defects.
  d They enabled us to eliminate a number of incurable genetic diseases.

3 During the 1990s, people in gene therapy research always spoke realistically about the progress they had made and about the obstacles that remained.
   True or False?

4 In paragraph 5, the writer gives a general cause and effect explanation of serious problems with early gene-therapy research. Reread the paragraph. Then complete the cause and effect diagram with sentences A–C. Write the correct letter in each box.

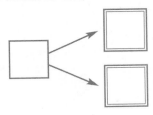

A Not many of the clinical trials were successful.
B Researchers started clinical trials before they had adequately assessed the possible risks and benefits.
C A participant in one trial died.

5 A chain of cause and effect explains why researchers in the 1990s sometimes conducted clinical trials too early. Reread paragraph 6 for its details. Then complete the cause and effect diagram with sentences A–D. Write the correct letter in each box.

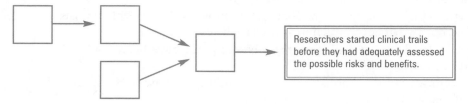

Researchers started clinical trails before they had adequately assessed the possible risks and benefits.

A Researchers wanted their funding to continue because their jobs depended on it.
B To satisfy their investors, biotech companies wanted profits as soon as possible.
C Under this pressure, researchers did not pay enough attention to safety.
D Biotech companies put pressure on researchers to conduct early clinical trials.

6 What does this article suggest about the state of gene therapy at the end of the twentieth century?
  a It was so successful that some treatments were becoming widely available.
  b It was successful enough that we could look forward to the availability of some genetic treatments in the future.
  c It experienced enough failures to cause serious doubts about gene therapy ever being worthwhile.
  d It was not receiving sufficient funding to conduct the basic research that was needed.

VOCABULARY STUDY: SYNONYMS

Find words in the article that are similar in meaning to the following.

  1 not working correctly *(adj)* Par. 1
  2 to receive from an earlier generation in one's family *(v)* Par. 2
  3 people who buy a share of a business in order to make a profit *(n)* Par. 3
  4 very dangerous *(adj)* Par. 3
  5 a method of doing something, often in medicine *(n)* Par. 3
  6 to work; to operate *(v)* Par. 3
  7 to describe something as greater than it really is *(v)* Par. 4
  8 not to pay attention to someone or something *(v)* Par. 4
  9 able to do something *(adj)* Par. 5
 10 something that protects the human body from disease *(n)* Par. 5
 11 with the purpose of making money *(adj)* Par. 6
 12 money that is available for a project *(n)* Par. 6
 13 expected before it happens *(adj)* Par. 6
 14 having a good reason *(adj)* Par. 7
 15 to get something you want by working for it *(v)* Par. 7

VOCABULARY STUDY: WORDS IN CONTEXT

Complete the sentences with words from the list below. If necessary, review the words in the Key Vocabulary from the Readings on page 248.

assess	conduct	eliminate	fatal	cautious
profit	potential	evidence	determine	ignore

1 Before researchers start to test new treatments on human subjects, they need to _____ the possible risks to their subjects.

2 In assessing risks to their human subjects, researchers should be extremely _____. It's better to overstate than to understate the possible dangers.

3 In 1967, the World Health Organization began a program whose goal was to _____ smallpox. In 1979, doctors treated the last case of wild smallpox.

4 Malaria is a disease that can be _____ if it is not treated in time. It kills over a million children under five every year.

5 After a new drug is developed and tested on animals, the next step is to _____ clinical trials with human subjects.

6 One purpose of clinical trials is to _____ if a new drug is beneficial for the treatment of a medical condition.

7 This new discovery has the _____ to revolutionize the treatment of disease. However, it may take years before we know if our hopes are justified.

8 A low fever in a child is usually not a cause for alarm. But don't _____ it! Keep an eye on the fever. If it gets worse, call your doctor.

9 Drug companies often invest millions of dollars to research a new drug before they start making a _____ from selling the drug.

10 The results of genetic tests are now used as _____ in criminal trials. Sometimes such tests can show conclusively who did or did not commit the crime.

BEYOND THE READING

Research

Do Internet or library research to find additional, up-to-date information on one of these questions.

- What are the new developments in gene therapy research today?
- What questions about gene therapy are people discussing today?

Discussion

Discuss the following situation and questions with a partner. Justify your answers.

- A biotechnology company wants to begin human testing of a gene therapy procedure that it has developed.

  1 Who should decide if the procedure is ready for testing?
  2 Who should conduct the tests?
  3 Who should pay for the tests?

Writing

Write a short report on the results of your research or your discussion.

READING 4
AIDS — NOT SOMEONE ELSE'S PROBLEM

GETTING INTO THE TOPIC
Activating what you know about a topic before you start reading is a good strategy. Work with a partner and share what you already know by discussing the following questions.

1 When was AIDS first recognized and named as a disease?
2 What can cause someone to get AIDS?
3 What are some of the symptoms of AIDS?
4 What is the treatment for AIDS?

GETTING A FIRST IDEA ABOUT THE ARTICLE
Read the first sentence of paragraph 1. Decide what the topic of the paragraph will be and then match your idea to one of the topics below. Write the number of the paragraph in the blank. Then do the same for paragraphs 2–6.

_____ A The spread of HIV/AIDS in the United States

_____ B The results of early research into HIV/AIDS

_____ C The first appearance of AIDS in the United States

_____ D Reasons for the slow reaction to the appearance of AIDS in the United States

_____ E A discussion of how to solve the problem of HIV/AIDS

_____ F The global spread of HIV/AIDS

WHILE YOU READ
As you read the article, stop at the end of each sentence that contains boldface text and follow the instructions in the box in the margin.

AIDS – Not Someone Else's Problem

By the late 1970s, an unusual health problem was beginning to appear in the United States. Healthy young people, most of them white homosexual males, started to suffer from infections that doctors had rarely seen. In some cases, treatment was not effective and the infections worsened. In other cases, the infections were successfully treated but they recurred. In all cases, the patients weakened and ultimately died. Their infections were symptoms of a condition that was unknown at that time. In 1982, the condition came to be known as AIDS (acquired immune-deficiency syndrome). 1

Scan forward. Highlight the words that show you where to look for each of these reasons. Then come back and continue reading for the main idea.

In these early days, the response to AIDS in the United States was slow – for at least **three reasons**. First, many medical experts disregarded the possibility that it was a completely new disease. Second, problems at the Centers for Disease Control slowed this important organization's reaction to the situation. Third, the White House did not feel comfortable talking about the two behaviors that seemed to be associated with the disease – illegal drug use and homosexual sex. From 1981 to 1984, in fact, the government prevented its top health official, the surgeon general, from making any public statements on AIDS. 2

However, in spite of the slow government response, medical science began to provide answers to basic questions about the disease. By 1982, research had established that the condition was transmitted through blood-to-blood contact with an infected person. The most common transmission routes also became clear: unprotected sexual contact with an infected person, the use of contaminated hypodermic needles in illegal drug use, and contact between an infected mother and her child during pregnancy. Another advance came in 1983, when French scientists identified the cause of AIDS – a virus that attacks the human immune system. They named it HIV (human immune-deficiency virus). Finally, in 1985, U.S. researchers developed the first blood test to identify the virus. 3

Scan forward and highlight the words that identify these groups. Then come back and continue reading for the main idea.

Between 1984 and 1989, the number of annual cases of AIDS in the United States rose by an enormous 660 percent. After that, the rate of infection fell, but HIV/AIDS continued to spread into **other social groups**. For example, between 1989 and 1992, the number of American teenagers who were infected with the virus rose by 75 percent. In 2001, a government study in six major U.S. cities found that 30 percent of young, gay, African American men were HIV-positive. In the same year, African Americans made up 68 percent of new infections among women. By 2001, more than 420,000 Americans had died of the disease and over 900,000 others were living with HIV/AIDS. 4

Scan forward and highlight 4–5 words or phrases that show the worldwide nature of the problem. Then come back and continue reading for the main idea.

Statistics show that HIV/AIDS quickly became **a worldwide problem**. By 1985, it had begun to kill large numbers of young, educated adults in sub-Saharan Africa. By 2000, experts estimate, it had left 12 million children without parents. In South Africa the rate of HIV infection was a catastrophic 25 percent of the adult heterosexual population. In South and Southeast Asia, the estimated number of people with HIV/AIDS increased from 600,000 to 5.8 million within the last decade of the twentieth century. In the countries of the former Soviet 5

FIGURE 1.3 Estimated Number of HIV/AIDS Cases at the End of 2003

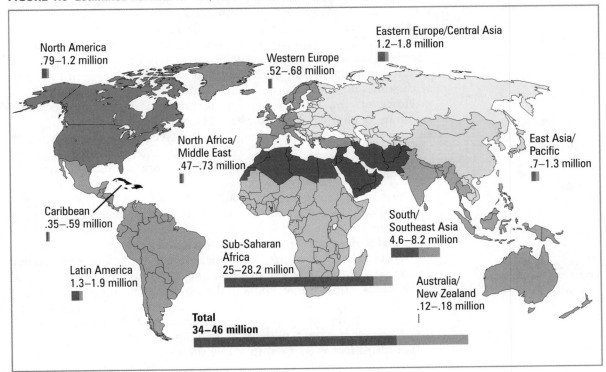

Union, 700,000 people were living with HIV/AIDS in 2000, an increase of 55 percent over the estimated figures for 1999. Worldwide, by 2004, AIDS had killed more than 21 million men, women, and children. Furthermore, between 34 and 46 million people were living with HIV/AIDS (see Figure 1.3). These numbers left no doubt that HIV/AIDS was a truly global epidemic.

Where should we look to find an answer to this global catastrophe? **6** Research into the disease has been continuing since the mid-1980s, when AIDS became a high priority in Western nations. Enormous sums of money have been made available to fund AIDS research – the U.S government alone contributed $2.1 billion in the year 2000. And the research has produced some advances. Antiviral drugs that were introduced in the mid-1990s proved to be effective in slowing the development of AIDS in some HIV-infected patients. By 2001, a number of experimental vaccines were in development.

However, despite some encouraging progress, most experts were **7** not optimistic that a complete answer to HIV/AIDS would appear soon – **for at least two reasons**. First, the antiviral drugs in use by 2001 were not effective in all cases and were certainly not a cure. Second, developing an effective vaccine will be very difficult, perhaps even impossible, because the virus is capable of changing very rapidly, up to 100,000 times faster than the influenza virus, and because it directly attacks the human immune system.

Under these circumstances, the only realistic response to the **8** AIDS crisis is to make treatments more accessible and affordable, and

Cause and Effect Marker! You already know the effect. Draw a simple cause and effect arrow diagram in the margin as you read on.

to emphasize prevention. At first sight, the task of developing effective prevention programs appears simple. For one thing, despite some success in treating the symptoms, AIDS remains a fatal disease. This fact should be a sufficient incentive to avoid becoming infected. In addition, we know how to prevent most cases of HIV/AIDS – people should avoid having unprotected sex or sharing a hypodermic needle with someone who might already be infected.

How many factors? Scan forward and highlight the words that help you answer this question. Then come back and continue reading for the main idea.

However, the task of developing prevention programs is made much more complex by **a number of factors**. First, because HIV/AIDS threatens so many people worldwide, effective programs of prevention are enormously expensive. Often the countries that most urgently need such programs are the least capable of organizing and financing them. 9

The second factor results from attitudes to sexual behavior, the main method of transmission for HIV. People are often unwilling to speak openly about sex, especially sexual behavior that societies tend to regard as less acceptable – homosexual sex, sex with prostitutes, sex with multiple partners, and underage sex. We see **this reluctance** not only in individuals but also among governments and other social institutions, including schools and churches. These institutions are not always willing to speak plainly and directly to people about the link between high-risk sexual behavior and HIV/AIDS. In fact, a common first response has been to deny that the disease could be a problem. 10

Check back for the meaning of *this reluctance*. Highlight it.

The third factor that complicates the task of developing effective prevention programs is a false sense of security about HIV/AIDS among the general population. People still tend to regard it as a disease that is exclusive to homosexual men and illegal-drug users. The majority of people believe that they have no contact with either of **these groups**. Even among high-risk sections of the U.S. population, by the year 2000 there were signs of a false sense of security in younger people who were disregarding warnings about unsafe sexual behavior. Perhaps they were being unrealistically optimistic about AIDS treatments. The statistics, however, show that such attitudes can have fatal consequences. 11

Check back for the meaning of *these groups*. Highlight it.

If they are to defeat HIV/AIDS, health experts must get the public to accept two basic facts. First, everyone is at risk; second, the risk decreases greatly if people avoid illegal drugs and follow the rules for safe sexual behavior. As the epidemic develops, however, experts do not underestimate the enormous obstacles that stand in the way of their completing the task. 12

MAIN IDEA CHECK

Here are the main ideas of each paragraph in the article. Match each paragraph to its main idea. The first one has been done for you as an example.

Paragraphs 1–6

_____ A Researchers soon began to provide basic information about AIDS – its cause, transmission, and diagnosis.

_1_ B In 1982, researchers identified an unknown illness that had appeared in the United States in the late 1970s and named it AIDS.

_____ C There are at least three reasons why the U.S. government and medical experts reacted slowly to AIDS.

_____ D Research into HIV/AIDS has received a lot of funding and has made some progress towards treating and preventing the disease.

_____ E In the United States, HIV/AIDS at first spread very rapidly and then slowed but continued to infect new victims.

_____ F HIV/AIDS quickly spread, and by the end of the twentieth century was an enormous global problem.

Paragraphs 7–12

_____ G Another obstacle to effective prevention of HIV/AIDS is people's reluctance to speak openly about sexual behavior, especially less socially acceptable behavior.

_____ H One of the major obstacles to developing effective prevention programs for HIV/AIDS is their high cost.

_____ I Experts know that persuading people to change their AIDS-related attitudes and behaviors will be very difficult.

_____ J By 2001, most HIV/AIDS experts did not believe that an effective treatment or vaccine for the disease would appear in the near future.

_____ K A final obstacle to successful prevention is that many people mistakenly believe they are not at risk for HIV/AIDS.

_____ L Because HIV/AIDS is fatal and because we know how to prevent infections, the task of developing prevention programs would seem easy.

A CLOSER LOOK

Look back at the article to answer the following questions.

1 Reread paragraph 2. Then complete this cause and effect diagram with sentences A–D. Write the correct letter in each box.

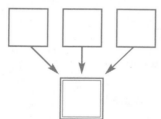

A The government was reluctant to talk openly about AIDS.

B There were problems at the Centers for Disease Control.

C In the United States, the early response to AIDS was slow.

D Medical experts were not expecting a new infectious disease.

2 After reading paragraphs 1 and 2, you would be justified in believing that politics helped to determine the early U.S. response to AIDS. True or False?

3 Identify the way, according to the article, in which a person could *not* have become infected with the AIDS virus in the early 1980s.

a Through sexual contact with an infected person

b Before birth, from his or her mother

c By sharing a drug needle with an infected person

d By living in the same house as an infected person

4 The history of AIDS shows that heterosexual sex carries no risk of AIDS. True or False?

5 Reread paragraph 7. Then complete this cause and effect diagram with sentences A–E. Write the correct letter in each box.

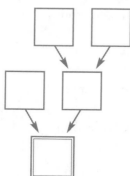

A Experts do not expect an answer for AIDS soon.

B HIV can change very fast.

C Developing an AIDS vaccine will be very difficult, perhaps impossible.

D HIV attacks the human immune system.

E Medication to fight HIV/AIDS does not work in every case, nor is it a cure.

6 Reread paragraphs 9–11. Then complete the cause and effect diagram with sentences A–D. Write the correct letter in each box.

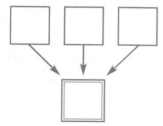

A The majority of people believe that they are not at risk for HIV/AIDS.

B Society is often not willing to discuss the sexual behaviors that place people at high risk for HIV/AIDS.

C It is very difficult to develop effective prevention programs for HIV/AIDS.

D The costs of education and prevention for HIV/AIDS are extremely high.

VOCABULARY STUDY: SYNONYMS

Find words in the article that are similar in meaning to the following.

1 a condition that is caused by a bacteria or a virus in the body *(n)* Par. 1

2 finally *(adv)* Par. 1

3 to give people something that is needed *(v)* Par. 3

4 to determine the truth about something *(v)* Par. 3

5 containing dangerous bacteria, viruses, or poisons *(adj)* Par. 3

6 yearly *(adj)* Par. 4

7 to calculate something without having exact information *(v)* Par. 5

8 disastrous *(adj)* Par. 5

9 worldwide *(adj)* Par. 5

10 situation *(n)* Par. 8

11 something that encourages people to do something *(n)* Par. 8

12 a piece of work that a person has to do *(n)* Par. 9

13 difficult to deal with *(adj)* Par. 9

14 against the law *(adj)* Par. 12

15 to think that something is smaller than it really is *(v)* Par. 12

VOCABULARY REVIEW: SAME OR DIFFERENT

The following pairs of sentences contain vocabulary from Readings 3 and 4. Write
S in the blank if the two sentences have the same meaning. Write *D* if the
meanings are different.

_____ 1 In spite of the considerable advances that medicine has made in the last sixty years, we still have not eliminated many infectious diseases.

Many communicable diseases have disappeared because of what has been achieved in medicine in the last sixty years.

_____ 2 The World Health Organization has reduced the number of cases of infectious diseases in developing countries through mass immunization programs.

By vaccinating enormous numbers of people in developing countries, the World Health Organization has eliminated many infectious diseases there.

_____ 3 One of the obstacles to developing an effective response to the HIV/AIDS epidemic is people's unwillingness to be honest about their sexual behavior.

People are reluctant to be honest about their sexual behavior; this is one factor that makes it difficult to develop successful programs to fight HIV/AIDS.

_____ 4 Scientists are cautiously optimistic that the next decade will see the development of effective genetic treatments for a number of fatal diseases.

Scientists are reluctant to predict that genetic medicine will be able to treat any fatal diseases within the next ten years.

_____ 5 In a number of countries, providing adequate sanitation and clean water is the top priority for the health care systems.

In some countries, contaminated water and a lack of access to adequate sanitation are the two most urgent problems the health care systems must solve.

_____ 6 The first important task for HIV/AIDS researchers was to determine how the virus was transmitted.

Establishing how the HIV/AIDS virus spread was the first priority for researchers.

_____ 7 Medical science is developing new, more effective vaccines for certain diseases.

Medical researchers are developing new, more effective drugs for the treatment of certain diseases.

_____ 8 A reluctance to see a doctor for regular physical examinations or at the first sign of symptoms may explain why low-income Americans survive heart disease and cancer less frequently than others.

Low-income Americans have a higher death rate from cancer and heart disease than others, perhaps because they are less willing to have regular physical examinations or to see a doctor when symptoms first occur.

BEYOND THE READING

Research

Do Internet or library research to find additional, up-to-date information on HIV/AIDS. Here are some possible topics.

- AIDS in a specific country or community
- Recent developments in AIDS research

Discussion

Discuss the following situation with a partner:

- You are a doctor. A patient of yours, who is a student, tells you that he has discovered that his roommate is HIV-positive. He is very concerned and wants your advice. What would you tell him?

Writing

Write a short report on the results of your research or your discussion.

SKILLS AND STRATEGIES 3
PASSIVE SENTENCES

Because passive sentences are common in academic writing, you need to recognize and understand them quickly. The passive allows writers to focus on an action without saying who performed the action. It also allows them to change the order of ideas in a sentence.

EXAMPLES & EXPLANATIONS

Examples

In the 1990s, university researchers and scientists in biotechnology companies **made** considerable progress in the field of gene therapy.

In the 1990s, considerable progress **was made** in the field of gene therapy.

In the 1990s, considerable progress **was made** in the field of gene therapy **by** university researchers and scientists in biotechnology companies.

Explanations

In active sentences, the subject identifies who performed the action (the agent). In this sentence, the agent is *university researchers and scientists in biotechnology companies*.

In passive sentences, writers can focus on what happened and do not need to identify the agent if that information is unknown or not important.

If they wish, writers can choose to identify the agent in a **by + noun phrase**.

THE LANGUAGE OF THE PASSIVE

The Passive Marker has two parts, which always appear in the same order. However, these markers will not always be next to each other. Between them, you may see other words – e.g., subjects in questions, negatives, and adverbs.

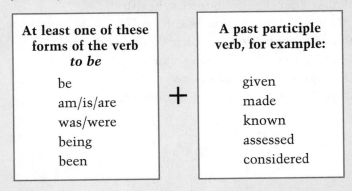

At least one of these forms of the verb *to be*		A past participle verb, for example:
be am/is/are was/were being been	**+**	given made known assessed considered

STRATEGIES

Use these strategies to help you identify passive sentences.

- If you see one of the eight forms of the verb *to be*, scan forward for a past participle verb.
- If you identify a past participle verb, scan back to see if there is one of the eight *to be* markers.
- If you see a *by* + agent phrase, scan back for a passive verb.

SKILL PRACTICE 1

Read the following short texts and underline all examples of the passive you find.

1 Much better methods of diagnosis and treatment have been developed over the last twenty-five years. The contribution of these advances should not be ignored when we consider why fewer Americans are dying of heart disease today.

2 It has been conclusively shown that certain factors in our day-to-day lives contribute to heart disease. Stress, diet, smoking, and insufficient exercise all have been linked to the development of the disease.

3 Since the 1980s, the task of developing an effective response to AIDS has been made more difficult by governments that have refused to take the disease seriously. Western governments, for example, did not quickly recognize AIDS as a major threat to public health. In the 1990s, similar reactions were seen from other governments as the disease began to appear across the world.

4 People are reluctant to speak openly about HIV/AIDS because the disease is most often transmitted by behaviors that tend to be considered socially unacceptable, such as homosexual sex, sex with multiple partners, underage sex, and illegal drug use.

5 To solve the most urgent health problems of developing countries, health experts recommend that priority should be given to primary health care. Primary health care emphasizes both disease prevention and early diagnosis and treatment. Many deadly diseases can be prevented if clean water and childhood vaccinations are provided. Others, such as malaria, are much less dangerous if they are diagnosed and treated soon after patients are infected.

SKILL PRACTICE 2

Decide which form of the verb, the active or the passive, correctly completes each sentence.

1 In the trial, a number of seriously ill patients _____ with a new cancer drug.
   a are being treated   b are treating

2 At first, the governments of most countries _____ the dangers of HIV/AIDS to public health.
   a were underestimated   b underestimated

3 Unlike traditional drugs, which attack all cells, this new drug _____ to attack cancer cells exclusively.
   a has been developed   b has developed

4 What _____ in the field of gene therapy in the last ten years?
   a has been achieved   b has achieved

5 _____ that deaths from heart disease will increase in poorer countries over the next thirty years.
   a It is expected   b It expects

6 In 1999, an eighteen-year-old participant, Jesse Gelsinger, died in a gene-therapy experiment. His death showed that the researchers _____ the risks of their procedure.
   a had not been adequately assessed   b had not adequately assessed

7 Since AIDS first appeared, governments _____ enormous sums of money for research into the disease.
   a have been spent   b have spent

8 Some married couples decide not to have children after they _____ that their children would run a 50 percent risk of inheriting the gene for Huntington's disease, a rare but fatal neurological disorder.
   a are informed   b inform

9 Because of rising costs in the 1990s, the British government _____ the number of hospital beds that were available for patients.
   a was reduced   b reduced

10 In 1985, the World Health Organization decided to work toward eliminating polio in the Americas. The goal _____ in 1999, when the last case of polio was successfully treated in Peru.
   a was achieved   b achieved

SKILL PRACTICE 3

In each of the following short texts, work with a partner to identify a clause in the second sentence that would benefit if the writer used the passive instead of the active. Then rewrite the sentence in the passive and discuss why the passive is better.

1 "How could it happen?" is the question that most people asked after the *Titanic* disaster. Experts who have used the latest scientific methods to examine all the available evidence have identified four main causes.

2 In 2000, the world faced the difficult task of developing an effective response to a growing HIV/AIDS epidemic. Governments who refused to take the disease seriously or who claimed that it did not exist in their countries made the task even more difficult.

3 Extremely high death rates, like those that are associated with HIV/AIDS, are not new in history. Bubonic plague, a disease that fleas transmit from rats to people, killed 35 percent of Europe's population in the fourteenth century.

4 Clinical trials of new medical treatments should not begin until the risks and benefits to patients have been adequately assessed. Experts who are not working on these research projects and who have no financial interest in their success or failure should make such assessments.

5 Heart disease is associated with certain factors in our daily lives. Researchers in many countries and in a number of scientific fields have linked stress, diet, tobacco, and lack of exercise to the development of the disease.

MAIN READING

BETTER HEALTH FOR EVERYONE: HEALTH CARE IN TWO WORLDS

GETTING INTO THE TOPIC

Read the title of this article. Work with a partner and discuss the health care
system of a country you are familiar with.

1 How do people pay for their health care?
2 What are the strengths and weaknesses of the health care system?
3 How could the health care system be improved?
4 If you are familiar with the health care system of another country, how is that
  system better or worse?

GETTING A FIRST IDEA ABOUT THE ARTICLE

You can quickly develop an idea of the topics and organization of a longer article
by reading the section headings and the introduction (especially its final
paragraph) and by examining the illustrations.

Read the section headings, look at the illustrations, and scan the introduction of
this article. Then complete the chart by matching each topic with the section
that deals with it. Some sections may have more than one topic. Write the
number of the section (I–IV) in the blank.

SECTION	TOPIC
	The chances of getting good health care in the rich nations of the world
	Solutions to health care problems in less developed countries
	Different health care issues in different parts of the world
	Solutions to the health care problems in wealthy countries
	The high cost of health care and its impact on possible solutions

WHILE YOU READ

Read the article section by section. Stop after each sentence that contains
boldface text and follow the instructions in the box in the margin. After you read
each section, answer the Main Idea Check and A Closer Look questions, which
can be found on pages 49–53.

Better Health for Everyone: Health Care in Two Worlds

I. ONE EARTH – TWO WORLDS OF HEALTH

"How can we provide the best health care for our people?" This is 1 a question that every responsible society is attempting to answer. In the wealthier nations, doctors and patients demand that the health care systems provide the highest standard of service regardless of cost. If certain drugs or procedures are not immediately available to patients, angry complaints are heard. In the poorer countries, however, the priorities seem very different. Here an estimated 1.7 million children die annually from treatable infections; from common, curable diarrhea; and from infectious diseases like measles and whooping cough – diseases that have almost completely disappeared in the industrial nations. In the developing countries, it is believed, about 80 percent of all illnesses are the result of contaminated water and inadequate sanitation.

It seems, therefore, that there are two worlds of medicine and that 2 these two worlds have **nothing in common** with each other. The industrial world is concerned about illnesses like heart disease and cancer, which are often still incurable; the developing world is concerned about illnesses that would disappear if basic health programs could be afforded. One world seeks to provide the latest, most advanced treatments for the small section of the population who are ill; the other has difficulty providing, for the majority of its people, things the industrial world takes for granted – clean drinking water, vaccines, and the drugs essential to medical care. The immediate problems that face these two worlds seem very different. However, when we examine the challenges and possible solutions, we see almost as many similarities among nations as differences.

In this paragraph do you expect to read about (a) similarities or (b) differences?

II. HEALTH CARE COSTS AND ACCESS IN THE WEALTHIER COUNTRIES

Although the health care available in the wealthy countries is the 3 best in the world, their health care systems are experiencing serious problems. By far the most urgent, complex difficulty is financial. Medical costs are already enormously high. For example, in Germany in 1995, total health care spending stood at $210 billion. In the United States, total spending in 2000 was more than $910 billion. Even more problematic, health care costs increased very rapidly. In the United States, for example, the rate of increase for 2001 was a troubling 11 percent.

Responses to rising costs caused access to health care to be 4 reduced rather than maintained or increased. For example, in Britain, a country which provides publically funded health care to all its citizens, the government was reluctant, for political reasons, to increase the tax burden on the population and so had no additional money to invest in the country's health care system. As costs rose and funding did not, it became necessary to reduce services. The

Check figures for 2010

Scan forward and find at least three effects of rising costs and number them. Then come back and continue reading for the main idea.

number of hospital beds fell; less high-tech equipment was bought; and fewer doctors and nurses were hired. As a result, there were waits of six months or longer for modern diagnostic procedures like MRIs and colonoscopies, and the most up-to-date treatments were not available to every seriously ill patient who needed them. For some types of nonemergency procedures, such as cataract and hip-replacement surgery, patients had to wait for up to three years.

In the United States, where most health insurance is provided by 5 employers, access to quality health care has also been reduced. In response to rising health care costs, the cost of insurance has increased. As a result, employers have found it difficult to maintain earlier levels of health care benefits. Many employers have had to reduce health care coverage for their employees, while others no longer can afford to provide any health insurance and have eliminated it completely. As a result, from 1987, the number of Americans without health insurance increased steadily; by 2002, an estimated 43 million people were uninsured. The changes affected almost everyone in some way, but clearly hit lower-income families harder.

The continuing rise in the costs of health care is **attributable to a** 6 **number of factors**. One of these, according to critics of our health care systems, is our emphasis on *crisis care*, the treatment of disease after it has become serious. According to the critics, however, such an approach to health care tends to ignore a basic fact: crisis care is usually more expensive and often less effective than prevention or treatment after an early diagnosis. For today's killers, such as cardiovascular disease, breast cancer, and colon cancer, early diagnosis can greatly increase recovery rates and reduce the need for expensive crisis care later.

A second factor behind rising health care costs is that people are 7 living considerably longer than they used to. Average life expectancy

> How many factors? Quickly scan paragraphs 6–8. Highlight the words that show you where to look for these factors.

FIGURE 1.4 Percent of U.S. Population by Age Group: Past, present, and future

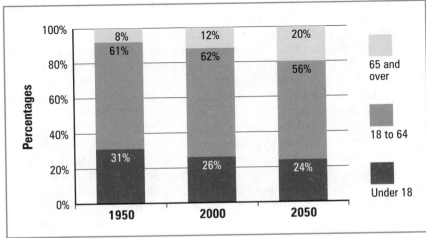

As the number and percentage of older people increase, so too will spending on health care.

in industrial countries rose through most of the 1900s and reached 77 years of age by the end of the century. Many people are surviving into their eighties and nineties. Because older people tend to require the services of the health care system more often than younger people, health care spending has increased.

A third reason for increasing costs is found in the public's attitude toward medicine. Today, many people demand that their health care systems provide them with the best treatment available, regardless of cost. Consider, for example, the question of bone marrow transplants. By 2000, research had established that **this procedure**, which then cost more than $700,000, could be an effective treatment for some types of leukemia. A majority of the public want this treatment to be available to all leukemia patients. Such a demand explains why health care providers invest enormous sums of money in the latest equipment for diagnosis and treatment. A similar demand also explains why researchers continue to develop expensive technology, procedures, and drugs. **8**

Is there a solution to the problem of reduced access to health care? To answer this question, we must first answer a more basic one: Is it possible to bring about change in any of **the three factors that have been identified**? **9**

It should be possible to reduce the emphasis on crisis care that is typical of Western health care systems. We need to give greater priority to *primary health care*, which emphasizes the prevention and early diagnosis of disease through education and regular visits to a primary care doctor. In fact, many countries have already started to focus on primary health care – with good results. For example, as a result of publicity about the factors that can contribute to heart disease, many people have made changes in the way they choose to live. As a result of greater public awareness, many more people are being tested regularly for breast and colon cancer and are paying closer attention to their blood pressure. **10**

On the other hand, there is evidence that primary health care should be made more accessible to the considerable number of people it is not yet reaching, especially the young, the poor, and the less educated. For example, in spite of the information available about healthy nutrition, many Western countries, including the United States and the United Kingdom, are experiencing a growth in the rate of youth obesity, a condition that may be associated with diabetes later in life. In the United States and many European countries, the death rate from diabetes, unlike the death rate from heart disease, rose in the last decades of the twentieth century. **11**

The other two factors that drive up health care costs, however, are much less open to change. First, people in the industrial world are living longer. Second, it is natural that people will continue to demand, for themselves and their families, the best health care that science can provide. These two facts of life point to one conclusion: people will need to pay more – in taxes or insurance – to fund the quality of health care they demand. **12**

Check back for the meaning of *this procedure*. Highlight it.

Scan back through paragraphs 6–8 and number each of these three factors. Then come back and read paragraph 10.

As you continue to read, find these two factors and mark them *Factor 2* and *Factor 3*.

III. COSTS AND PRIORITIES: MEETING HEALTH CARE NEEDS IN POORER NATIONS

At first sight, developing and developed nations may seem to have 13
very different problems and priorities in health care. **In three areas**,
however, they have a great deal in common. The first of these is
HIV/AIDS, which was identified as a major problem in the United
States in the 1980s. By 2003, an estimated 38 million people in developing countries were living with HIV/AIDS, 90 percent of all global
infections.

Second, cardiovascular diseases (CVD), illnesses of the heart and 14
circulatory system, are no longer seen as exclusive to the wealthy
nations. CVD is increasing in many developing countries as lifestyles
change. Consider the recent history of Singapore, which has become
one of the wealthier developed nations of the world. Between 1940
and 1979, while life expectancy rose from forty to seventy years of
age, deaths from infectious diseases fell from 40 percent to 12 percent
of total deaths. At the same time, however, deaths from cardiovascular
diseases rose from 5 percent to 32 percent of all deaths. Similar
changes are expected worldwide as other developing nations move
away from traditional lifestyles. In 2001, the World Health Organization
(WHO) predicted that CVD would be the leading cause of death in
developing countries within ten years.

The health care systems of industrialized and developing countries 15
have a third area of common concern: a tendency to focus on crisis
care. Although they have less money to spend for health care, developing countries clearly have inherited the Western tendency to give
priority to treating disease after it has developed. Recent statistics
show that about 80 percent of health care funds in developing countries
are spent to train doctors and to build hospitals.

We have already seen that an emphasis on crisis care creates problems 16
for the industrial countries. Because crisis care is incapable of meeting
the different health care priorities of poorer nations, **it has even more
disastrous consequences there**. As Table 1.1 shows, in the world's

Scan forward through the text and highlight only the words that identify each of these areas. Number each area. Then come back and continue reading for the main idea.

Check back and highlight the meaning of *it*.

TABLE 1.1 Health Care in Wealthier and Poorer Nations

		Type of country	
		Wealthier*	Poorer†
Population with access to	safe water	99.0%	51.0%
	sanitation	97.0%	34.0%
Annual health spending per person		$2,331	$23
Population per doctor		365:1	6,903:1
Percent of children dying before age 5		0.6%	12.0%

* Australia, Belgium, Denmark, Finland, France, Germany, Holland, Sweden, Switzerland, USA
† Cameroon, Haiti, India, Laos, Mali, Nicaragua, Nigeria, Pakistan, Yemen, Zimbabwe

FUN.—August 18, 1866.

DEATH'S DISPENSARY.

OPEN TO THE POOR, GRATIS, BY PERMISSION OF THE PARISH.

This sketch records the 1866 cholera epidemic in London. Today, water-borne diseases are still a serious problem in many developing countries (see Table 1.1 on page 45).

poorest nations, children under five die at a rate that is twenty times greater than in the world's wealthiest countries. The diseases that kill them include malaria, which is controllable and treatable if it is diagnosed early. Among the other killer diseases are the so-called vaccine-preventable diseases (measles, whooping cough, diphtheria, tetanus, polio, and tuberculosis), which killed 2.1 million children in 1990. They also include simple diarrhea, which kills enormous numbers of young children and which is caused by contaminated water and food.

Although **these killer diseases** are no longer real problems for the wealthier countries, they were a major cause of death in the nineteenth and early twentiety centuries. Ultimately they were brought under control not by crisis care, but by prevention; in other words, when safe water, adequate sanitation, and mass immunization programs became available.

17

Check back for the names of *these killer diseases*. Highlight them.

There is, however, **a second reason** why infectious diseases remain 18 such an enormous problem in poorer countries. Effective public health programs are often far too expensive for these countries – even with some international assistance. As evidence of this, consider Table 1.1, which shows that the world's poorest countries cannot afford to meet even the basic health needs of their people.

To solve the most urgent health problems of developing countries, 19 experts have recommended that priority should be given to primary health care. **This approach to health care**, as we have seen, emphasizes health maintenance through disease prevention and control. Many of the developing world's deadliest diseases, the experts point out, can be prevented if clean water and adequate sanitation are provided. Other diseases can be prevented by mass vaccination programs. Still others can be controlled by effective health education that gives people information about ways to avoid malaria-carrying mosquitoes or about the importance of nutrition, especially for pregnant women and young children.

Primary health care, as we have seen, does not merely focus on 20 prevention and ignore the treatment of disease. Another priority for poorer nations is to provide timely diagnoses and basic treatment for the general populations instead of technologically advanced and expensive treatment for a few wealthy people. Under international programs, the governments of developing countries are given incentives to build community health centers and train health workers. Patients receive immediate attention from doctors, nurses, and health workers who have the necessary diagnostic training and equipment and have an adequate supply of drugs. These local health centers are much more accessible to people who need treatment than a few hospitals in the larger cities.

If poorer countries can offer **this type of health care**, the health of 21 their general populations will improve rapidly. A number of developing countries have already shown that primary health care programs can be successful. Cuba eliminated polio in 1972, even before the disease was eliminated in the United States. In 1974, the World Health Organization began a program to immunize the world's children against six vaccine-preventable diseases during their first year of life. By 1994, the vaccinations were protecting 80 percent of children and the annual number of child deaths had fallen by 3 million. Another WHO program, whose goal was to wipe out polio in the Americas, began in 1985. The goal was achieved in 1991. In that year, nearly 2 million children in Peru were vaccinated in one week after polio had been diagnosed in a two-year-old boy. The boy, Luis Fermin, recovered and proved to be the last case of polio in the Americas.

Similar successes have been achieved in the fight against diseases 22 for which no effective vaccines are available. In one area of Nigeria, deaths from diarrhea fell by 82 percent after local health workers learned to use oral rehydration therapy (ORT), a simple treatment that does not depend on complex hospital equipment or expensive drugs. By 1990, according to United Nations estimates, ORT was saving the lives of 1 million children annually. In 1992, Brazil conducted a program of malaria control that emphasized early diagnosis and

Check back to refresh your memory of the first reason. Mark it *Reason 1*. Then come back and continue reading to identify the second reason.

Check back for the meaning of *This approach to health care*. Highlight it.

Check back for the meaning of *this type of health care*. Highlight it.

The phrase *Similar successes* looks back and points forward. Highlight an example of a success in paragraph 21. Then continue reading paragraph 22 and highlight another example of a success.

treatment as well as preventing the transmission of the disease – for example, by the use of bed nets that were treated with insecticide. By 1996, malaria-related fatalities had fallen by 21 percent; in addition, an estimated 1.8 million infections and over 100,000 deaths had been prevented.

IV. A FOCUS ON THE BOTTOM LINE

Both wealthier and poorer nations would benefit if greater priority 23 were given to providing primary health care. A number of nations have already had success in informing people about the risks of CVD and AIDS. More programs of this type should produce even better results, especially if they are developed for less educated and less affluent social groups. In the wealthier countries, better access to a primary care provider would help many people lead healthier lives. In the poorer nations, of course, primary health care must include attention to basic problems of public health. Here, there is still an urgent need for much wider access to clean water, to adequate sanitation, to vaccines, to health education, and to basic medical care before the killer diseases are finally under control.

Can the world develop the needed programs of primary health 24 care? The success of WHO programs shows that we have the expertise to do so. **However, to give an honest answer,** we must not ignore the major obstacle to developing such programs – their enormous cost. In the poorer nations, providing the necessary water and sanitation demands equipment, materials, and expertise that these countries cannot afford. Primary health care programs require large numbers of trained medical workers as well as enormous supplies of vaccines, essential drugs, and basic medical equipment. Poorer countries simply do not have the resources that are necessary for **such programs**. They will therefore need massive economic and technical help from the wealthier countries.

The wealthier nations, however, have their own problems. Access 25 to high-quality health care is being reduced; at the same time, health care costs are rising and there is considerable discussion about how to pay for health care and how much to pay. In these circumstances, two basic questions remain unanswered: What kind of health care systems are the wealthy nations able and willing to fund for themselves? And how much help are these countries, who are having problems meeting the rising health care expectations of their own populations, willing to provide to other nations?

The first answer to the question in sentence 1 is positive. Do you now expect to read (a) another positive answer or (b) a less positive answer?

Check back for the meaning of *such programs*. Highlight it.

SECTION I: One Earth – Two Worlds of Health

MAIN IDEA CHECK

Here are the main ideas of each paragraph in this section of the article. Match each paragraph to its main idea. Write the number of the paragraph in the blank.

Paragraphs 1–2

_2_ A In examining health care problems and solutions, the article will show both similarities and differences between the poorer and the wealthier nations.

_1_ B In the wealthier countries, providing the best health care seems to be a very different task than in the poorer nations.

SECTION II: Health Care Costs and Access in the Wealthier Countries

MAIN IDEA CHECK

Here are the main ideas of each paragraph in this section of the article. Match each paragraph to its main idea. Write the number of the paragraph in the blank.

Paragraphs 3–8

_4_ A In a system of publicly funded health care, responses to increasing costs have reduced people's access to health care.

_5_ B In a system of employer-provided health insurance, responses to increasing costs have reduced people's access to health care.

_3_ C The high cost of health care is a major problem for the industrial countries.

_8_ D The public demands the best possible health care; this is another reason why health care costs continue to rise.

_7_ E Health care costs are high partly because an increasing number of people are living longer.

_6_ F In the health care systems of industrial countries, an emphasis on crisis care is one reason why the costs are high and continue to increase.

Paragraphs 9–12

_10_ G A greater emphasis on primary health care, which is part of the solution to high costs, is already having a positive effect on people's attitudes and behavior.

_12_ H We need to accept the fact that medical costs will continue to increase because of an aging population and our demand for high-quality health care.

_9_ I Solutions to the problem of increasing health care costs depend on whether we can change any of the factors that are driving the increase.

_11_ J There is evidence that many people need better access to important services in primary health care.

A CLOSER LOOK

Look back at Section II of the article to answer the following questions.

1 Reread paragraphs 3–5. Then complete the diagram with sentences A–C. Write the correct letter in each box.

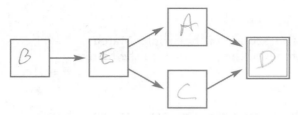

A Good health care becomes less accessible.
B Health care costs are high and rising fast.
C The providers of health insurance try to cut their expenses.

2 Reread paragraph 5. Then complete the diagram with sentences A–E. Write the correct letter in each box.

A Many employers reduce health benefits for their employees.
B Health care costs increase.
C Some employers can no longer provide health insurance for their workers.
D More patients are unable to get quality health care when they need it.
E The costs of medical insurance increase.

3 Why does the writer use the examples of Britain and the United States in paragraphs 4 and 5?

a To show that the British health service is not as good as the U.S. health care system

b To show that great advances have been made in health care in the industrial countries

c To show that rising costs ultimately cause health care to become less accessible to patients

d To show that a system of public health insurance is better than a system of employer-provided health insurance

4 Reread paragraphs 6–8. Then complete the cause and effect diagram with sentences A–F. Write the correct letter in each box.

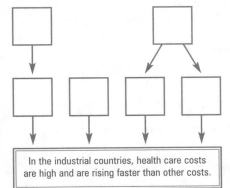

In the industrial countries, health care costs are high and are rising faster than other costs.

A Health care tends to emphasize crisis care, the treatment of disease after it becomes serious.

B Life expectancy continues to increase.

C Research continues and provides new, often expensive, drugs, medical procedures, and technology.

D To recover their costs, health care providers need to increase charges for patients.

E Larger numbers of older people create an increased demand for health care.

F The public demands the very best health care.

5 What two responses does the writer suggest for dealing with the increase in health care costs in wealthy countries?

SECTION III: Costs and Priorities: Meeting Health Care Needs in Poorer Nations

MAIN IDEA CHECK

Here are the main ideas of each paragraph in this section of the article. Match each paragraph to its main idea. Write the number of the paragraph in the blank.

Paragraphs 13–17

_14_ A Cardiovascular disease, which is usually associated with the industrial countries, is becoming a problem in developing nations.

_16_ B An emphasis on crisis care cannot solve the most urgent health problems of developing countries.

_13_ C HIV/AIDS is one problem that wealthy and poor countries have in common.

_17_ D The diseases that face developing countries today were once problems in the wealthier countries but were finally controlled by prevention.

_15_ E The health care systems of the developing world, like those of wealthier countries, tend to emphasize crisis care.

Paragraphs 18–22

_20_ F Primary health care also provides better access to early diagnosis and treatment of common diseases.

_18_ G Diarrhea, malaria, and infectious diseases remain a major problem because developing nations cannot afford to fund effective programs of basic health care.

_22_ H Primary health care programs can be successful in fighting diseases like malaria and diarrhea, for which no vaccines exist.

19   I   As a solution to their most urgent needs, developing countries need to focus on providing primary health care.

21   J   Experience shows that primary health care can have a major impact on the problem of vaccine-preventable diseases.

A CLOSER LOOK

Look back at Section III of the article to answer the following questions.

1   Why does the writer mention Singapore in the third sentence of paragraph 14?

    a   To show that life can improve for developing countries

    b   To show that we can expect CVD to increase as countries develop

    c   To show that Singapore is no longer a developing country

    d   To show that infectious diseases are no longer a major problem in Singapore

2   In which way(s) are the health problems of developing countries and those of the industrial nations similar? Circle all that apply.

    a   HIV/AIDS is a threat in both groups of nations.

    b   Vaccine-preventable diseases are no longer a problem in either type of country.

    c   Some problems in both groups are associated with the emphasis on crisis care.

    d   The answer to many of the problems in both types of countries is greater access to safe water and better sanitation.

3   Reread paragraphs 16–19 to identify the main cause and effect connections that explain the massive health problems in developing countries. Then complete the cause and effect diagram with sentences A–D. Write the correct letter in each box.

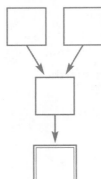

A   Funding for public health programs and primary health care is inadequate.

B   Death rates for children under five are extremely high.

C   Resources are very limited in poor developing countries.

D   Health care systems in poor developing countries have tended to focus on crisis care.

4   Why does the writer mention Cuban and World Health Organization programs in paragraph 21?

    a   To show that primary health care programs can be successful against vaccine-preventable diseases

    b   To show that primary health care could also help people in the United States

    c   To show that polio is no longer a problem in some parts of the developing world

    d   To show how close the world was to eliminating polio in 1991

MAIN IDEA CHECK

Here are the main ideas of each paragraph in this section of the article. Match each paragraph to its main idea. Write the number of the paragraph in the blank.

Paragraphs 23–25

_____ A Because wealthier countries have difficulty funding the heath care their people demand, it is not clear how much financial assistance they can afford to give for health care in poorer countries.

_____ B Providing greater access to primary health care would improve people's health in both poorer and wealthier countries.

_____ C The task of developing effective programs of primary health care is made very difficult, especially in poorer countries, by the enormous cost of such programs.

A CLOSER LOOK

Look back at Section IV of the article to answer the following questions.

1 According to the conclusion (paragraphs 23–25) of the article, what do the health care systems of industrial countries and developing nations have in common? Circle all that apply.

  a They are facing the same threats to the health of their populations.

  b They would benefit from greater attention to primary health care.

  c Their most urgent need is to improve the quality of their water.

  d They are having problems funding adequate health care.

2 Is the writer sure that the health care problems of the world will be solved? Give evidence from the article's conclusion to support your answer.

BEYOND THE READING

Research

Do Internet or library research to find additional, up-to-date information on a topic in health care that interests you. Here are two suggestions.

  ▢ A health problem in the news at present
  ▢ Recent advances in medical treatment or research

Discussion

Discuss the following with a partner.

  ▢ The health care system in your country – its strengths and weaknesses

Writing

Write a short report on the results of your research or your discussion.

MAKING CONNECTIONS

The vocabulary in these two exercises comes from all the readings in Unit 1. The exercises will help you see how writers make connections across sentences in a text.

EXERCISE 1: CONNECTIONS BETWEEN SENTENCES

Read the numbered sentence. Then choose and circle the sentence, a or b, that logically follows. Then, from the box, decide how the sentence you chose connects to the first. Write *A*, *B*, or *C* to identify the connection.

A It describes a result of what is reported in the first sentence.

B It describes a better response to a problem than the response in the first sentence.

C It adds specific details to support the more general information in the first sentence.

_C_ 1 Heart disease is often associated with a person's lifestyle.

   a Smoking, a nutritionally poor diet, stress, and insufficient exercise are all factors that contribute to the development of the disease.

   b Modern technology allows doctors to perform surgery on patients who are suffering from heart disease.

_B_ 2 Experience has shown conclusively that we cannot afford to wait until heart disease and cancer are established and then rely exclusively on drugs and surgery to fight them.

   a Surgeons, for example, can perform complex operations on many seriously ill patients.

   b We need to provide access to procedures for early diagnosis and to information on prevention.

_A_ 3 Historically, mass immunization has made it possible to control, and sometimes even eliminate, some infectious diseases.

   a Influenza, for example, is still common and is estimated to cause ten thousand deaths annually in the United States.

   b In countries where an effective vaccine has been available since the late 1950s, for example, there have been few or no cases of polio.

_A_ 4 In the 1990s, governments, research institutions, biotechnology companies, and investors became aware of the huge potential – economic, scientific, and commercial – of genetic research.

   a This realization led to an enormous growth of interest in, and financial support for, the research.

   b This pessimism prevented researchers from making the advances they had thought possible in genetic medicine.

<u>C</u> 5 A 2002 United Nations study on AIDS awareness and behavior provided evidence that the existing AIDS education programs were often <u>ineffective</u>.

   a The study showed that such programs had reduced ignorance about the disease and about ways to prevent its transmission.

   <u>b</u> In six African nations with such programs, about 50 percent of women respondents still did not know that HIV/AIDS can be transmitted through sexual contact.

EXERCISE 2: CONNECTIONS WITHIN PARAGRAPHS

Make a clear paragraph by putting sentences A, B, and C into the best order after the numbered sentence. Write the letters in the correct order. The boldface words help you identify continuing ideas.

1 The death rate from cardiovascular disease (CVD), which includes heart disease, high blood pressure, and strokes, has been falling since the 1960s, with a decrease of 35% in the last twenty years. ____ ____ ____

A	B	C
A **second factor** is the recent advances that have considerably improved the diagnosis and treatment of CVD.	To what can we attribute **this encouraging development**?	**One factor** is people's willingness to make lifestyle changes in order to reduce their risk of CVD.

2 Although many patients benefit from advances in heart surgery, critics have concluded that an overemphasis on the surgical treatment of cardiovascular disease has at least two considerable disadvantages. ____ ____ ____

A	B	C
It attracts financial resources away from the prevention programs that, according to experts, are urgently needed.	To recover the enormous costs of the necessary expertise and equipment, hospitals raise their charges for all patients.	**It** is **also** a factor in the increasing costs of health care.

3 In a number of cases, early experimental treatments achieved results that justified cautious optimism about the potential of gene therapy. ____ ____ ____

A	B	C
In **the same year**, other teams of researchers reported the encouraging results of gene therapy in patients who were suffering from hemophilia and skin cancer.	In 2000, **for example**, French doctors reported success with a procedure in which they introduced a normally functioning gene into three babies who suffered from a fatal immune deficiency.	Ten months later, **the children's** immune systems appeared to be functioning normally, evidence that **the normal gene** had taken over the work of the defective one.

4 The task of developing an effective program to prevent AIDS is made more complex by a number of factors. ___ ___ ___

A **This reluctance** can frequently be seen in the early responses of governments to the growing threat of AIDS.

B For example, in spite of evidence that the disease was spreading rapidly, the White House did not allow its own surgeon general to make public statements about AIDS for four years.

C **The main obstacle** is people's reluctance to speak openly about the ways HIV/AIDS is most often transmitted – through unprotected sex and through contaminated needles in illegal drug use.

5 A greater focus on primary health care (PHC) would benefit public health in the United States. ___ ___ ___

A For the same reason, **their** children frequently do not complete their programs of vaccination.

B Because many low-income **Americans** cannot afford annual physical examinations, they tend to be diagnosed with serious diseases late, when survival rates are lower.

C Both of **these problems** would be helped by more emphasis on PHC, which provides patients with easy access to regular assessments of their health needs.

Living in a
Multicultural Society

SKILLS AND STRATEGIES 4-6
- Main Ideas
- Unfavored and Favored Views
- Reduced Relative Clauses

READINGS
- The Age of Immigration
- Who Are Today's Immigrants?
- Views on Multiculturalism
- Experimental Evidence on the Nature of Prejudice
- The Challenge of Diversity

SKILLS AND STRATEGIES 4
MAIN IDEAS

The main idea is the most important idea that a writer expresses in a paragraph. Often, but not always, the main idea is stated clearly in one sentence. The other sentences in the paragraph usually support the main idea by providing details. Identifying main ideas helps your academic reading.

EXAMPLES & EXPLANATIONS

Good readers form hypotheses, or careful guesses, about the main idea of a paragraph as they are reading the first sentence. As they read further, they keep testing to see whether their hypothesis is correct or needs to be changed.

Example

To answer the urgent health care needs of developing countries, experts argue, we should give priority to primary health care (PHC).[1] PHC emphasizes the prevention of disease.[2] Many deadly diseases, the experts point out, can be prevented if clean water and adequate sanitation are provided.[3] Many other illnesses can be prevented by mass vaccination programs.[4]

Explanation

A good reader will find the paragraph's main idea by developing and testing hypotheses in the following way.

"After reading sentence 1, my first hypothesis (H_1) for the main idea of this paragraph is: *To respond to the most serious health problems in developing countries, we need to focus on primary health care (PHC)*.

"Sentence 2 gives more information about PHC. I need to revise my first hypothesis. Perhaps the main idea is: *PHC, which stresses prevention, is the best response to the worst health problems in developing countries*. Let me try this as my revised hypothesis (H_2).

"Sentence 3 gives me an example of how deadly diseases can be prevented. Therefore, I can continue with my revised hypothesis (H_2).

"Sentence 4 gives another example of successful disease prevention. I can keep the revised hypothesis (H_2)."

STRATEGIES

These three strategies will help you identify main ideas.

- Start looking for the main idea as soon as you begin reading a paragraph. Use the strategy called Early Hypothesis Formation and Testing (EHFT). (See the flowchart on the opposite page for how this works.)
- If you are still unsure of the main idea when you finish a paragraph, look for examples and ask yourself, "What idea do these examples support?"
- At the beginning of a paragraph, writers may repeat an important idea from the previous paragraph. This continuing idea can help you identify the main idea of the previous paragraph.

Early Hypothesis Formation and Testing

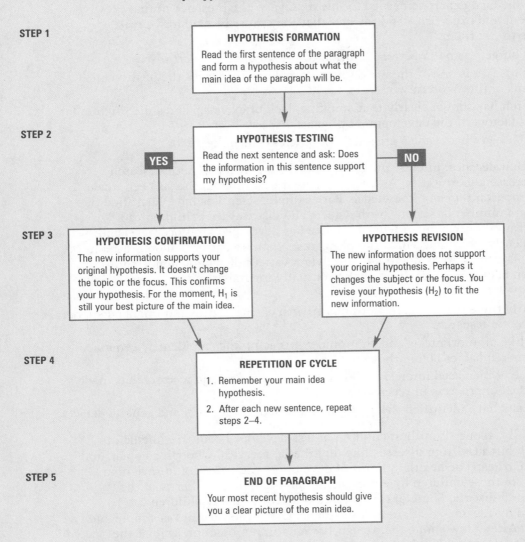

STEP 1

HYPOTHESIS FORMATION

Read the first sentence of the paragraph and form a hypothesis about what the main idea of the paragraph will be.

STEP 2

HYPOTHESIS TESTING

Read the next sentence and ask: Does the information in this sentence support my hypothesis?

YES

NO

STEP 3

HYPOTHESIS CONFIRMATION

The new information supports your original hypothesis. It doesn't change the topic or the focus. This confirms your hypothesis. For the moment, H_1 is still your best picture of the main idea.

HYPOTHESIS REVISION

The new information does not support your original hypothesis. Perhaps it changes the subject or the focus. You revise your hypothesis (H_2) to fit the new information.

STEP 4

REPETITION OF CYCLE

1. Remember your main idea hypothesis.
2. After each new sentence, repeat steps 2–4.

STEP 5

END OF PARAGRAPH

Your most recent hypothesis should give you a clear picture of the main idea.

SKILL PRACTICE 1

Use the EHFT strategy as you read each paragraph. Highlight your first hypothesis for the main idea. Then, when necessary, circle any words that cause you to revise your hypothesis. Finally, choose the sentence (a–d) that best matches your final main idea hypothesis.

1   Heart surgery, in spite of the enormous progress it has made since the 1970s, still has a number of weaknesses as an answer to heart disease. First, the exciting world of heart surgery attracts research and public interest away from the question of preventing heart disease. Second, it attracts money that could be used instead for programs to educate the public about the factors that contribute to heart disease – smoking, a lack of regular exercise, and fat in our diet. Third, the emphasis on the surgical treatment of heart disease may cause

doctors to perform unnecessary surgery. In a hospital that has the equipment and the medical expertise needed for heart surgery, the presence of that equipment and expertise – and the fact that they must be paid for – creates pressure to use them.

a Heart surgery is not a perfect solution to the problem of heart disease.

b Heart disease is one of the most serious problems that faces the health care systems of the Western world.

c Research has shown clearly that smoking, lack of exercise, and a diet high in fat are all factors in the development of heart disease.

d Heart surgery has made a great deal of progress since the 1970s.

2   In recent decades, interest in, and financial support for, genetic research have increased enormously. As a result, a great deal of progress has been made in this important area of knowledge. For example, scientists have identified the genes for a number of serious birth defects and diseases that children can inherit from their parents. Medical science has developed amniocentesis and, more recently, chorionic villus sampling, tests that are performed on pregnant women. The tests allow doctors to discover a variety of genetic abnormalities in unborn babies, abnormalities that are usually incurable and often result in death.

a Recently there has been an enormous growth of interest in, and financial support for, genetic research.

b Tests like amniocentesis and chorionic villus sampling can identify genetic problems in babies before they are born.

c Because of increased interest and financial support, genetic research has made a great deal of progress in recent years.

d Scientists have identified the genes for some serious diseases and genetic defects.

3   Annually, about 12 million children in less-developed countries die before their fifth birthday from diseases like diphtheria, measles, whooping cough, and simple diarrhea. The health systems of developing countries could save many, if not all, of these children by emphasizing the prevention rather than the treatment of disease. Some of the diseases that kill so many children can be prevented by vaccines that are now available. Using the vaccines is simple and effective. After a few shots, the patient has a natural protection against the disease. On the other hand, treating the diseases after they occur is often not effective; it is expensive and difficult and requires drugs, facilities, and the medical expertise that many developing countries cannot provide. Other killer diseases, such as simple diarrhea, are closely associated with unhygienic living conditions and can easily be prevented if clean water and adequate sanitation are provided.

a Diseases like diarrhea are no longer a serious problem in the industrial world because of new drugs and other improvements in medical treatment.

b In developing countries, 12 million children die before their fifth birthday from diphtheria, whooping cough, polio, measles, and diarrhea.

c Vaccines are very effective against many of the diseases that kill children in developing countries.

d If the health systems of developing countries emphasized disease prevention, they could save many of the 12 million children who die every year.

SKILL PRACTICE 2

For each numbered item, use the EHFT strategy as you read the first paragraph. Then, in the first sentence of the next paragraph, identify the continuing idea that might help you recognize the main idea of the first paragraph. Finally, choose the sentence (a–d) that best expresses the main idea of the paragraph.

1   What can be done to fight cardiovascular disease (CVD)? The surgical treatment of heart disease continues to benefit patients in countries where the necessary expertise, equipment, and other resources are available. However, by itself such treatment is not an adequate response to CVD – for at least two reasons. First, surgery is enormously expensive and is a burden even for the rich nations that can afford to offer it. For developing countries, which often do not have the necessary financial, technological, or human resources, large treatment programs are simply not possible. Second, where the resources are available, an emphasis on the surgical treatment of CVD can sometimes result in the ineffective use of those resources. In the late 1980s, for example, a government report found that only 15 percent of patients benefited from a type of heart operation that doctors were performing more than 100,000 times a year in the United States.
    For these reasons, health experts have concluded that a global strategy to fight CVD must emphasize prevention of the disease through community and government programs.

a The surgical treatment of heart disease is one solution to the global problem of cardiovascular disease.

b Developing countries simply do not have the resources to fight CVD with surgery.

c Heart surgery is very expensive and a financial burden even to those wealthier countries that can afford to offer it.

d Surgery alone is not the answer to global CVD because it is very expensive and may use resources ineffectively.

2   The health care systems of developing countries have another quality in common with those of wealthier nations: a tendency to focus on treatment. Developing countries have inherited the Western preference for treatment. Although they have much less money to spend for health care, their systems also give priority to treatment. Recent statistics show that about 80 percent of health care funds in developing countries are spent to train doctors and to build hospitals.
    There are two reasons for this emphasis on treatment.

a There are two reasons why developing countries focus on treatment in their health care systems.

b Like those in wealthier countries, the health care systems of developing countries also emphasize the treatment of disease.

c Developing countries spend the major part of their health care funds to train doctors and build hospitals.

d The health care systems of developing countries are similar to those of wealthier countries.

3   There are two reasons for this emphasis on treatment. First, many doctors in developing countries have received their medical training in the industrial countries or in systems that follow Western traditions. As a result, they tend to have attitudes that are typical of Western medicine. Naturally, the type of system they want for their own countries is the kind that seems successful in the West. Therefore, they support a system that focuses on treatment, even though it may not be the most realistic answer to the public health problems in their countries.

The second reason for the emphasis on treatment in developing countries is a commercial one.

a Doctors in developing countries tend to have their training in the wealthier countries or in systems that follow Western traditions.

b There are two reasons for the emphasis on treatment in the health care systems of developing countries.

c A health care system that emphasizes treatment may not be the best answer to the health problems of developing countries.

d One reason for the emphasis on treatment in developing countries is the Western-style medical training of their doctors.

4   A number of developing countries have already shown that primary health care programs can be successful. Cuba eliminated polio in 1972, even before the disease was eliminated in the United States. In 1974, the World Health Organization began a program to immunize the world's children against six common vaccine-preventable diseases during their first year of life. By 1994, the vaccinations were protecting 80 percent of children and the annual number of child deaths had fallen by 3 million. Another WHO program, whose goal was to wipe out polio in the Americas, began in 1985. The goal was achieved in 1991. In that year, nearly 2 million children in Peru were vaccinated in one week after polio had been diagnosed in a two-year-old boy. The boy, Luis Fermin, recovered and proved to be the last case of polio in the Americas.

Similar successes are to be found in diseases for which no effective vaccines are available.

a Primary health care programs have been very effective in fighting vaccine-preventable diseases in some poorer nations.

b Cuba eliminated polio before the United States achieved the same goal.

c By 1994, the World Health Organization had succeeded in vaccinating 80 percent of the world's children against six killer diseases.

d The World Health Organization program gave the polio vaccine to 2 million children in Peru.

READING 1
THE AGE OF IMMIGRATION

GETTING INTO THE TOPIC
It is a good idea to look at illustrations to get an idea of the topic of an article. Look at the photograph in this article and discuss the following questions with a partner.

1 When do you think the immigrants in the photograph arrived in the United States, and where did they come from?
2 How was the journey across the Atlantic for the majority of these immigrants?
3 How was life in the United States for this generation of immigrants?

GETTING A FIRST IDEA ABOUT THE ARTICLE
You will understand an article more easily if you can get an idea of its organization and content before you start reading. A quick way to do this is to read the first sentence of each paragraph. First sentences can help you because they often introduce the ideas that the writer will develop and explain in that paragraph.

For each paragraph, read the first sentence and think of a question that you expect this paragraph to answer. Then choose the question below that is most like your question. The first paragraph has been done for you as an example.

_____ A What kinds of linguistic, cultural, and educational backgrounds did the immigrants have?

__1__ B Why is the period 1820–1920 called the most significant in U.S. immigration?

_____ C What was achieved by the sacrifices of new immigrants?

__2__ D What reasons did immigrants have for leaving Europe?

_____ E What sacrifices did immigrants have to make?

_____ F What economic difficulties caused people to emigrate to the United States?

_____ G What was the second major development that occurred in the later generations of immigrant families?

WHILE YOU READ
As you read the article, stop at the end of each sentence that contains boldface text and follow the instructions in the box in the margin.

The Age of Immigration

European immigration to the United States has been continuous 1
since 1607, but the most significant period of such immigration
occurred between 1820 and 1920. During this time, a total of 32 million
immigrants arrived in the country in successive waves. For the first
seventy years, almost all came from northwestern Europe, especially
from Britain, Ireland, Scandinavia, and Germany. (See Figure 2.1.)
Then, as the flow of immigrants from these countries declined, large
numbers of people began to make the journey across the Atlantic
from Italy, Hungary, Poland, Russia, Greece, and other countries of
southern and eastern Europe. (See Table 2.1.)

Scan forward through the paragraph and number the factors. Then come back and continue reading for the main idea.

A number of factors lay behind people's decision to leave their 2
European homes. Some people were escaping from political oppression
in their homelands. Others, especially in Britain and Germany, had
acquired technical skills that allowed them to seek jobs on the open
market. For still others, threats to their physical survival were a factor.
The start of the great period of Irish immigration (1845–1900), for
example, is associated with a disease that destroyed the potato crop
and caused starvation throughout Ireland. The Jews of eastern Europe
saw moving to North America as a way to escape widespread prejudice
and violence in which thousands of Jews were murdered.

Scan the paragraph and highlight words or short phrases that suggest *economic hardship*. Then come back and continue reading.

Although each immigrant had his or her reasons for leaving home, 3
one factor – **economic hardship** – was behind most of the decisions to
risk an uncertain future in America. Nineteenth-century Europe was
a continent in economic transition. The old agricultural system that
depended on large numbers of unskilled workers was disintegrating
and leaving many of the workers unemployed. Other workers found
themselves replaced by steam-driven machines. The population was
increasing and crowding into the towns and cities that industrialization
was creating. This transition created unemployment and poverty for
masses of people – conditions that led many to consider starting a
new life in a new country.

What does *However* suggest about the main idea of the paragraph? Should you (a) keep your first hypothesis (H$_1$) or (b) change it?

Immigrants brought with them a wide diversity of languages, 4
cultures, and educational backgrounds. **However**, whether Irish or
Italian, educated or illiterate, skilled or unskilled, industrial worker
or teacher, farm worker or lawyer, most immigrants had two qualities
in common. First, because the great majority were between fifteen
and thirty-five years old, most had the energy of youth. Second, they

TABLE 2.1 The Age of Immigration 1820–1920: Immigrant totals and origins

Region of Origin	1820–1890	1891–1920
Northwest Europe*	12.5 million	4.6 million
South and East Europe†	1.1 million	11.4 million

* Belgium, France, Germany, Ireland, Netherlands, Scandinavia, Switzerland,
United Kingdom
† Austria-Hungary, Greece, Italy, Poland, Portugal, Russia, Spain

These European immigrants are on their way to the United States in 1910.

were willing to make sacrifices for their future in a country they considered the land of opportunity.

And considerable sacrifices were demanded from them. They left 5 home with little more than a suitcase to carry their possessions. In the United States, both men and women worked long hours for low wages. The majority lived in unhealthy conditions in the overcrowded immigrant neighborhoods of the large cities of the Northeast, Great Lakes, and midwestern states. They suffered widespread discrimination as each wave of new immigrants met many of the same prejudices and fears that earlier immigrants had experienced. Some of the least fortunate arrived during the Civil War, were immediately persuaded to join the Union army, and were killed in the fighting. Few of the first generation managed to achieve the prosperity that was the dream of every immigrant.

The result of the first generation's sacrifices first became visible in 6 the generations that followed. Within three generations, most non-English-speaking immigrant families had acquired a new first language. The children and grandchildren of immigrants who spoke Swedish, German, Italian, and more than twenty other languages became native speakers of English. This process of language shift is one of the most significant features of immigration history in the

As you continue reading, answer this question: "Does the paragraph describe (a) positive or (b) negative aspects of immigrants' lives?"

Read the first sentence of paragraph 7 and highlight the continuing idea in it. Use this idea to help you identify the main idea of paragraph 6.

7

United States. Although the process did not guarantee these generations would become wealthy and successful, it was essential for economic advancement and for **full integration into the mainstream of society**.

The shift to English was accompanied by another change that took 7 place in second-generation immigrant families. While first-generation immigrants still tended to think of themselves as Irish, English, Italian, or German, their children and grandchildren clearly considered themselves American. A story that was told by an English immigrant symbolizes a process that must have taken place in most immigrant households. One day the immigrant's son came home from school, where his class had been learning about the American Revolution. He explained to his English-born father what had happened in words similar to these: **"You had the king's army, and we had only a bunch of farmers, but we beat you anyway."** Out of the diversity of more than thirty countries and almost as many languages, a generation appeared that felt itself to be truly American.

Highlight the sentence in the paragraph that this story illustrates.

MAIN IDEA CHECK

Here are the main ideas of each paragraph in the article. Match each paragraph to its main idea. Write the number of the paragraph in the blank.

___2___ A Immigrants had a number of different reasons for wanting to leave home.

___6___ B Within three generations, immigrant families spoke English as their first language, a development that was necessary for their economic progress and full membership in American society.

___4___ C In spite of their differences, the great majority of immigrants were young and ready to make sacrifices for a better future.

___7___ D The second and third generations of immigrant families thought of themselves as Americans.

___1___ E Thirty-two million immigrants came to the United States from all over Europe between 1820 and 1920.

___3___ F Difficult economic conditions in their native country were the main reason why Europeans decided to move to the United States.

___5___ G In the United States, the lives of many immigrants were very difficult.

A CLOSER LOOK

Look back at the article to answer the following questions.

1 The highest number of German, Irish, British, and Scandinavian immigrants arrived after 1890. True or False?

2 Some immigrants left their home countries in Europe because of political oppression. True or False?

3 What brought about difficult economic conditions in nineteenth-century Europe?

   a An increase in population

   b The change to an industrial society

   c The decline of traditional agriculture

   (d) All of the above

4 In paragraph 5, why does the writer report the working conditions of immigrants in the United States, the prejudice they experienced, and their unhealthy living conditions?

   a To show the improvements that occurred in immigrants' lives in the United States

   b To show the sacrifices that immigrants made to establish new lives in the United States

   c To show the way Americans took advantage of new immigrants

   d To show that discrimination was common in the United States at that time

5 What, in the writer's opinion, is the significance of language shift in immigrant families?

   a It made it certain that later generations would become prosperous members of U.S. society.

   b It is an example of a sacrifice that immigrants were expected to make.

   c It was necessary for economic success and acceptance into U.S. society.

   d It was not a factor that influenced whether an immigrant family was successful or not.

VOCABULARY STUDY: SYNONYMS

Find words in the article that are similar in meaning to the following.

1 important (adj) Par. 1 *significant*

2 to get away from a threat (v) Par. 2 *escape*

3 to get something by learning (v) Par. 2 *acquired*

4 a hunger that can lead to death (n) Par. 2 *famine*

5 behavior that is intended to hurt people (n) Par. 2 *threat*

6 unable to read or write (adj) Par. 4 *illiterate*

7 things that a person gives up for something more important (n) Par. 4 *sacrifice*

8 things that belong to a person (n) Par. 5 *possessions*

9 the unfair treatment of a group of people (n) Par. 5 *discrimination*

10 an unfair opinion that a person forms before having enough information (n) Par. 5 *prejudice*

11 financial success (n) Par. 5 *prosperity*

12 people from a similar age group (n) Par. 6 *generation*

13 able to be seen (adj) Par. 6 *visible*

14 a typical quality of something (n) Par. 6 *characteristic feature*

15 to promise that something will happen (v) Par. 6 *guarantee*

VOCABULARY STUDY: WORDS IN CONTEXT

Complete the sentences with words from the list below. If necessary, review the words in the Key Vocabulary from the Readings on page 251.

process	oppression	integrated	diversity	in transition
hardships	in succession	declined	flow	symbol

1 Language shift is the technical name for the _process_ by which a group of people move from one first language to a new first language.

2 You know that an immigrant family is becoming _integrated_ into its new society if language shift takes place in its second or third generation.

3 One feature of Indian society is the _diversity_ of languages that are spoken there. The country has more than 1,600 different languages.

4 Many immigrants to America left Europe to escape the religious _opression_ that caused friends and family members to suffer.

5 Nineteenth-century Europe was a continent _in transition_. Machines were replacing workers in agriculture and unemployment was rising.

6 The Statue of Liberty may be the world's best-known _symbol_ of freedom. For millions of immigrants, it signified the hope of a better future.

7 For three years _in succession_ in the 1840s, a new disease destroyed the potatoes in Ireland.

8 In the late 1840s, the _flow_ of Irish immigrants into the United States became very strong.

9 Before 1840, the population of Ireland had reached over 8 million. Then it _declined_ rapidly and by 1890 it was only 5 million.

10 Life in America had its own _hardships_ for Irish immigrants in the 1850s. Because of anti-Irish prejudice, they had difficulties getting good jobs.

BEYOND THE READING

Research
Do Internet or library research to find information on one of these subjects:
- Immigration (past and present) from your country into the United States
- Immigration (past and present) into your own country from other countries

Discussion
Discuss the following question with a partner.
- What difficulties might an immigrant or a visitor to your country experience?

Writing
Write a short report on the results of your research or your discussion.

READING 2
WHO ARE TODAY'S IMMIGRANTS?

GETTING INTO THE TOPIC

Read the article's title and examine the figure on page 70. Then discuss the following questions with a partner.

1 Why are many of today's immigrants to the United States not from Europe but from other parts of the world?
2 What might today's immigrants have in common with the European immigrants of the nineteenth and twentieth centuries?

GETTING A FIRST IDEA ABOUT THE ARTICLE

Read the first sentence of paragraph 1. Think of a question that you expect this paragraph to answer and match it to a question below. Continue in the same way for paragraphs 2–5. Write the number of the paragraph in the blank.

_____ A How do today's immigrants differ from earlier European immigrants?

_____ B Why are ethnic communities important for today's immigrants to the United States?

_____ C In what ways is life in the United States difficult for today's immigrants?

_____ D What is the significance of ethnic neighborhoods in today's United States?

_____ E Who are these new immigrants to the United States?

WHILE YOU READ

As you read the article, stop at the end of each sentence that contains boldface text and follow the instructions in the box in the margin.

Who Are Today's Immigrants?

Today a new first generation of immigrants is pursuing its dream **1** of a new life in the United States. The backgrounds and experiences of these immigrants are **in some ways different** from those of the typical European immigrant of the nineteenth and early twentieth centuries. Although Europeans are still arriving, the majority of contemporary immigrants come from Asia and Latin America (see Figure 2.1) and include refugees from war-torn parts of the world. In addition, some writers have claimed that a greater proportion of the new immigrants are well-educated, but this claim has been challenged and remains unproven. However, it is clear that many of the better-trained, more prosperous immigrants are not moving into ethnic neighborhoods but instead favor middle-class suburbs. Lastly, the United States of the twenty-first century is no longer expanding its industrial base. Nor is it creating the number of factory jobs that were available for the earlier immigrants.

The differences between modern immigrants and earlier European **2** immigrants cannot be ignored in any thorough analysis of the topic. The differences, **however**, should not be interpreted to mean that the lives and attitudes of modern immigrants are completely different from those of the Europeans who preceded them. In fact, today's immigrants in many ways are following the patterns that were established by earlier immigrants.

Although some new immigrants live in middle-class suburbs, **3** Asian and Latin ethnic neighborhoods are alive and well in cities across the United States. For many of today's immigrants, these neighborhoods function in the same way as immigrant neighborhoods traditionally functioned for Europeans – as the place to find employment or start a business that serves the ethnic community.

For immigrants who don't live in ethnic neighborhoods, the **4** immigrant community remains **an important part of their working and social lives**. Although its members may not live near each other, the community provides a network of connections and contacts like those in ethnic neighborhoods. Thus, although an ethnic community may not be identified with a specific neighborhood, for the new immigrants, it functions as ethnic neighborhoods have traditionally

Scan forward and highlight words that introduce each of these differences. Number the differences. Then come back and continue reading the article.

Will the article now focus on (a) the differences between past and present immigrants or (b) the similarities?

As you continue reading, look for specific examples that support the general idea in this sentence. Number them.

FIGURE 2.1 Origins of Immigrants to the United States: 1901–1910 and 1991–2000

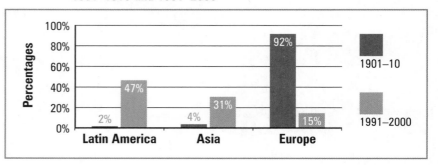

functioned. It supports them by providing opportunities to socialize and attend religious services with people who know their language and culture. Further, for more recent immigrants wishing to establish businesses, it is a source of both financing and labor. And finally, through the ethnic community, new immigrants can find employers who are willing to hire non-English speakers.

Finally, the new immigrants are also like those of a hundred years 5 ago **in their willingness to make sacrifices.** In their businesses, they work long hours to compete with economically stronger businesses. Some workers accept jobs of lower status than the jobs they had at home. Some, especially those who open stores in neighborhoods that are populated mainly by other ethnic groups, face the hostility of people who may resent their economic success or their mere presence in the neighborhood. For today's new immigrants, as it was for the generations of Europeans who preceded them, adjusting to life in their new country has its own challenges and hardships.

> As you continue reading, number each example that supports the general idea in this sentence.

MAIN IDEA CHECK

Here are the main ideas of each paragraph in the article. Match each paragraph to its main idea. Write the number of the paragraph in the blank.

_____ A The ethnic community is as important for the new immigrants as it was for earlier European immigrants.

_____ B New ethnic neighborhoods are functioning the way the earlier European neighborhoods once did.

_____ C Today's immigrants to the United States are somewhat different from the European immigrants of many years ago.

_____ D Modern immigrants make sacrifices to live in the United States.

_____ E The lives of today's immigrants are similar in many ways to those of the European immigrants who came to the United States in the nineteenth and early twentieth centuries.

A CLOSER LOOK

Look back at the article to answer the following questions.

1 It has been established that there are more well-educated professionals among today's immigrants than there were among the earlier European immigrants. True or False?

2 For which purpose(s) do modern immigrants use the networks in their immigrant communities? Circle all that apply.

   a To look for business loans

   b To find employees for their businesses

   c To spend their free time

   d To find jobs for themselves

3 Some of today's first-generation immigrants live in nonethnic neighborhoods. True or False?

4 What experience(s) do today's immigrants have in common with the European immigrants of the nineteenth and early twentieth centuries? Circle all that apply.

a Difficulty adjusting to life in the United States
b The support of immigrant communities
c Their countries of origin
d The need to make sacrifices
e Jobs in traditional industries
f Jobs and homes in ethnic neighborhoods

5 The writer is more interested in the similarities between today's immigrants and earlier European immigrants than in the differences. True or False?

VOCABULARY STUDY: SYNONYMS

Find words in the article that are similar in meaning to the following.

1 to try to reach *(v)* Par. 1
2 existing today *(adj)* Par. 1
3 to say or write that something is true without proving it *(v)* Par. 1
4 to question if something is really true *(v)* Par. 1
5 an examination of something in order to understand it *(n)* Par. 2
6 to explain the meaning of something *(v)* Par. 2
7 to be before someone or something *(v)* Par. 2
8 a group of people with something in common *(n)* Par. 3
9 a group of connected things or people *(n)* Par. 4
10 workers *(n)* Par. 4
11 to employ; to give someone a job *(v)* Par. 4
12 importance in society *(n)* Par. 5
13 strong feelings of dislike *(n)* Par. 5
14 to feel angry because of being treated unfairly *(v)* Par. 5
15 to change in order to fit new circumstances *(v)* Par. 5

VOCABULARY REVIEW: SAME OR DIFFERENT

The following pairs of sentences contain vocabulary from Readings 1 and 2. Write *S* in the blank if the two sentences have the same meaning. Write *D* if the meanings are different.

_____ 1 The flow of immigrants into the United States from Europe declined significantly after 1925.

After 1925, there was a significant expansion of European immigration to the United States.

_____ 2 The process of adjustment to a new culture can be a difficult experience.

Getting used to life in a new culture can be a real challenge.

_____ 3 It generally took two or three generations before non-English-speaking immigrant families were a fully integrated part of American society.

For immigrant families who did not speak English, the process of full integration into American society was not usually completed until the second or third generation.

_____ 4 Contemporary immigrants tend to look to their ethnic communities as places to find jobs or employees to work for them.

For today's immigrants, their ethnic communities function as a source of employers willing to hire them or of labor for their own businesses.

_____ 5 An analysis of the language that immigrants choose to speak shows a clear pattern: within three generations, most families have shifted to English.

By analyzing English and finding patterns in it, successive generations of immigrants have been able to acquire English.

_____ 6 After 1970, the proportion of immigrants from Asia who entered the United States was much greater than in the preceding decades of the century.

The flow of Asian immigrants into the United States declined considerably in the last decades of the twentieth century.

_____ 7 A few immigrants, unable to make the transition to U.S. culture, returned home.

A small number of immigrants returned home after failing to become prosperous in America.

_____ 8 In the past, competition for jobs caused different ethnic groups to be hostile toward, and resentful of, each other.

In the past, groups of different ethnic backgrounds competed for work; this caused hostility and resentment to develop between them.

BEYOND THE READING

Research
Do Internet or library research to find additional, up-to-date information on culture shock.

Discussion
Discuss the following questions with a partner:
- If you are studying English outside your native country: In which ways does the behavior of a speaker of English seem strange to you? How have you changed since you've been living in this country?
- If you are studying English in your native country: In addition to learning your language, what are the most important social behaviors you would advise English speakers to learn in order to get along well in your culture?

Writing
Write a short report on the results of your research or your discussion.

SKILLS AND STRATEGIES 5
UNFAVORED AND FAVORED VIEWS

Writers sometimes present two different views on an issue. The first view may be common; the second view, however, is the one that the writer considers better, or *favors*. Recognizing and understanding this type of organization will improve your academic reading.

EXAMPLES & EXPLANATIONS

Example

It seems to be a reasonable assumption that the health care problems in developing nations are very different from those that face industrial countries.[1] However, we would be seriously mistaken if we accept this assumption.[2] In fact, the reality is that health care systems throughout the world are facing many of the same general challenges and some of the same specific problems.[3] AIDS, for example, is a major threat in both industrial and developing countries.[4]

Explanation

Sentence 1 contains an idea about differences in health care problems for developing and industrial countries. The word *assumption* is a View Marker, a word that tells readers to expect an opinion, not a fact.

Sentence 2 begins with *However,* a Contrast Marker. It tells readers to expect information that disagrees with sentence 1. The word *mistaken* is an Assessment Marker, a word that judges (here negatively) the view that is expressed in the first sentence.

Sentence 3 offers a different view of health care problems around the world – that they are often the same. The words *in fact* and *reality* emphasize that the second view, the writer's favored view, represents the truth.

Sentence 4 contains an example to support the favored view.

THE LANGUAGE OF UNFAVORED AND FAVORED VIEWS

A text that contains unfavored and favored views first introduces views and then assesses them. In such texts, therefore, we find View Markers, Contrast Markers, and Assessment Markers.

VIEW MARKERS			
VERBS		**NOUNS**	
to accuse	to criticize	accusation	doubt
to allege	to doubt	allegation	idea
to argue	to imagine	analysis	impression
to assume	to interpret	argument	interpretation
to believe	to perceive	assumption	judgment
to blame	to regard	belief	notion
to charge	to seem	blame	opinion
to claim	to suggest	charge	perception
to conclude	to think	claim	theory
to consider	to view	conclusion	thought
		criticism	view

CONTRAST MARKERS

but
however
in theory . . . in practice
on the other hand
yet

ASSESSMENT MARKERS

NOUNS

accuracy	(mis)interpretation
defect	mistake
error	myth
fallacy	shortcoming
fault	trap
flaw	validity
illusion	weakness
(mis)conception	

ADJECTIVES

defective	(in)accurate
erroneous	(un)convincing
false	(in)correct
faulty	(un)justified
flawed	(un)reasonable
flawless	(un)sound
illusory	(in)valid
mistaken	(un)warranted
questionable	weak

+ other positive and negative adjectives
or phrases – good, excellent, poor, and
terrible

STRATEGIES

Here are three strategies to help you recognize and understand texts that are
organized around unfavored and favored views.

- Look for View Markers. Use them to establish that you are reading
  about beliefs, not facts.
- Look for Contrast Markers. Use them to identify where the first view
  ends.
- Look for Assessment Markers. Use them to identify the unfavored and
  the favored views.

SKILL PRACTICE 1

In the following sentences, circle the View Markers and highlight the opinions. The first one has been done for you as an example.

1 At the end of their (analysis,) the authors (conclude) that political oppression is increasing in some parts of the world.

2 Although the government would like you to believe that its programs are helping the economy to recover, unemployment continues to rise and investment is falling.

3 Most people who have not lived in cultures other than their own assume that the rules for polite speech and behavior are universal.

4 People who watch a great deal of television tend to perceive the world as more violent than it really is.

5 A frequent allegation that is made about people between the ages of eighteen and twenty-five is that they have no interest in politics.

6 The latest statistics, which show an increase in the illiteracy rate, do not support the government's claim that its programs have brought about improvements in education.

7 The tendency of immigrants to live in their own ethnic communities is sometimes interpreted as evidence that they do not wish to become integrated into U.S. society.

8 The researchers argue that much more information is needed before anyone can adequately describe how people adjust to life in a new culture.

9 Relations between the company and its workers worsened after the employees charged that the company wanted to destroy their union.

10 Among Americans, a common perception is that most immigrants enter the United States illegally.

SKILL PRACTICE 2

Read the following short texts. Continue to look for View Markers, but circle the Contrast Markers and Assessment Markers. Then highlight the unfavored view. The first one has been done for you as an example.

1 There is a widespread belief that cardiovascular disease is a problem only in affluent societies and that it attacks mostly men. Studies from the 1990s, (however,) provide evidence that this view of CVD is (no longer valid.)

2 Some years ago, it was argued, usually by Western experts, that overpopulation in developing nations was one of the main causes of widespread poverty. According to more recent studies, however, this analysis of the relationship between poverty and overpopulation is seriously flawed.

3 Even before vaccination became available, people in the West considered measles to be a relatively minor childhood disease that was more of an inconvenience than a serious danger to health. But past and present experience shows that such an optimistic view of this highly infectious disease is unwarranted.

4 There is a tendency among nonexperts to regard primary health care in developing countries as exclusively for the prevention of disease. Yet a closer look at specific programs offers evidence to correct this common misperception.

5 The fact that some first-generation immigrants continue to speak their first languages might suggest that these immigrants and their families are unwilling to become a full part of their new society. Studies by social scientists, on the other hand, cast doubt on the validity of this conclusion.

SKILL PRACTICE 3

Read the following paragraphs and look for View Markers, Contrast Markers, and Assessment Markers. Then underline the unfavored view and highlight the favored view.

1 There is a widespread belief that cardiovascular disease is a problem only in affluent societies and that it attacks mostly men. This was perhaps true in the 1950s, when CVD was first identified as a major health risk. However, more recent studies indicate that this view of CVD is questionable. In many parts of the world, CVD is the leading cause of death among women under sixty-five. It is also becoming more common in less affluent countries and is expected to be the leading cause of death there by 2010.

2 Many people assume that the rules for polite social behavior are universal. They claim that all societies have the same rules, for example, for how and when to thank others. Yet research on intercultural communication shows that this apparently reasonable assumption is unjustified. In fact, the rules for social behavior may differ, sometimes widely, from culture to culture. Studies have established, for instance, that some Asian cultures do not give or expect to receive thanks while shopping, but Americans do.

3 Even before a measles vaccine became available, people in the West considered measles to be a relatively minor childhood disease that was more of an inconvenience than a danger to health. But past and present experience shows that such an optimistic view of this highly infectious disease is unwarranted. Measles, with its many complications – including diarrhea and pneumonia – is, in fact, potentially fatal. Before the vaccine became widely available late in the twentieth century, measles killed an estimated 8 million children annually. In 2000, the disease caused an estimated 700,000 deaths in developing countries.

READING 3
VIEWS ON MULTICULTURALISM

GETTING INTO THE TOPIC

Read the title of the article and then discuss the following questions with a partner.

1 What is "culture," and how and when do we acquire it?
2 What kinds of human behavior are influenced by culture?
3 What do you expect to see in a country that is described as "culturally diverse"?

GETTING A FIRST IDEA ABOUT THE ARTICLE

Read the first sentence of paragraph 1. Think of a question that you expect this paragraph to answer and match it to a question below. Continue in the same way for paragraphs 2–8. Write the number of the paragraph in the blank.

_____ A What evidence is there that multiculturalism is controversial?

_____ B What is a better explanation for the division of public opinion?

_____ C What evidence is there that the United States and Canada have become more culturally diverse?

_____ D Why is multiculturalism causing controversy?

_____ E What is another way to interpret multiculturalism?

_____ F What have the U.S. and Canadian governments done to encourage cultural diversity?

_____ G What evidence is there for claiming that Canadian society is divided on the issue of multiculturalism?

_____ H How do people who interpret multiculturalism this way feel about it?

WHILE YOU READ

As you read the article, stop at the end of each sentence that contains boldface text and follow the instructions in the box in the margin.

Views on Multiculturalism

Since the 1960s, Canada and the United States have become more culturally diverse than at any other time in their history. In 1957, for example, 95 percent of people who settled in Canada were European; thirty years later, 76 percent of immigrants were from Asia and elsewhere in the developing world. In the United States, between 1970 and 2000 the foreign-born population doubled and experienced significant changes in ethnic makeup. In 1970, 59 percent of the foreign-born population were European, while 27 percent were from Latin America and Asia. By 2000, the proportions were very different. Of the 31.1 million foreign-born, 78 percent were Latino and Asian, whereas Europeans made up only 16 percent of the total. (See Table 2.2 for historical shifts in immigration patterns.)

1

Also since the 1960s, the governments of the United States and Canada have supported cultural diversity by developing a policy that is often called **multiculturalism**. Both countries, for example, shifted from immigration laws that favored Europeans (and admitted few people from other parts of the world) to more open, fairer policies. In the United States, the Bilingual Education Acts of 1968 and 1978 provided funds to educate the children of non-English-speaking immigrants. In the Multiculturalism Act of 1988, the Canadian government committed itself to the idea that all citizens had the right to preserve their cultural inheritance. It also established a Ministry for Multiculturalism.

2

As you continue to read this paragraph, number the examples that support the idea of this sentence.

Multiculturalism, however, is **a controversial issue in both countries**. In the United States, multiculturalism is closely associated with bilingual education – public school programs that use the native language of immigrant children to teach them math, science, and social studies. These programs have caused disagreement both within immigrant communities and in the wider American public. In the 1990s, for example, public opinion polls showed Americans were divided on bilingual education, sometimes equally, sometimes with a majority opposed to it. By 2003, small majorities in California, Arizona, and Massachusetts had voted not to allow any more state funds to be spent on **bilingual education**.

3

Scan forward and highlight a phrase that shows where the writer starts to deal with the controversy in each country. Mark the passage *U.S.* or *Canada*. Then come back and continue reading.

Read the first sentence of paragraph 4. Highlight the continuing idea. Use this idea to help you identify the main idea in paragraph 3.

TABLE 2.2 Immigration to Canada and the United States: Changes in immigrant region of origin 1960–2000

	Canada		United States	
	Europe	Elsewhere*	Europe	Elsewhere*
1961–1970	74%	26%	39%	61%
1991–2000	21%	79%	15%	85%

*Canadian figures do not include immigration from the U.S.; U.S. figures do not include immigration from Canada.

Use the strategies for identifying organization by unfavored and favored views. Scan for View, Contrast, and Assessment Markers and circle them. Then come back and continue reading.

In Canada, similar divisions on the issue of multiculturalism are also visible. A 1988 public opinion poll found that approximately 60 percent were in favor of encouraging immigrants to assimilate into Canadian culture, whereas 38 percent thought that immigrants should be encouraged to retain their cultural traditions. Support for assimilation was strongest, at 73 percent, among Canadians with low educational levels; however, such support was also found among 52 percent of university graduates. 4

Why is multiculturalism such a divisive issue? Some people argue that the poll results and the votes against bilingual education are empirical evidence of a growing racism in U.S. and Canadian society. Yet such an interpretation appears unjustified. In both countries, polls in 2002 showed that large majorities of Americans (75 percent) and Canadians (77 percent) believed that immigration has benefited their countries. In Canada, the 1988 poll also showed that approximately 80 percent of Canadians disapproved of using country of origin as a way to select immigrants. Such responses would be highly unlikely to occur in societies in which racist attitudes were widespread. 5

There is a more likely explanation why public opinion seems divided on the issue of multiculturalism. Because the concept has never been clearly defined, people inevitably use their own experiences to arrive at a definition. Different experiences lead to **different interpretations of multiculturalism.** 6

Scan paragraphs 7 and 8. Circle the earliest View Marker in each paragraph and one Contrast Marker. Mark them *View 1* and *View 2*. Then come back and continue reading.

One common interpretation of multiculturalism is that society should encourage immigrants to retain their own culture and language. Under this definition, multiculturalism seems to imply that immigrant families need not adapt to the culture of their new country. Canadians and Americans who interpret multiculturalism in this way oppose it, perhaps justifiably. Common sense tells them that people cannot be full members of a new society if they are not willing to adapt and use the new society's cultural rules at least some of the time. 7

On the other hand, many people interpret multiculturalism differently. For them it means accepting American or Canadian cultural traditions for public behavior and retaining their own culture in private life. If multiculturalism were explicitly defined in this way, much of the controversy would probably disappear. This definition, after all, reflects the experience of earlier first-generation immigrants to the United States and Canada. Later generations, however, considered themselves fully integrated North Americans. 8

MAIN IDEA CHECK

Here are the main ideas of each paragraph in the article. Match each paragraph to its main idea. Write the number of the paragraph in the blank.

Paragraphs 1–4

_____ A Multiculturalism, with its focus on maintaining immigrant language and culture, is a divisive issue in Canada.

_____ B Canada and the United States have become more culturally and ethnically diverse than ever before.

_____ C Multiculturalism, with its focus on maintaining immigrant language and culture, is a divisive issue in the United States.

_____ D Cultural diversity in the United States and Canada is supported by a government policy that is called multiculturalism.

Paragraphs 5–8

_____ E A better explanation for the controversy is that multiculturalism, because it has never been defined, means different things to different people.

_____ F The lack of support for multiculturalism among many Americans and Canadians should not be interpreted as evidence of racism in these two countries.

_____ G For many people, multiculturalism means that immigrants may retain their native culture for their private lives, but should acquire the new culture's rules for their public lives.

_____ H Canadian and American opponents of multiculturalism reject it because it seems to ignore the need to adapt to the new society.

A CLOSER LOOK

Look back at the article to answer the following questions.

1 Why does the writer include the statistical details in paragraph 1?
   a To show that the majority of Americans and Canadians are of European origin
   b To show how Canadian and U.S. immigration policy has changed
   c To show that the United States and Canada are becoming more culturally diverse
   d To show that immigration policies in the United States and Canada no longer discriminate against non-Europeans

2 According to opinion polls, large majorities of Americans support all the government programs that are associated with multiculturalism. True or False?

3 What evidence does the writer use to argue against the claim that racism is the reason for the public's opposition to government policies on multiculturalism? Circle all that apply.

a A number of U.S. states voted to discontinue funding for bilingual education.

b Most Canadians and Americans believe that immigration has had a positive effect on their country.

c About 80 percent of Canadians don't want country of origin to be a factor in deciding who is allowed to immigrate to Canada.

d Only 38 percent of Canadians believe that immigrants should be encouraged to retain their cultural traditions.

4 The writer is sure that everyone in Canada and the United States is in agreement on the meaning of the term *multiculturalism*. True or False?

5 Why does the writer introduce the topic of earlier U.S. and Canadian immigrants in paragraph 8? Circle all that apply.

a To show that multiculturalism, under one definition, does not prevent immigrant families from becoming assimilated into their new society

b To show that the behavior of immigrants differs in Canada and the United States

c To show that multiculturalism is a danger for society in general

d To show that the definition of multiculturalism in paragraph 8 reflects the experiences of real people

6 The article implies that the writer prefers to define *multiculturalism* in a specific way. Identify the writer's preferred definition.

VOCABULARY STUDY: SYNONYMS

Find words in the article that are similar in meaning to the following.

1 other places *(adv)* Par. 1
2 to allow someone to enter *(v)* Par. 2
3 to prevent something from being changed, damaged, or destroyed *(v)* Par. 2
4 causing deep disagreement *(adj)* Par. 3
5 a report of people's opinion on a topic *(n)* Par. 4
6 to keep something; not to give up something *(v)* Par. 4
7 based on what a person sees or experiences *(adj)* Par. 5
8 the belief that some races of people are better than others *(n)* Par. 5
9 about; not exactly *(adv)* Par. 5
10 to choose *(v)* Par. 5
11 not probable *(adj)* Par. 5
12 not avoidable; certain to happen *(adv)* Par. 6
13 to disagree with something *(v)* Par. 7
14 to change in order to fit new conditions; to adjust *(v)* Par. 7
15 clearly and completely shown or expressed *(adv)* Par. 8

VOCABULARY STUDY: WORDS IN CONTEXT

Complete the sentences with words from the list below. If necessary, review the words in the Key Vocabulary from the Readings on page 254.

policy	approves of	assimilate	settled	native
committed	issue	likely	racial	reflect

1 There is good news for the government. The latest opinion polls show that 65 percent of the public _____ the way it is running the country.

2 The majority of nineteenth-century immigrants _____ in the cities of the East and Midwest, but some moved west into areas that were populated by Native Americans.

3 The immigration _____ of the United States changed during the twentieth century. Until 1965, it favored Europeans, but then it became fairer and more open.

4 When Europeans settled in the Americas and elsewhere, they often oppressed the _____ people they found there.

5 In a few generations, most European immigrants were able to _____ fully into U.S. society. The Old Order Amish, however, still live, work, and marry within their own communities.

6 Only 35 percent of the people feel that the president is doing a good job in the economy. These low approval figures _____ people's dissatisfaction with the latest unemployment numbers, the highest in twenty years.

7 The weak economy will be an important _____ in the next election.

8 In 2002, there was still evidence of _____ discrimination in the United States. African Americans were paying higher interest rates on mortgages than white homeowners with similar incomes and jobs.

9 In 1985, the World Health Organization _____ itself to eliminating polio in the Americas. In 1991, the goal was achieved.

10 If public support for the present government continues to fall, it is _____ to lose the election next year.

BEYOND THE READING

Research

Do Internet or library research to find additional, up-to-date information on bilingual education.

Discussion

Discuss the following situation with a partner:

■ You are a new immigrant to a country where English is the language of the large majority of the population. You have one child aged seven. For her education, which of the following two programs do you choose:

1 A bilingual education program? This program teaches all subjects, including your cultural history, in your native language. The program also provides one daily class of instruction in the English language.

2 The same program that English-speaking students take? This program pays no special attention to your cultural history. In addition, a tutor is available to give your child extra help with her learning.

Writing

Write a short report on the results of your research or your discussion.

READING 4
EXPERIMENTAL EVIDENCE ON THE NATURE OF PREJUDICE

GETTING INTO THE TOPIC

Read the title of the article. Then discuss the following questions with a partner.

1 What examples of prejudice have you read about or experienced?
2 Who was the prejudice directed against, and what consequences did it have for that person or group?

GETTING A FIRST IDEA ABOUT THE ARTICLE

Read the first sentence of paragraph 1. Think of a question that you expect this paragraph to answer and match it to a question below. Continue in the same way for paragraphs 2–6. Write the number of the paragraph in the blank.

_____ A What is the writer's attitude to this assumption?

_____ B What did the experiment attempt to test?

_____ C What questions will the next section of the chapter help to answer?

_____ D What is the connection between prejudice and relations between social groups?

_____ E Why do people persist in their prejudices?

_____ F What significance is there in the fact that the student teachers misjudged the language of the African American and Mexican American children?

WHILE YOU READ

As you read the article, stop at the end of each sentence that contains boldface text and follow the instructions in the box in the margin.

Experimental Evidence on the Nature of Prejudice

Most people will acknowledge that the relations between different 1
ethnic and racial groups is a potential source of problems for culturally
diverse societies. Most rational people will also agree that prejudice
contributes to the misunderstandings, intolerance, and even hostility
that may develop and persist between such groups. Thus, if society's
goal is to minimize these problems, a necessary step is to address the
issue of prejudice.

A good starting point for our examination of prejudice is **an** 2
experiment that is often cited in education textbooks. The experiment,
which was conducted some time ago, sought to determine the potential
effects of prejudice on the judgments of future U.S. schoolteachers.
The researchers made three videotapes, each of a different child in
conversation with an adult. On each tape, the camera was behind the
child so that his mouth was not visible. However, it was obvious
from the tapes that the children were speaking and that they were
racially different: one was white, one was African American, the third
was Mexican American. A sound track was added to each videotape.
It contained the same conversation in English, with the same two
voices, a child's and an adult's. Each tape was then played to one of three
groups of student teachers. Their task was to evaluate the correctness
of the speech of the child they had seen on the videotape. Correctness
was defined as "closeness to good Standard English," which is, of
course, the type of English that schools seek to teach.

Although they actually heard the same child's voice, the student 3
teachers judged each child's English differently. They perceived the
African American and Mexican American children's English to be
less like Standard English than the language on the videotape with
the white child. (See Figure 2.2.) These results may be interpreted as
demonstrating the existence of a specific prejudice in the student

> Four important elements of experimental research are: the research question, methodology, results, and interpretation of the results. Scan paragraphs 2–3 and label each element.

FIGURE 2.2 Ethnic Prejudice and Perceptions of Children's Speech

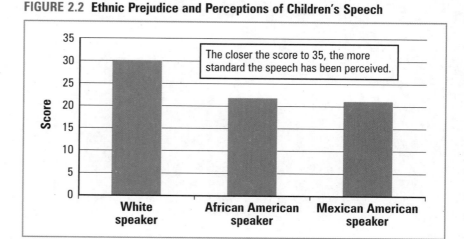

The closer the score to 35, the more standard the speech has been perceived.

teachers – a bias in favor of the language of white children. Because the English on the videotapes was identical, it is clear that the student teachers were basing their evaluations of the children's speech on a previously formed opinion – that Mexican Americans and African Americans don't speak Standard English as well as white Americans. In addition, this specific prejudice was strong enough to prevent the student teachers from perceiving the objective reality on the videotapes. Although the sound track contained no evidence to justify differences in their assessment of the three children's speech, the student teachers responded as if they had heard such evidence.

Since prejudice is associated with insufficient knowledge, we often **assume** that we can reduce it simply by replacing ignorance with knowledge. But such an assumption is unjustified. In the experiment that is described in the preceding paragraphs, prejudice successfully resisted change. The student teachers heard evidence on the sound track that contradicted some of their previously held ideas, but they did not revise these beliefs. Instead, they persisted in them and erroneously found the English on one tape to be superior to the same English **on the other two tapes.**

Thus, the immediate problem seems to be the persistence of prejudice. To address this problem rationally, we must first find answers to the following questions: Under what circumstances does prejudice resist change? Are there different kinds of prejudice, and, if so, are some types more persistent than others? Under what circumstances can prejudices be changed or eliminated?

In the next section of this chapter, we will consider research that may help suggest answers to **these questions**. Yet, from what we have seen so far, one fact seems clear: finding a remedy for social prejudice will be a complex and challenging task.

> View Marker! Scan this paragraph for a Contrast Marker and an Assessment Marker. Circle them. Then come back and continue reading.

> Highlight a continuing idea in the first sentence of paragraph 5. Use this to confirm the main idea of paragraph 4.

> Check back for the meaning of *these questions*. Number the questions.

MAIN IDEA CHECK

Here are the main ideas of each paragraph in the article. Match each paragraph to its main idea. Write the number of the paragraph in the blank.

_____ A The experiment shows that providing people with correct information will probably not be sufficient to reduce prejudice and its effects.

_____ B If we want to adequately address the problem of why prejudice resists change, we need answers to a number of questions.

_____ C The paragraph describes an experiment to identify how prejudice might influence the judgment of future schoolteachers.

_____ D To reduce racial intolerance and hostility, we need to understand prejudice.

_____ E The paragraph prepares the reader for the next section of the chapter.

_____ F The student teachers showed the effects of unconscious prejudice when they judged the English of the African American and Mexican American children to be inferior to that of the white child.

A CLOSER LOOK

Look back at the article to answer the following questions.

1 In the experiment that is described in paragraph 2, what were the student teachers explicitly asked to do?

  a To judge the correctness of the child's English

  b To guess the racial background of the child

  c To say what the child was talking about

  d To identify their own prejudices

2 On the videotapes, the three children had different accents. True or False?

3 What were the results of the experiment?

  a The student teachers judged the speech of the African American child and Mexican American child to be superior to that of the white child.

  b The student teachers gave lower evaluations to the speech on the videotapes with the African American child and the Mexican American child.

  c The white child expressed himself better in Standard English than the African American child or the Mexican American child.

  d There were no differences in the student teachers' assessments of the language they heard on the three videotapes.

4 What conclusion(s) does the article draw from the results of the experiment? Circle all that apply.

  a Mexican Americans and African Americans don't speak Standard English as well as Americans of European origin.

  b Prejudice can influence the way people perceive the world around them.

  c The student teachers were prejudiced.

  d We can eliminate or at least reduce prejudice simply by providing the information that the prejudiced person does not have.

5 The results of the experiment imply that some students could become victims of biased teachers. True or False?

6 What more general conclusion(s) does the writer want readers to draw from the discussion of this experiment? Circle all that apply.

  a Prejudices can be resistant to change.

  b To understand prejudice, we need to do more research.

  c Solving the problem of prejudice is not as simple as some people might think.

  d Giving people objective information will guarantee a reduction in their prejudices.

VOCABULARY STUDY: SYNONYMS

Find words in the article that are similar in meaning to the following.

1 to agree that something is true *(v)* Par. 1
2 unwillingness to accept ideas or behavior different from one's own *(n)* Par. 1
3 not to stop in a situation where stopping is expected *(v)* Par. 1
4 to make something as small as possible *(v)* Par. 1
5 to try; to have as a goal *(v)* Par. 2
6 easy to see or understand *(adj)* Par. 2
7 to judge; to assess *(v)* Par. 2
8 in reality *(adv)* Par. 3
9 to see or hear in a particular way *(v)* Par. 3
10 to believe that something is true, without having proof *(v)* Par. 4
11 to say or be the opposite of another idea *(v)* Par. 4
12 better *(adj)* Par. 4
13 to try to answer or solve *(v)* Par. 5
14 with the use of logical thought *(adv)* Par. 5
15 to remain unaffected by something; to fight against it *(v)* Par. 5

VOCABULARY REVIEW: SAME OR DIFFERENT

The following pairs of sentences contain vocabulary from Readings 3 and 4. Write
S if the two sentences have the same meaning. Write *D* if the meanings are
different.

_____ 1 Approximately 9 million immigrants were legally admitted to the country in the last decade of the twentieth century.

In the 1990s, the total number of legal immigrants entering the county was about 9 million.

_____ 2 Recent empirical research has demonstrated that the assimilation of immigrant families is completed within two generations.

The claim that immigrant families assimilate within two generations has been contradicted by recent empirical studies.

_____ 3 It is unlikely that we can change the views of prejudiced people simply by providing information that contradicts their ideas.

Just supplying information that demonstrates their views are mistaken will probably not cause biased people to change these views.

_____ 4 The television program contained an objective analysis of the effects of the government's immigration policy.

The television program included an unbiased examination of the impact of the government's immigration policy.

_____ 5 The latest polls reflect approval of the government's immigration policy by a majority of the public.

The latest polls indicate that most people are not in favor of the government's policy on immigration.

_____ 6 Empirical studies demonstrate that immigrants and native-born Americans are not likely to compete for the same jobs.

According to empirical research, immigrants and native-born Americans tend to compete for the same types of employment.

_____ 7 The experiment suggests that a prejudice is likely to persist even though objective reality contradicts the biased view.

The implication of the experiment is that providing objective information is unlikely to be a sufficient remedy for prejudice.

_____ 8 When people hear first-generation immigrants still using their native language, some may doubt the immigrants' commitment to becoming fully integrated members of their new community.

Because they continue to use their native language, first-generation immigrants may be perceived as not really serious about participating fully in their new community.

BEYOND THE READING

Research
Do some research and identify a group that has suffered from prejudice in your country or in the country where you are studying English. Find someone from that group to interview about the causes and effects of the prejudice.

Discussion
Discuss the following question with a partner.
- How can a society work to reduce prejudice?

Writing
Write a short report on the results of your research or your discussion.

SKILLS AND STRATEGIES 6
REDUCED RELATIVE CLAUSES

To add variety to their writing and to avoid having too many clauses that begin with *who, which,* or *that,* writers can use reduced relative clauses. Learning to recognize and understand these clauses will help your reading of academic English.

EXAMPLES & EXPLANATIONS

Example

Only a small percentage of **immigrants arriving** in the United States ever returned to live in their native countries.

Explanation

Noun + verb -*ing*. To understand reduced relative clauses with this pattern, you can produce the full clause by making these changes:

- Before the verb-*ing,* add *that* or *who.*
- Drop the *-ing.*
- Give this verb the tense of the other verb(s) in the sentence.

*Only a small percentage of immigrants **who arrived** in the United States ever returned to live in their native countries.*

Today's immigrants are following the **patterns established** by earlier immigrants.

Noun + past participle. To understand reduced relative clauses with this pattern, you can produce the full clause by making these changes:

- Before the past participle, add *that/who.*
- After *that/who,* add *is/are* or *was/were.*

*Today's immigrants are following the patterns **that were established** by earlier immigrants.*

Many of **the drugs being used** in medicine today are extremely expensive.

Noun + *being* + past participle. To understand reduced relative clauses with this pattern, you can produce the full clause by making these changes:

- Before *being,* add *that/who.*
- After *that/who,* add *is/are* or *was/were.*

*Many of the drugs **that are being used** in medicine today are extremely expensive.*

THE LANGUAGE OF REDUCED RELATIVE CLAUSES

Here are the markers for reduced relative clauses.

> noun + verb-*ing*
> noun + past participle
> noun + *being* + past participle
> ↑
> A negative or an adverb
> may follow the noun.

STRATEGIES

Here are three strategies to help you recognize and understand sentences that contain reduced relative clauses.

- Look for the markers of reduced relative clauses.
- Until you can easily understand reduced relative clauses, change them to full relative clauses. Use the explanations shown on page 91.
- In most verbs, the past participle is the same as the simple past tense. So ask yourself: "Is this a main verb in the simple past or a past participle in a reduced relative clause?"

SKILL PRACTICE 1

In the following sentences, highlight the reduced relative clauses. Some sentences have more than one. The first one has been done for you as an example.

1 The major problem facing health care systems is the increasing cost of medical care.

2 In the nineteenth century, Europeans wanting to immigrate to the United States could do so as long as they were not criminals and did not have any infectious disease.

3 The behavior described in the previous paragraph is typical of the behavior of people experiencing culture shock.

4 In the nineteenth century, the economic hardship created by the transition from agricultural to industrial economies was a major reason for European immigration to the United States.

5 Acquiring an adequate knowledge of English is one of the first tasks facing many immigrants coming to the United States and Canada.

6 Two studies recently published in Europe focus on the health risks faced by overweight children.

7 Most democratic nations with diverse populations have laws explicitly intended to protect ethnic and religious minorities from discrimination.

8 By the year 2000, the discrimination suffered by African Americans since the end of slavery had lessened considerably but had not disappeared.

9 In the 1980s, a large proportion of the immigrants settling in Los Angeles were from developing countries troubled by poverty and high unemployment.

10 By changing the laws governing immigration, in 1965 the U.S. Congress ended the biased system giving preference to Europeans and discriminating against other nationalities.

SKILL PRACTICE 2

In the following sentences, highlight the reduced relative clauses. Then circle the verb of the main clause of the sentence. The first one has been done for you as an example.

1 The economic hardships <mark>caused by the decline in agricultural economies</mark> (created) a huge increase in European immigration to the United States.

2 Economic hardship caused many nineteenth-century Europeans wanting a better life to immigrate to the United States.

3 The frustration resulting from an inability to communicate easily and effectively is a common experience among newcomers to the United States.

4 Research showing evidence of language shift in the second and third generations of recent immigrant groups suggests that their experience is similar to that of nineteenth- and early-twentieth-century groups.

5 This analysis of problems associated with immigration concludes that three steps are necessary if we are to achieve a transition to a more diverse society.

6 A complaint frequently directed at immigrants is that they are unwilling to assimilate – to become full members of U.S. society.

7 In the experiment, the race of the child appearing in the videotape activated a prejudice in the student teachers watching the tape.

8 The sacrifices made by first-generation immigrants to the United States were sometimes greater than any immediate benefits they experienced.

9 The frustration sometimes experienced by newcomers to the United States may often result from an inability to communicate easily and effectively.

10 In the latest opinion poll, the percentage of voters giving the president a favorable evaluation fell by 15 points, to 54 percent.

SKILL PRACTICE 3

Rewrite the following sentences by replacing each full relative clause with a reduced relative clause. Some sentences have more than one relative clause. The first one has been done for you as an example.

1 The government acknowledged that researchers had reported only 6 percent of the serious side effects that were experienced by patients in one type of gene therapy.

The government acknowledged that researchers had reported only 6 percent of the serious side effects experienced by patients in one type of gene therapy.

2 Gene therapy may be able to help people who are suffering from Parkinson's disease.

3 A sound track that contained the same conversation with the same two voices was added to each videotape.

4 Under a law that was passed in 1980, refugees are no longer counted in the annual total of immigrants who are admitted to the United States.

5 The procedures that have been outlined by the National Institutes of Health are intended to make sure that researchers follow the rules that require them to report all negative side effects that are observed in clinical trials.

MAIN READING
THE CHALLENGE OF DIVERSITY

GETTING INTO THE TOPIC

Look at the illustrations and photos accompanying "The Challenge of Diversity" and discuss the following questions with a partner.

1 What region of the world did most of the students in 1926 come from? If you saw a similar photo from 2004, what differences would you expect?
2 In the 1946 cartoon, why was President Truman unhappy with the immigration policy in effect then? What was the cartoonist's attitude toward the policy?
3 In the 1885 leaflet, what connection could there be between immigration and "Ruinous Business and Labor Competition"? Who might have produced this leaflet?

GETTING A FIRST IDEA ABOUT THE ARTICLE

For information about the organization and topics of this article, read the section headings, look at the illustrations, and scan the introduction. Then complete the chart by matching each topic with the section that deals with it. Some sections may have more than one topic. Write the number of the section (I–V) in the blank.

SECTION	TOPIC
	Problems associated with immigration and diversity
	How Americans feel about immigration
	The causes of cultural and ethnic diversity in the United States
	An overview of the content and organization of the article
	Solutions to problems associated with immigration and diversity
	Some misconceptions about immigrants
	A description of U.S. immigration policy

WHILE YOU READ

Read the article section by section. Stop after each sentence that contains boldface text and follow the instructions in the box in the margin. After you read each section, answer the Main Idea Check and A Closer Look questions, which can be found on pages 102–107.

The Challenge of Diversity

I. INTRODUCTION

Today in the United States, a social experiment that began in the early nineteenth century is continuing: the development of a truly multicultural and multiethnic society. Immigrants continue to flow into the country; in the 1990s alone, over 3.9 million settled in New York, Los Angeles, San Francisco, Miami and Chicago. As an illustration of the increasing cultural diversity of these areas, consider the following statistic. In 2003, San Francisco County reported that forty-five languages other than English were spoken natively by students in the county's schools. Interestingly, only an estimated 3 percent of these students were of European origin; the large majority were **from Asia and Latin America**.

Such ethnic diversity will be an even more significant feature of life in the United States as the twenty-first century progresses. If recent immigration and population patterns persist, the total Asian and Hispanic population will rise from its 2003 level of approximately 52 million to 96 million by 2030. By the same year, according to government estimates, Asians and Hispanics will make up 26 percent of the total population, up from 17 percent in 2003.

The experiment in multiculturalism, however, is **controversial**. Its supporters point to the country's history as a nation of immigrants and argue that cultural and ethnic diversity has always been a source of strength in American society. Opinion polls, for example, repeatedly show that large numbers of Americans believe that immigration has benefited the country. However, many others are opposed to continuing the experiment. They feel that present government policies will inevitably lead to the development of large ethnic groups who are not interested in becoming part of the national community. The presence of such groups, according to the opponents of multiculturalism, could, over time, result in social disorder and ultimately the disintegration of society. To see the potential dangers of encouraging diversity, they argue, we need only look at recent history in the former Yugoslavia, where a once-multicultural society disintegrated during years of ethnic hostility, violence, **and civil war**.

Read the first sentence of paragraph 2. Highlight the continuing idea and use it to help you identify the main idea of paragraph 1.

Two opposing attitudes toward multiculturalism will be described. Scan forward and highlight where the writer begins to describe each view. Then come back and continue reading.

Read the first sentence of paragraph 4 and highlight the continuing idea. Use this idea to help you identify the main idea of paragraph 3.

This photograph shows schoolchildren in a New York City public school classroom in 1926. Notice that most of the children are from Europe; by contrast, most of the immigrant children in today's U.S. public schools come from Latin America and Asia.

Because of the emotion produced by this controversy, there is 4 clearly a need for a rational analysis of ethnic and cultural diversity in the United States. As a first step in providing such an analysis, this article identifies immigration policy as the main factor behind the present level of diversity. It then evaluates the justification for some common worries about immigration before identifying the real problems associated with the issue. Finally, it offers suggestions on how these problems might be addressed.

II. THE ORIGINS OF U.S. CULTURAL DIVERSITY

The most significant and most obvious **factor** behind the growth of 5 cultural diversity in the United States is, of course, the country's immigration policy. Immigration policy, in turn, reflects the political and social thinking of the period during which the policy came into existence.

Between 1921 and 1965, immigration was controlled by laws 6 favoring newcomers from Europe and placing obstacles in the way of immigration from elsewhere. The laws also restricted the annual number of immigrants to approximately 150,000. The result was a considerable decline in the flow of immigrants, down from the enormous numbers of the period 1880–1920, and a U.S. population that remained almost completely **European in origin**.

For forty years, this immigration policy was not effectively chal- 7 lenged. In the 1960s, however, the United States was changing. By then, many Americans had become aware of the discrimination suffered by African Americans and of the need to make such discrimination illegal. The public's awareness caused politicians to realize that the civil rights of all racial minorities should be protected; this realization, in turn, led naturally to a reexamination of the contemporary immigration laws. In their clear preference for European immigrants, the laws were obvious examples of the discrimination that many Americans were beginning to reject.

In 1965, Congress approved **major changes in the laws governing** 8 **immigration.** The new law eliminated the system giving preference to Europeans and discriminating against other nationalities. At the same time, it raised the annual number of legal immigrants to 290,000, and established a new principle for U.S. immigration – family reunification. Under this principle, priority was given to admitting the immediate family members of recent immigrants.

Later changes to the 1965 immigration law had the effect of 9 increasing the number of people who could be admitted annually. From 1980, refugees were no longer considered immigrants and a 20,000 per-country limit was established worldwide. Ten years later, the annual limit of immigrant visas was increased to 675,000, including a total of 140,000 for people who had specific job skills that would immediately benefit the U.S. economy.

The 1965 immigration law and its later adjustments had an enormous 10 impact on the volume and ethnic character of immigration. In the last three decades of the century, the overall immigration rate almost doubled. Close to 31 million legal immigrants entered the country – almost as many as the 32 million who arrived between 1900 and

Draw a simple cause and effect arrow diagram for this paragraph.

Read the first sentence of paragraph 7 and highlight the continuing idea. Use this idea to help you identify the main idea of paragraph 6.

Number these changes as you find them in the paragraph.

"What Happened To The One We Used To Have?"

U.S. IMMIGRATION POLICY

HERBLOCK
©1946 THE WASHINGTON POST

In 1946, many Americans, including President Harry Truman (the man in the white hat), wanted fairer and less restrictive immigration policies. (© Herblock; from *The Herblock Book* [Beacon Press, 1952])

1960. In the new total, the proportion of Europeans averaged 19 percent, a significant decline from the 70 percent in the earlier period. At the same time, the proportion of immigrants from Latin America and the Caribbean climbed from 13 percent to 45 percent of total U.S. immigration, while Asian immigration rose from 4 percent to 34 percent of the total.

III. IMMIGRATION: PERCEPTIONS AND ATTITUDES

Throughout U.S. history, there has always been some degree of 11 hostility to immigrants, especially if they arrive in large enough numbers to attract the attention of American-born citizens or even of earlier immigrants. Some proportion of public opinion – local, regional, and national – has looked with disfavor on Catholics and Jews, on Germans, Swedes, Koreans, Italians, Chinese, Cubans, Mexicans, and other groups. Since the continuing opposition to immigration is probably due to fears about how it might change U.S. society for the worse, two questions suggest themselves: (1) What are these fears? and (2) How justified are such fears today?

Scan paragraphs 12–14. Circle the View Markers and highlight two Assessment Markers. Mark each paragraph as *Views* or *Assessment.* Then come back and continue reading here.

One recurrent fear (see the illustration on page 99) is that immigrants 12 take jobs away from native-born workers, a belief that is shared by 53 percent of Americans, according to a 1990 poll. Since immigrants are willing to work for lower wages, the charge goes, employers lay off native-born workers and hire immigrants in their place. This allegation is often combined with the charge that newcomers immediately go on government assistance and remain dependent on welfare payments for a long period of time. Thus, the argument goes, they take more out of the economy than they ever contribute to it.

Is there objective evidence that the charges outlined in the preceding 13 paragraph are warranted? Empirical studies have not yet provided a conclusive answer to the question of whether immigrants are a cost or a benefit to the economy. On the one hand, some researchers conclude that newcomers are a burden on the economy because they are more likely to use welfare and to displace native-born unskilled workers. On the other hand, other researchers claim that these negative conclusions are unwarranted. Their numbers show that the economy profits from immigrants.

Use the View Marker you have circled to identify the view in paragraph 14. Underline this view.

Another charge traditionally directed at immigrants is that they 14 are unwilling to assimilate and become part of U.S. society. As evidence for this, opponents cite the tendency of immigrants to settle in their ethnic neighborhoods – in the Chinatowns, Little Saigons, Manilatowns, and Koreatowns of major U.S. cities. Further evidence may be provided by the language behavior of first-generation immigrants: they continue to use their native languages and thus seem to be demonstrating an unwillingness to learn English.

To assess the validity of this charge, we need to reconsider **the** 15 **evidence that seems to support it** and to provide additional evidence that the critics of immigration have ignored. It is true that new immigrants tend to settle in their ethnic neighborhoods. It is a mistake to conclude, however, that the newcomers therefore have no interest in becoming part of American society. The same tendency did not prevent Italians, Germans, Swedes, European Jews, or other earlier immigrant groups from completing the process of assimilation. In fact, the ethnic neighborhoods of the nineteenth and early twentieth centuries were a positive factor in immigrants' adjustment to life in the United States. They enabled adults to develop a supportive social life in the new country. Just as important, these communities offered a network of contacts through which newcomers learned about employment opportunities that would make them productive, contributing members of their new nation. By helping their residents establish themselves, the European neighborhoods and communities supported the ultimate assimilation of immigrant families into the mainstream of American life. There is every reason to believe that Asian and Latin neighborhoods will do the same for today's newcomers.

Scan paragraphs 15–17 and highlight at least one Contrast and one Assessment Marker in each paragraph. Then come back and continue reading.

Look for unfavored and favored view organization in the first three sentences of this paragraph. In the margin, identify the unfavored view and mark it *UV,* and identify the favored view and mark it *FV.*

It is also true that new arrivals to the United States continue to 16 use their native language. Again, however, it is an error to conclude that their children and grandchildren will live outside the mainstream, English-speaking society. Research has shown that immigrant communities typically take three generations to complete *language shift,* the process by which a group takes a different language as their native language. Usually, first-generation adult immigrants acquire some English, but few master the language. Their children, educated mostly in U.S. schools, are typically bilingual in English and their parents' native language, although their abilities in that language may be limited. The third generation, the grandchildren of the original immigrants, are typically monolingual English speakers. With a few exceptions, this pattern was followed by the European immigrants of the nineteenth and early twentieth centuries. **A similar pattern** is visible in recent immigrant communities in which the language behavior of two or three generations can be studied.

According to the historical evidence from the nineteenth and early 17 twentieth centuries, full assimilation into mainstream American society, like language shift, takes time to complete. If we ignore this fact, we might conclude from the behavior of today's first-generation immigrants that their children and grandchildren will continue to speak imperfect English and lead lives separate from the mainstream. **That conclusion**, however, would be wrong.

In fact, the available evidence shows that, like earlier immigrants, 18 recent newcomers are learning English and slowly assimilating into mainstream society. Although the American-born children or grandchildren of European immigrants have retained some parts of their native culture, they are now fully integrated into American life. U.S. society, for its part, has been enriched by the immigrants who have contributed to it. Similarly, we can expect today's immigrant families to become full members of tomorrow's society and to add something of their culture to it.

Check back for the meaning of *a similar pattern*. The pattern has three clear parts. Highlight the two or three words that introduce each part and number them.

Check back for the meaning of *That conclusion*. Highlight it.

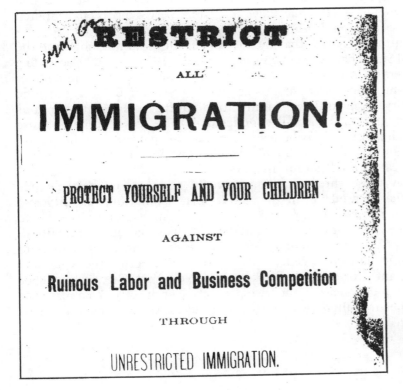

An 1885 leaflet appeals to fears that immigrants will take jobs away from American workers – fears that still exist today.

IV. THE CHALLENGE

The preceding section has demonstrated that some of the fears 19
about modern immigration are the result of misperceptions and
misinterpretations of immigrant behavior. However, it would be a
mistake to assume that cultural diversity is problem-free. The truth
is that immigration, as well as being of long-term benefit to U.S.
society, has the potential to create its own immediate problems or to
worsen existing ones. Immigration raises **complex issues** that must
be considered and brings real challenges that must be addressed.

Scan this section. Highlight the short phrases that show where the writer introduces each issue; number them. Then come back and continue reading.

One of these issues is how to avoid the unintended consequences 20
of admitting skilled and unskilled workers from overseas in order to
satisfy the immediate demands of the country's economy. The
United States already has large numbers of people living in poverty
because they are poorly educated, sometimes illiterate, and without
marketable skills. Resentment among members of this group, sometimes called the underclass, will increase as they watch immigrants
achieve what they cannot – success and acceptance into mainstream
society. This despair and resentment can only hurt the nation.

A second problem results from the tendency of immigrants to settle 21
disproportionately in a few areas of the United States. As a consequence
of this tendency, the cost of providing services to immigrants falls
disproportionately on a limited number of communities. To cover
the costs of providing the additional services, the local or state government responds in one or both of two ways: raise taxes and/or reduce
the level of the services enjoyed by the community. **Either response**
has the potential to create a negative reaction against immigrants. By
2002, for example, citizens in three states had voted to end state and
local funding for bilingual education, which serves mostly the children
of first-generation immigrants.

Check back for the meaning of *Either response*. Highlight and number each response.

A third problem is that the number of illegal immigrants into the 22
United States has been growing since the late 1970s. By 2000, according
to government estimates, there were 6 million illegal immigrants in
the country and the number was increasing by 275,000 per year. The
publicity given to illegal immigration affects American perceptions
of immigration. In a poll conducted in 2001, 53 percent of those
responding mistakenly believed that most people entering the United
States did so illegally. Such a belief must inevitably affect public
attitudes toward legal immigrants.

What these three problems have in common is their obvious 23
potential to **produce**, in the native-born population, hostility and
resentment toward immigrants. In the past, such feelings have led to
violence between native-born and foreign-born groups, especially in
places where immigrant numbers were high and during times of
economic hardship. Violence between native-born Americans and
immigrants, for example, broke out in New York City in the 1850s
after a rapid increase in the Irish population of the city. Such reactions
could occur again if we do nothing to address the circumstances that
produce them.

Draw a simple cause and effect arrow diagram for this sentence.

V. RESPONDING TO THE CHALLENGE

This analysis of problems associated with immigration suggests 24 that at least three steps are necessary if there is to be a relatively smooth transition to a more diverse society in the United States in the twenty-first century.

Two of the issues we have identified have **fairly obvious solutions.** 25 First, to address the problem of a large underclass that is potentially resentful of the success of newcomers, the federal government should offer programs of education and training, in order to integrate as many of this underclass as possible into American society. In this way, resentment against immigrants will be minimized, and the potential for tension and violence between ethnic and racial groups will be significantly reduced.

Second, to ease the financial burden on areas where immigrants 26 disproportionately settle, Congress should direct sufficient federal funds to these areas to cover the costs of providing services to the newcomers. In this way, native-born residents will have less justification for complaining that their tax dollars are being spent for the benefit of strangers.

Addressing the problem of illegal immigration is a much more diffi- 27 cult task. The United States shares a long border with Mexico, where economic conditions cause many people to risk crossing the border illegally in order to feed their families. Stopping the flow of such immigrants will be impossible until the social and economic conditions creating it no longer exist. However, the flow can be reduced with better border security and increased identification of U.S. businesses that break the law by hiring illegal immigrants.

In the United States of the twenty-first century, the immigrant and 28 the native-born communities need time to learn about each other and gradually to adjust to each other. **This process** is not new. In the past, successive generations of immigrant families were changed by society and, at the same time, helped to change society. The three steps suggested support the process today. By making ethnic hostility less likely, they help produce conditions in which understanding and acceptance can replace ignorance and intolerance. The result should be a more fully integrated multiethnic society.

> As you read paragraphs 25–27, highlight the sentences (one in paragraphs 25 and 26 and two in paragraph 27) that describe solutions.

> Check back for the meaning of *This process*. Highlight it.

SECTION I: Introduction

MAIN IDEA CHECK

Here are the main ideas of each paragraph in this section of the article. Match each paragraph to its main idea. Write the number of the paragraph in the blank.

Paragraphs 1–4

_____ A Public opinion in the United States is divided on the issue of multiculturalism.

_____ B The United States is continuing the process of becoming a multiethnic society.

_____ C This paragraph identifies the specific issues to be discussed in the rest of the article.

_____ D The United States of the future will be even more ethnically and culturally diverse than it is today.

SECTION II: The Origins of U.S. Cultural Diversity

MAIN IDEA CHECK

Here are the main ideas of each paragraph in this section of the article. Match each paragraph to its main idea. Write the number of the paragraph in the blank.

Paragraphs 5–10

_____ A Between 1921 and 1965, U.S. policy kept the numbers of immigrants low and was biased in favor of immigration from Europe.

_____ B Adjustments made later to the 1965 immigration law increased the number of people allowed to settle in the United States.

_____ C The realization, in the 1960s, that racial minorities in the United States suffered discrimination led Congress to reconsider the racially biased immigration laws.

_____ D Immigration policy is the most important determiner of ethnic and cultural diversity in the United States.

_____ E Immigration policy from 1965 to 2000 caused a considerable increase in immigration and changed its ethnic character.

_____ F In 1965, significant changes were made to the immigration law that favored Europeans.

A CLOSER LOOK

Look back at section II of the article to answer the following questions.

1 Between 1921 and 1965, U.S. immigration laws were biased in favor of non-Europeans. True or False?

2 This diagram shows the process of cause and effect that ended in the Immigration and Nationality Act of 1965. Reread paragraph 7. Then complete the diagram with sentences A–D. Write the correct letter in each box.

    A The 1965 act removed the bias in favor of Europeans and against people from other parts of the world.

    B People began to reconsider the existing immigration policy.

    C U.S. society became aware of the discrimination suffered by African Americans.

    D Politicians and the public came to believe that the rights of all ethnic minorities needed legal protection.

3 How did immigration policy change between 1965 and 2000? Circle all that apply.

    a The new laws eliminated the earlier obstacles to immigration from Asia and Latin America.

    b Family reunification became a guiding rule of the policy.

    c A large number of immigrant visas were reserved for workers who would benefit the U.S. economy.

    d Refugees and family members of immigrants already in the United States were no longer included in the annual count of immigrants.

4 How did immigration to the United States change from 1965 to 2000? Circle all that apply.

    a There was an enormous increase in the proportion of immigrants from Asia and Latin America.

    b The percentage of immigrants from Europe fell significantly.

    c The overall number of immigrants declined.

    d The number of Asian immigrants grew even faster than that of Latin American immigrants.

SECTION III: Immigration: Perceptions and Attitudes

MAIN IDEA CHECK

Here are the main ideas of each paragraph in this section of the article. Match each paragraph to its main idea. Write the number of the paragraph in the blank.

Paragraphs 11–14

_____ A Research has given contradictory answers to the question of whether immigrants help or hurt the U.S. economy.

_____ B In U.S. history, many new groups of immigrants have been met with hostility.

_____ C Because immigrants tend to live in ethnic neighborhoods and continue speaking their native language, immigration opponents claim that they are unwilling to really become a part of U.S. society.

_____ D It is a common belief that immigrants damage the U.S. economy.

Paragraphs 15–18

_____ E If people ignore the fact that assimilation and language shift take time, they may wrongly conclude that today's immigrant families will not become part of American society.

_____ F Research on language shift shows that first-generation immigrants may continue to use their native languages but that their children or grandchildren will be native speakers of English.

_____ G There is already evidence that contemporary immigrants, like the earlier European arrivals, are assimilating into U.S. society.

_____ H Because ethnic neighborhoods helped the assimilation of earlier European immigrants, we can reasonably assume that today's ethnic neighborhoods will do the same for today's immigrants.

A CLOSER LOOK

Look back at section III of the article to answer the following questions.

1 The anti-immigrant feeling that exists today among some Americans is a new phenomenon in U.S. history. True or False?

2 What has empirical research on the economic impact of immigration found? Circle all that apply.
   a Native-born unskilled workers may lose their jobs to immigrants.
   b There may be defects in research claiming that immigrants damage the economy.
   c Immigrants help the U.S. economy.
   d Immigrants take more money from the economy than they contribute to it.

3 One allegation made against today's immigrants is that they do not want to become integrated into U.S. society. What behavior do people cite as evidence to justify this charge? Circle all that apply.
   a Some new immigrants settle in their own ethnic neighborhoods in U.S. cities.
   b New immigrants are willing to work for lower wages than native-born Americans.
   c New immigrants continue to use their native language.
   d New immigrants take more money out of the economy than they contribute to it.

4 This article is about immigration today. So why, in paragraphs 15–18, does the writer include details about earlier European immigrants?

  a To provide evidence that ethnic neighborhoods do not prevent but help the assimilation of immigrants into American society

  b To demonstrate clearly that the lives of European immigrants were very different from the lives of today's immigrants

  c To show that American society was diverse even in the nineteenth and early twentieth centuries

  d To show that today's immigrants are unwilling to assimilate into U.S. society

5 If the English of an adult first-generation immigrant remains poor, we can assume that his or her family will not become integrated into U.S. society. True or False?

6 According to the writer, what happened as earlier, European immigrants assimilated into American society? Circle all that apply.

  a They lost all their native culture in the process of assimilation.

  b They lost some parts of their native culture and retained others.

  c They changed American culture in positive ways.

  d They shifted to English as their native language over several generations.

SECTION IV: The Challenge

MAIN IDEA CHECK

Here are the main ideas of each paragraph in this section of the article. Match each paragraph to its main idea. Write the number of the paragraph in the blank.

Paragraphs 19–23

_____ A We risk causing bitterness and resentment among poor unemployed Americans if we do nothing for them but at the same time admit large numbers of immigrants.

_____ B Media reports about the number of illegal immigrants are probably causing an increase in anti-immigrant feelings in the United States.

_____ C Although some fears about immigration are unjustified, there are problems associated with it.

_____ D Hostility and resentment toward immigrants have caused problems between immigrants and native-born Americans in the past and could do so again.

_____ E Immigrants tend to settle in a limited number of areas and can cause economic problems in those communities.

A CLOSER LOOK

Look back at section IV of the article to answer the following questions.

1 It can be clearly demonstrated that immigration causes no problems for U.S. society. True or False?

2 What specific problems does the writer believe are associated with immigration? Circle all that apply.

a Resentment increases among members of the native-born underclass who see immigrants achieving what they cannot.

b There is a decline in services to native-born Americans.

c Many new immigrants are unable to find work because they have no marketable skills.

d Immigrants are becoming a burden on some communities because of their tendency to settle in only a few areas of the United States.

3 According to the writer, which development(s) could cause resentment against immigrants in the communities where they settle? Circle all that apply.

a Taxes are increased to cover increased services to the immigrants.

b Services are reduced to save money that can be used for services to the immigrants.

c The immigrants successfully assimilate into society.

d Immigrants do not settle in similar numbers in every part of the United States.

4 In paragraph 23, why does the writer use the example of nineteenth-century violence in New York between immigrants and native-born Americans?

a To show that relations between these two groups are now better than in the nineteenth century

b To illustrate how difficult life could be for immigrants

c To show that bad feelings toward immigrants can lead to more serious social problems

d To show that racial and ethnic prejudice existed in nineteenth-century America

SECTION V: Responding to the Challenge

MAIN IDEA CHECK

Here are the main ideas of each paragraph in this section of the article. Match each paragraph to its main idea. Write the number of the paragraph in the blank.

Paragraphs 24–28

_____ A Illegal immigration can be reduced by increased border security and better identification of companies that employ illegal immigrants.

_____ B Education and training programs are needed so that members of the underclass can advance socially and economically.

_____ C The solutions suggested will give cultural understanding and tolerance time to grow and will help create a more integrated society.

_____ D The United States needs to take at least three steps to ease the way to a multiethnic society.

_____ E The federal government should provide adequate financial support for those regions where immigrants tend to settle.

A CLOSER LOOK

Look back at section V of the article to answer the following questions.

1 Reread paragraph 25. Then complete the cause and effect diagram with sentences A–D. Write the correct letter in each box.

A We reduce the possibility of ethnic tension and violence.
B We provide effective programs to educate and train the underclass.
C There are fewer reasons to feel resentful of immigrants' success.
D Members of the underclass become a real part of U.S society.

2 The writer implies that the United States by itself cannot solve the problem of illegal immigration. True or False?

3 What would help the United States today make a smooth transition to a more multicultural society of the future? Circle all that apply.
a The government needs to develop a better immigration policy.
b Immigrants and native-born residents need time to get to know each other.
c The government needs to recognize the problems associated with immigration and address these problems.
d Immigrants need to give up their traditions and adapt to U.S. culture as quickly as possible.

4 The writer appears to believe that native-born Americans and immigrants will influence and change each other in time. True or False?

BEYOND THE READING

Research
Do Internet or library research to find information about a first-generation immigrant to the United States or to your own country who has become successful and famous.

Discussion
Discuss the following question with a partner.
■ To help a multicultural society, the writer suggests, immigrants and native-born people must learn more about each other's cultural ways. How could such learning occur and be effective?

Writing
Write a short report on the results of your research or your discussion.

MAKING CONNECTIONS

The vocabulary in these two exercises comes from all the readings in Unit 2. The exercises will help you see how writers make connections across sentences in a text.

EXERCISE 1: CONNECTIONS BETWEEN SENTENCES

Read the numbered sentence. Then choose and circle the sentence, *a* or *b*, that logically follows it. Then, from the box, decide how the sentence you chose connects to the first. Write *A*, *B*, or *C* to identify the connection.

A It contains a correction to a view that is reported in the first sentence.
B It describes the cause of what is reported in the first sentence.
C It adds specific details to support the more general information in the first sentence.

_____ 1 One obvious quality possessed by most immigrants to the United States is their willingness to make sacrifices as they pursue the goal of a better life for themselves and their children.

    a They become part of an ethnic community where they make a network of contacts that is a source of support in their adjustment to their new lives.

    b A significant proportion of them accept jobs that place them in a lower economic and social status than they had achieved at home.

_____ 2 Because contemporary immigrants continue using their native language, some native-born residents of the United States perceive them as not really committed to becoming fully integrated members of American society.

    a Such a conclusion, however, is likely to be invalid, because it assumes – erroneously – that language shift should occur in the first generation of immigrants.

    b Their language use demonstrates that today's immigrants are acquiring English and are assimilating into mainstream American life just as well as earlier European immigrants.

_____ 3 Between 1965 and 2000, the United States became a much more diverse society – ethnically and racially – than it had been in the preceding one hundred years.

    a This development reflects the government's successful attempt to preserve the ethnic and racial character of the nation.

    b This development was the inevitable result of a shift from an immigration policy that was biased in favor of admitting Europeans to one that did not discriminate against people of other racial or ethnic backgrounds.

_____ 4 There is a widespread but erroneous belief that all immigrant parents favor bilingual education for their children.

    a Significant numbers of such parents, in fact, are opposed to bilingual education, especially programs whose priority is to help children retain their native culture.

    b By teaching subjects like math, science, and social studies in their native language, bilingual education seeks to help children make a better transition to American schools.

_____ 5 The Old Order Amish are often cited as an obvious example of an immigrant group that has successfully resisted assimilation into mainstream American society.

    a For two centuries, they have retained their native language and preserved their religion and culture by selecting marriage partners from inside their communities and by limiting contact with the English-speaking world.

    b Like most other early immigrant groups, in three generations they had shifted to English and had achieved full integration into American life.

EXERCISE 2: CONNECTIONS WITHIN PARAGRAPHS

Make a clear paragraph by putting sentences A, B, and C into the best order after the numbered sentence. Write the letters in the correct order. The boldface words help you identify continuing ideas.

1 In 1965, in an attempt to address discrimination in the country's immigration policy, the U.S. Congress approved major changes to the Immigration and Naturalization Law. _____ _____ _____

A	B	C
In addition, **it** gave priority to admitting the immediate family of recent immigrants.	**These two features of the law** have significantly increased the ethnic diversity of the United States.	**The new law** eliminated the bias in favor of immigrants from Europe.

2 Why do contemporary immigrants still follow the patterns established by earlier European immigrants and tend to settle disproportionately in a few metropolitan areas of the United States? _____ _____ _____

A	B	C
The primary reason is that immigrants perceive the ethnic communities **in these areas** as a source of support in the transition to a new life.	These new immigrants inevitably tend to move to areas of the country in which they already have a network of family support.	**A second reason** is that present immigration policy gives preference to admitting relatives of immigrants already in the United States.

3 There is a belief among some Americans that contemporary immigrants are not as committed to becoming fully integrated Americans as earlier immigrants were. ___ ___ ___

A **In this process**, the clear pattern is that the first generation acquires only some English, but their children and grandchildren will be native speakers of English.

B As evidence for **this conclusion**, they cite the tendency of first-generation immigrants to retain their native languages for use in private and in public.

C Their claim, however, is unwarranted because it does not acknowledge what empirical research has demonstrated about the process of language shift.

4 Through the 1990s, public opinion polls showed that a large majority of Americans believed that immigration should be reduced or maintained at the existing level. ___ ___ ___

A **This misperception** suggests a more likely explanation for the poll results: the public is opposed to illegal immigration, not immigration in general.

B **This claim**, however, is questionable because it does not address another poll finding – namely, the mistaken belief among many Americans that most immigrants arrive illegally.

C According to people seeking to change immigration policy, **these results** reflect strong public opposition to immigration in general.

5 One obvious cause of social prejudice against a minority group is that the majority community does not have correct information about the minority group. ___ ___ ___

A **The assumption**, however, ignores considerable empirical evidence that merely supplying **such objective information** will not reduce the prejudices directed against the minority group.

B **This causal connection** might lead us to assume that we can remedy the bias by simply providing the majority group with correct information that contradicts their prejudices.

C In fact, **these biases** are likely to persist until members of the groups actually get to know each other by working and socializing with each other.

Aspects of Language

SKILLS AND STRATEGIES 7
DEFINITION AND CLASSIFICATION

In textbooks, you are sure to meet unfamiliar technical words and their definitions. You will also find that writers use classification to divide general concepts into a number of different types. Identifying and understanding texts that contain definitions and classification will help your academic reading.

EXAMPLES & EXPLANATIONS

Examples

Phonetics is the study of the speech sounds used in human languages.

Matter is defined as anything that occupies space and has weight.

To predict future population growth, we need to establish **national fertility rates and mortality rates – i.e.,** the number of births and deaths per year in a country.

Some birth defects in unborn children are identifiable with **a sonogram, a picture** of the developing baby produced by sound waves.

We can identify six main **categories** of English consonants: stops, fricatives, affricates, nasals, liquids, and glides.

Explanations

Here a technical term is defined by the words that follow a form of the verb *to be*.

Here a technical term is defined after the verb phrase *is defined as*.

Here two technical terms are defined by the words that follow the marker *i.e.*, a Latin abbreviation for *that is*.

Here the definition appears in a noun phrase that follows the technical term. The phrase is always set off by a comma.

Here the word *categories* indicates that the writer is classifying the members of a larger group, *English consonants*, into six types.

THE LANGUAGE OF DEFINITION AND CLASSIFICATION

Here are some common Definition and Classification Markers.

DEFINITION MARKERS	
VERBS	OTHER
to be	*i.e.*
to define	*in other words*
to refer to	+ a comma between a technical term and its defining noun or noun phrase: ___ , _____

CLASSIFICATION MARKERS		
VERBS	NOUNS	
to categorize	*category*	*kind*
to classify	*class*	*part*
to distinguish	*component*	*section*
to divide	*division*	*sort*
to group	*group*	*type*

STRATEGIES

These strategies will help you recognize and understand texts that contain technical terms, definitions, and classification.

- ■ Expect writers to use technical terms and to define them in the text.
- ■ Expect writers to use common words and give them technical meanings.
- ■ Look for Definition Markers. They will help you identify both technical terms and their meanings.
- ■ Look for Classification Markers. They will help you identify both the general concept and its types.

SKILL PRACTICE 1

In the following sentences, circle the Definition Markers, highlight the technical terms, and underline the definitions. The first one has been done for you as an example.

1 Demand can be (defined) as the quantities of a product or service that are purchased during a certain period of time.

2 Internal migration – i.e., movements of people within a country – is determined largely by economic factors.

3 Voiceless sounds are sounds that are produced with no vibration of the vocal cords.

4 Some birth defects in unborn children can be diagnosed by amniocentesis, a procedure in which fluid is taken from the amniotic sac surrounding the child and analyzed.

5 Frustration may be defined as the unpleasant feelings that result when a desired goal is not achieved.

6 Prejudice is an unfair judgment that people make before they have all the facts.

7 Discrimination, on the other hand, is behavior in favor of or, more usually, against a person or a group and is often based on prejudice.

8 A disease may be endemic; in other words, it is always present in a community or in a region, but in relatively low numbers of cases.

9 A sudden outbreak of a disease affecting large numbers of people in a community or region during a given period of time is referred to as an epidemic.

10 Significance, a statement of how likely it is that a research result has occurred by chance and not as a result of some other factor, is a term in statistics.

SKILL PRACTICE 2

In the following paragraphs, circle the Classification Markers. Then draw a diagram showing the classification. The first one has been done for you as an example.

1   Nutritionists have determined that there are two main (types) of fats in food: saturated fats and unsaturated fats. Within unsaturated fats, we can (distinguish) between monounsaturated fats and polyunsaturated fats.

```
                ┌── saturated
      fats ─────┤                   ┌── monounsaturated
                └── unsaturated ─────┤
                                     └── polyunsaturated
```

2   In phonetics, we may distinguish between two approaches to speech sounds. On the one hand, we can focus on the way speech sounds are produced by the speaker. If we examine speech from this perspective, we are studying articulatory phonetics. On the other hand, speech creates waves of pressure that move through the air. If we study this aspect of speech sounds, our area of interest is called acoustic phonetics.

3   Perception, the complex process by which we make sense of incoming sensory information, seems to have at least two necessary components, selective attention and organization. Selective attention refers to our ability to focus our attention on one aspect of the massive amount of information that our senses are experiencing at a given moment. Organization refers to our ability to integrate the individual pieces of sensory information into an entire picture, or gestalt, which has meaning for us.

4   Status is usually defined by sociologists as the position of an individual in relation to other members of a group. Scientists distinguish two kinds of status. An individual has ascribed status, regardless of his or her abilities and wishes, by virtue of being born male or female and of being born into a given social class or racial and ethnic group. Achieved status, the other category, is a social position that an individual reaches through choice, ability, and competition.

5   Psychologists studying motivation and its effects on achievement have identified two types of motivation. One kind is intrinsic motivation, the desire to perform a task successfully for its own sake. For example, answer these questions: Are you working hard in this class because you enjoy learning? If you had the time, would you take more classes like this? If you answer "Yes" to these questions, then you are intrinsically motivated. The other type, extrinsic motivation, is a desire that results from outside incentives – the rewards or sanctions the individual may receive for doing or failing to do something. Are you working hard in this class to get a good grade or to be admitted to university so that you can get a good job later? If your answer to these questions is "Yes," then you are extrinsically motivated.

SKILL PRACTICE 3

Reread paragraphs 2–5 in Skill Practice 2 and highlight the definitions of the following terms.

1 acoustic phonetics
2 perception

3 selective attention
4 achieved status

5 extrinsic motivation
6 intrinsic motivation

READING 1
VARIATION IN LANGUAGE

GETTING INTO THE TOPIC
Read the title of this article and then discuss the following with a partner.

1 How do you know by talking to someone whether he or she is from your part of the country? Illustrate your answer with specific examples.
2 According to the article, we vary our language depending on who we are talking to. Think of some specific examples of how that is true in your culture.

GETTING A FIRST IDEA ABOUT THE ARTICLE
Read the first sentence of paragraph 1. Think of a question that you expect this paragraph to answer and match it to a question below. Continue in the same way for paragraphs 2–8. Write the number of the paragraph in the blank.

_____ A What are the two main types of linguistic variation?

_____ B What are the three main components of language?

_____ C Why might the idea of regional varieties be an easier concept for me to understand?

_____ D Do all native speakers of English use the same kind of English?

_____ E What is variation within the individual?

_____ F What evidence is there for differences in men's and women's language?

_____ G What are some examples of variation within the individual?

_____ H What are the variables that can be associated with a style switch?

WHILE YOU READ
As you read the article, stop at the end of each sentence that contains boldface text and follow the instructions in the box in the margin.

Variation in Language

You are most likely to find the topic of an article toward the end of an introduction. Highlight the words in paragraph 1 that give you the clearest idea of what to expect in this article.

"The English language," a phrase you may have frequently heard, gives the impression that English is a uniform system of communication used by all native speakers. Nothing could be further from the truth. The English spoken in the British Isles is recognizably different from that spoken in North America. Within the British Isles, the English of Scotland is not the same as the English spoken in England. Within the United States, the English of natives of New York State is very different from the versions of English spoken natively in Georgia or Texas. Like all languages, English varies extensively and systematically according to a number of social factors, including the region where the speaker was brought up. *Sociolinguistics*, the scientific study of that variation, seeks to observe, record, describe, and ultimately explain its occurrence.

The systematic variation that interests sociolinguists is found in each of the three main components of language. It is visible in the *lexicon* – i.e., the vocabulary of a language; in its *grammar* – i.e., the rules for combining words to form phrases and sentences; and in its *phonology* – i.e., the sounds of the language and the rules that govern their pronunciation.

What are these types? Scan this paragraph and the first sentences of the following paragraphs. Highlight and number the name of each type. Then come back and continue reading.

It is possible to distinguish between **two main types of linguistic variation**. The first of these, which we refer to as *between-group variation*, identifies a person as belonging to a specific group. Between-group variation can be illustrated by the regional differences mentioned earlier – in other words, those features of English that identify the speaker as a native of Scotland, New York, or Texas. Such variation produces regional varieties, often termed *dialects*, and other group varieties such as those that are associated with the speaker's gender, social class, or ethnic group.

Are any other between-group varieties discussed in detail? Scan forward and highlight their names. Then continue reading.

Among the between-group varieties, regional varieties are probably **the type most familiar to you**. Regardless of our native language, we can identify almost immediately if a stranger is not from our part of the country by the person's *accent* or regional pronunciation. In the United States, for example, the Standard American English pronunciation of the words "car" and "park" is KAR and PARK. Natives of

1

2

3

4

This American tourist and English policeman speak the same language, but distinctly different varieties of it.

Massachusetts, however, like many speakers in the United Kingdom, drop the "r" when it is not followed by a vowel and pronounce the words as KA and PAK. Regional differences are also reflected, but less frequently, in grammar and the lexicon. For example, speakers in the United Kingdom say, "We <u>haven't got</u> today's <u>post</u>," while U.S. speakers say, "We <u>don't have</u> today's <u>mail</u>."

Research has also confirmed the existence of *gender varieties*, the English used by men and women. For example, in both British English and American English, men tend to use the non-Standard pronunciation -IN of the *-ing* ending – e.g., "I'm eatin'" – more often than women do. Men also tend to use non-Standard grammatical forms more frequently than women. Thus the following are more likely to be spoken by a male: "I done it yesterday," "I didn't see nothin'," and "I ain't seen him today." Women are more likely to use the Standard English equivalents: "I did it yesterday," "I didn't see anything," and "I haven't seen him today." **These tendencies** are often referred to as the *sociolinguistic gender pattern*.

5

Check back for the meaning of *These tendencies*. Highlight the first two words of each sentence that introduces a new tendency. Then number each tendency.

The second main type of linguistic variation can be labeled *variation within the individual*. It occurs within the language of all speakers and is associated with changes in the *social situations* in which individuals find themselves. Variation within the individual, also referred to as *style shifting*, allows the speaker to use the style or level of language that is perceived to be appropriate to a situation. The style used by the speaker for a given situation lies somewhere on a continuum that extends from very casual to extremely formal.

6

In studying variation within the individual, sociolinguists seek both to record the linguistic changes that signal a style shift has taken place and to identify the relevant components of the situation, or variables, with which the shift is associated. **These variables** include the different *roles* an individual might play; for example, an individual can go from being a parent (at breakfast) to being a teacher and a colleague (at work). Such roles are closely connected to the relationship between an individual and the person to whom he or she is speaking – a close friend, a peer, a superior, a subordinate at work, or a stranger. Another variable in the situation is the *setting*, the physical environment in which the interaction occurs. For example, you may talk with a friend during a formal class discussion and later in the cafeteria. The setting is likely to influence the style you use.

7

Scan forward and highlight the technical name of each variable the writer identifies. Then come back and continue reading.

Research has offered evidence of phonological, grammatical, and lexical variation within the individual. Here, however, we will focus on the lexical variation in *forms of address* – **i.e.,** the names or titles individuals use when they address others. Imagine that you are talking to a professor, Dr. Mary Cooper. She is also a close family friend and not significantly older than you, and she is teaching one of your classes. You could address her in one of two ways, as "Dr. Cooper" or "Mary." Your choice, however, is clearly determined by the situation you find yourself in. If you speak to her in a class you are taking, your role is that of a student. The appropriate form to use is "Dr. Cooper." If you are talking about vacation plans with her at home, the setting, the topic, and your role have changed. In this situation, the appropriate form of address is "Mary."

8

Definition Marker! Highlight the technical term and underline its definition.

MAIN IDEA CHECK

Here are the main ideas of each paragraph in the article. Match each paragraph to its main idea. Write the number of the paragraph in the blank.

Paragraphs 1–5

_____ A Linguistic variation can be found in people's pronunciation, grammar, and vocabulary.

_____ B One of the two main types of linguistic variation is between-group variation.

_____ C The English spoken by men is different from that spoken by women, with men tending to use non-Standard forms more often than women.

_____ D All languages vary, and sociolinguistics is the scientific study of that variation.

_____ E Regional dialects are probably the best-known type of between-group linguistic variation.

Paragraphs 6–8

_____ F Linguistic variation within the individual is associated with changes in the situation in which the individual finds himself or herself.

_____ G Variation within the individual is the second main type of linguistic variation.

_____ H Linguistic variation within the individual is exemplified in the different ways an individual might address others.

A CLOSER LOOK

Look back at the article to answer the following questions.

1 If the English spoken by one group of people differs from that of another group, which circumstance(s) might explain the differences? Circle all that apply.
  a The place they were born and raised
  b Their gender
  c Their ethnic background
  d Their social class – i.e., whether working class or middle class

2 Which characteristic(s) would you expect to occur more often in American male speech than in American female speech? Circle all that apply.
  a Use of double negatives like "I don't know nothin' about that"
  b Phonological and grammatical forms that are typical of Standard English
  c Use of forms like "playin'" rather than "playing"
  d A preference for the form "She doesn't know" over the form "She don't know"

3 People adjust their language for different listeners. True or False?

4 Name the three factors mentioned in the article that could cause a speaker to shift language styles.

5 Draw a classification diagram that shows the two main types of language variation and any sub-types mentioned in the article.

6 List at least six technical concepts introduced in this article and give their definitions.

VOCABULARY STUDY: SYNONYMS

Find words in the article that are similar in meaning to the following.

1 an idea produced in the mind by some experience *(n)* Par. 1
2 without any differences *(adj)* Par. 1
3 a different form of the same thing *(n)* Par. 1
4 a lot; a great deal *(adv)* Par. 1
5 to watch closely and carefully *(v)* Par. 1
6 to identify something as different from something else *(v)* Par. 3
7 widely accepted and used *(adj)* Par. 4
8 to give something a name *(v)* Par. 6
9 informal and relaxed *(adj)* Par. 6
10 suitable for official, public situations *(adj)* Par. 6
11 the ways in which a person is expected to behave in a particular situation *(n)* Par. 7
12 a person of the same age or the same status in a group *(n)* Par. 7
13 a person whose position or status is lower *(n)* Par. 7
14 the circumstances and surroundings in which persons find themselves and which may influence them *(n)* Par. 7
15 a type of spoken communication *(n)* Par. 7

VOCABULARY STUDY: WORDS IN CONTEXT

Complete the sentences with words from the list below. If necessary, review the words in the Key Vocabulary from the Readings on page 257.

| combine | vary | relevant to | gender | equivalent |
| refers to | component | colleagues | appropriate | phrase |

1 The teacher advised me that I could improve my paper by cutting out three paragraphs that were not _____ the topic.

2 Knowing the grammar rules of our native language enables us to _____ words to form phrases and phrases to form sentences.

3 In British English, *lift* is the _____ of the American English *elevator*.

4 In the United States, it is illegal for an employer to use a person's
_____ as a reason for not promoting the worker to a position of
more responsibility.

5 When you write, it is a good idea to _____ the length of your
sentences. It makes your text less boring and easier to read.

6 A CD player is an essential _____ of a sound system.

7 "Government of the people, by the people, for the people" is a famous
_____ from a speech by Abraham Lincoln.

8 John has just retired after thirty-five years at the university. His
_____ in the Chemistry Department have named a new lab for
him.

9 The term *between-group variation* _____ linguistic changes that
distinguish members of one group from those of another group.

10 Asking questions in class is considered _____ behavior for
students in some cultures. In other cultures, the same behavior is not
acceptable.

BEYOND THE READING

Research
Find some examples of pronunciation, grammar, or vocabulary to illustrate one of
the following:
- Differences between standard American and British English
- Differences between standard American and Canadian English
- Differences between standard American and Australian English

Discussion
A speaker of American English says: "I ain't doin' nothin'." With a partner, discuss
the conclusion(s) you feel justified in making about the speaker.
- The speaker is more likely to be female than male.
- The speaker has good competence in Standard English.
- The statement is more likely to have occurred in an informal setting.

Writing
Write a short report on the results of your research or your discussion.

READING 2
SOCIOLINGUISTIC RULES OF SPEAKING

GETTING INTO THE TOPIC
Discuss the following questions with a partner.

1 What do you think a "sociolinguist" studies and researches?
2 What English-language behavior have you observed that would be strange, inappropriate, or impolite in your country?

GETTING A FIRST IDEA ABOUT THE ARTICLE
Before doing the activity below, read the first paragraph of the article.

Read the first sentence of paragraph 2. Think of a question that you expect this paragraph to answer and match it to a question below. Continue in the same way for paragraphs 3–7. Write the number of the paragraph in the blank.

_____ A What are examples of the way sociolinguistic rules can vary across cultures?

_____ B What will this conversation show me?

_____ C What do rules for socially appropriate speech look like?

_____ D Why should second language learners pay attention to this information?

_____ E Different cultures have different sociolinguistic rules for similar situations, but now what?

_____ F What else will the example of the American host and the foreign student show me?

WHILE YOU READ
As you read the article, stop at the end of each sentence that contains boldface text and follow the instructions in the box in the margin.

Sociolinguistic Rules of Speaking

Traditional linguistic research has focused most of its attention 1
on exploring *linguistic competence* – i.e., the rules that govern the
grammar, vocabulary, and pronunciation of a language. This approach
may have reinforced a widespread but erroneous **belief** about second
language learning – namely, that acquiring linguistic competence
will be enough for you to become an effective communicator in the
second language. Of course, you need this knowledge in order to
produce correct speech in that second language. Sociolinguists argue,
however, that linguistic competence by no means guarantees successful communication. Its crucial shortcoming is that it does not ensure
that you can understand and produce socially appropriate speech in
the second language.

View Marker! Scan the
paragraph. Highlight
Contrast Markers,
Assessment Markers, and
any other View Markers
you find.

Now go back and underline
and label the unfavored
and the favored view in
paragraph 1.

To see what sociolinguists mean, consider the following conversa- 2
tion and its outcome. This conversation between a U.S. host and a
foreign student is hypothetical, but the same type of situation has
been documented and discussed in the research literature (Rubin
1983; Thomas 1983).

> *U.S. Host:* Would you like some more dessert? Do have some!
> *Student:*　No, thank you very much.

> The host changes the topic of conversation and doesn't mention dessert
> again. The student really did want more dessert but was trying to appear
> polite by refusing. He remains hungry and might even feel offended
> because the host has not repeated the offer.

Clearly, the speech of each participant is linguistically correct. What
is equally clear, however, is that a breakdown of communication has
occurred in the situation. The student has communicated to the host
a false impression of his wishes: he does, in fact, want more dessert.
The host, for her part, has interpreted the refusal as a genuine one.
On the other hand, the host, attempting to be attentive and polite,
might somehow be giving the opposite impression to the student.
Neither participant in the conversation realizes, though, that there
has been a misunderstanding.

Technical term! As you
continue reading, look for its
definition and highlight it.

For sociolinguists, such misunderstandings offer **evidence for the** 3
existence of *sociolinguistic rules of speaking*. Just as the grammar,
vocabulary, and phonological rules of our linguistic competence help
us produce linguistically correct speech, the sociolinguistic rules
enable us to understand and produce socially and culturally appropriate
speech. They are acquired and applied, usually unconsciously, by
members of a given culture. In our example, the host is following a
sociolinguistic rule in his culture which states that offers of more
food are made once, or at most, twice. The student, on the other
hand, applies a rule from his own culture which states that you
should never accept the first offer, or even the second offer, of more
food. In his culture, it is polite to wait until the third or fourth offer,
which he knows will come.

There is extensive empirical data to support both the claim that 4
sociolinguistic rules of speaking exist and that **they may differ from**

Not knowing the sociolinguistic rules of a language may lead to misunderstandings in social situations, such as dinner table talk.

culture to culture. Christopher (1982) reports the relative unwillingness in Japanese culture (compared with American culture) to directly refuse a request from someone. According to Apte (1974), south Asians, unlike Americans and Europeans, do not thank shopkeepers, close friends, or family members. Others researchers have suggested that cultures differ in how and how often they apologize (Cohen and Olshtain 1981; Cohen and Olshtain 1983; Olshtain, 1983).

From the evidence presented in the preceding paragraph, it is clear that different cultures have different standards for what is socially appropriate linguistic behavior in similar circumstances. While thanking, apologizing, accepting, and refusing are probably universal activities, the rules for when and how to perform such actions may differ greatly from culture to culture. Does it follow, however, that second language learners need to master the rules of the culture whose language they are learning? 5

To address **this question**, let us return to the example of the foreign student and the U.S. host. Both follow the rules of politeness of their own society; both are unaware that there are other ways to show politeness. What is especially significant is that the student is already beginning to judge the host negatively. Reactions like this are relatively common in situations in which intercultural miscommunication occurs. One typical response is to jump to a conclusion and to attribute a negative quality – in this case, lack of politeness – to the person whose language was understood linguistically but misinterpreted sociolinguistically. 6

Learners of a second language, therefore, need to be aware that the rules for polite interaction are not universal. Students should be able to identify situations in which the rules of the cultures are different; they must also be ready to modify their speech to conform to the sociolinguistic conventions of the society they are in. Accomplishing **these two tasks** is not simple, but failure to do so will lead to misunderstandings that may have negative consequences for those who are involved. 7

As you read, identify examples of cultural differences in sociolinguistic rules. Label each example with a word that describes the type of speech behavior, e.g., *offering*.

Use the continuing ideas in this paragraph to help you remember paragraphs 3–4. Then highlight the one sentence that contains new ideas.

Check back and highlight the meaning of *this question*.

Check back to identify *these two tasks*. Highlight them and label them T₁ and T₂.

References

Apte, M. L. 1974. "Thank you" and South Asian languages: A comparative sociolinguistic study. *International Journal of the Sociology of Language* 3, pp. 67–89.

Christopher, R. C. 1982. The Japanese mind: The Goliath explained. New York: Simon and Schuster.

Cohen, A. D., and Olshtain, E. 1981. Developing a measure of sociolinguistic competence: The case of apology. *Language Learning* 31 (3), pp. 113–34.

Cohen, A. D., and Olshtain, E. 1983. Apology: A speech act set. In N. Wolfson and E. Judd (Eds.), *Sociolinguistics and language acquisition*. Rowley, MA: Newbury House.

Olshtain, E. 1983. Sociocultural competence and language transfer: The case of apology. In S. Gass and L. Selinker (Eds.), *Language transfer in language learning*. Rowley, MA: Newbury House.

Rubin, J. 1983. How to tell when someone is saying "no" revisited. In N. Wolfson and E. Judd (Eds.), *Sociolinguistics and language acquisition*. Rowley, MA: Newbury House.

Thomas, J. 1983. Cross cultural pragmatic failure. *Applied Linguistics* 4 (2), pp. 91–109.

MAIN IDEA CHECK

Here are the main ideas of each paragraph in the article. Match each paragraph to its main idea. Write the number of the paragraph in the blank.

Paragraphs 1–4

_____ A Empirical research has demonstrated the existence of rules for socially appropriate speech and of cultural differences in these rules.

_____ B This paragraph offers an example of a situation in which people fail to communicate effectively, although their speech is without linguistic errors.

_____ C According to sociolinguists, just having good linguistic competence in a second language is not enough for a second language learner.

_____ D Scientists conclude that there are rules for socially and culturally appropriate speech because miscommunication occurs between people whose speech is correct phonologically, grammatically, and semantically.

Paragraphs 5–7

_____ E To avoid the potentially serious consequences of intercultural miscommunication, second language learners should be prepared to identify and use the sociolinguistic rules of the new culture.

_____ F Do differences in sociolinguistic rules mean that second language learners need to learn rules for appropriate speech in the new language?

_____ G Because they are unaware of differences in rules for polite behavior, people may unjustifiably form a negative opinion about a person from another culture.

A CLOSER LOOK

Look back at the article to answer the following questions.

1 According to language experts, all you need for effective communication in a second language is to know its pronunciation, grammar, and vocabulary.
True or False?

2 What comment about the situation in paragraph 2 is justified?
   a The student did not want any more dessert.
   b The student was using the sociolinguistic rules of his own culture.
   c The host was following international rules for politeness.
   d The student did not comprehend the linguistic meaning of the host's question.

3 People in some cultures may not express thanks as often as Americans do.
True or False?

4 According to the passage, what outcome(s) can we expect when linguistically competent speakers of English as a second language (ESL) ignore sociolinguistic rules in talking with native speakers of English? Circle all that apply.
   a Native speakers of English may consider the ESL speakers rude.
   b The ESL speakers may unintentionally and unknowingly offend their listeners.
   c The native speakers of English will ignore the sociolinguistic errors of the ESL speakers.
   d The ESL speakers may get the wrong impression of native speakers and judge them negatively.

5 Scan to find definitions for the following concepts.
   a Sociolinguistic rules of speaking
   b Linguistic competence

VOCABULARY STUDY: SYNONYMS

Find words in the article that are similar in meaning to the following.

1 a specific way to deal with or study something *(n)* Par. 1
2 to make something stronger *(v)* Par. 1
3 incorrect *(adj)* Par. 1
4 weakness; flaw *(n)* Par. 1
5 to record information about something *(v)* Par. 2
6 failure *(n)* Par. 2
7 real *(adj)* Par. 2
8 a person taking part in an activity *(n)* Par. 2
9 a statement that something is true *(n)* Par. 4
10 existing in all cultures *(adj)* Par. 5
11 in comparison with other cases *(adv)* Par. 6
12 to change *(v)* Par. 7

13 to act in the way that is expected *(v)* Par. 7

14 to finish something successfully *(v)* Par. 7

15 to be a part of a situation *(v)* Par. 7

VOCABULARY REVIEW: SAME OR DIFFERENT

The following pairs of sentences contain vocabulary from Readings 1 and 2. Write *S* in the blank if the two sentences have the same meaning. Write *D* if the meanings are different.

_____ 1 To what extent is competence in the English language a requirement for this job?

How is a knowledge of English relevant to this work?

_____ 2 We can address these shortcomings by making some relatively simple modifications.

We have no means of making the changes that could address these flaws.

_____ 3 In recent speeches, the president has mentioned the crucial role played by immigrants in the history of the United States.

Lately in speeches, the president has referred to the great historical importance of immigrants for the United States.

_____ 4 Most social groups expect their members to conform to the behavioral conventions of the group.

Membership in the majority of social groups involves the expectation that individuals will follow the group's rules of behavior.

_____ 5 Applying the rules for apologies in your culture in interactions with English speakers will ensure that you give people the wrong impression.

It is an error to ignore your cultural conventions for apologizing when you are talking with speakers of English.

_____ 6 The company's version of the case claims that the employee was fired from his position for using inappropriate phrases that offended his colleagues.

According to the company, the reason for the employee's dismissal was that he used unacceptable language that was offensive to his coworkers.

_____ 7 These documents give the impression that educational standards in this country have declined in the last twenty-five years.

Most of the data in the extensive literature shows that levels of educational achievement have remained fairly uniform for the last twenty-five years.

_____ 8 There is extensive data in the literature to support the observation that the rules for socially appropriate linguistic behavior vary from culture to culture.

Different societies have different conventions for socially acceptable speech; this conclusion is supported by a great deal of published research.

BEYOND THE READING

Research

Find an example of a social situation in your country in which English speakers may not know how to behave, nor the right things to say. Describe the situation and describe the behavior and language that English speakers will need to know for it.

Discussion

Discuss one of the following questions, depending on your learning situation.

- If you are studying English in an English-speaking country: What in the language of native English speakers seems strange or impolite to you? For example, do they surprise you sometimes when they apologize, express thanks, say "No," or pay you compliments?
- What have you heard English speakers say when using your own language that seems strange or impolite? In other words, what mistakes do they make in sociolinguistic rules of speaking?

Writing

Write a short report on the results of your research or your discussion.

SKILLS AND STRATEGIES 8

TABLES AND ILLUSTRATIONS

Textbooks often use tables, charts, and other graphic material to give information. Examining this material before you read and while you read will help your academic reading.

EXAMPLES & EXPLANATIONS

Example

U.S. Immigrant Totals by Region of Origin 1901–1910 and 1991–2000

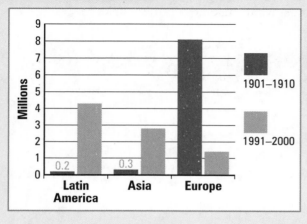

Explanation

If you examine this chart before reading the article that accompanies it, you can gain a great deal of information. You learn about:

- the origins of immigrants to the United States at the start and at the end of the twentieth century.
- the decline in the number of European immigrants and the increase in the number of Latin American and Asian immigrants.

Charts cannot tell you everything, however. This chart, for example, does not tell you *why* the numbers changed.

STRATEGIES

These strategies will help you use graphic material effectively in your reading.

- ■ Before you read a text, look at any graphic material that is included with it.
- ■ Quickly decide how much of the graphic material you can understand without reading the text.
- ■ While you read the text, look for references to the graphic material, such as "see Table 2."

SKILL PRACTICE 1

Answer the following questions from the information displayed in Table 1.

TABLE 1 International Phonetic Alphabet (IPA): English consonants

Symbols	Examples	Symbols	Examples
p	poor, soap	f	feet, safe
b	best, job	v	van, leave
t	ten, wet	θ	three, both
d	day, mad	ð	the, mother
k	king, can, lick	s	see, science
g	go, leg	z	zoo, games
h	hold, head	ʃ	she, sure, fish
m	most, game	ʒ	pleasure
n	no, seven	ʧ	chin, watch
ŋ	playing, sink	ʤ	jump, judge
l	left, fall	w	wet, weather
r	read, four	j	year, onion

1 Write the IPA symbol for the sound at the beginning of these words.

a came _____

b shoe _____

c tin _____

d cheap _____

2 Are the sounds at the beginning of *then* and *throw* the same (*S*) or different (*D*)? _____

3 What IPA symbol would you use for the sound at the end of these words?

a fetch _____

b five _____

c eating _____

d eleven _____

4 Which two sounds in English never occur at the beginning of words?

a _____

b _____

SKILL PRACTICE 2

Not all information, of course, can be found in figures and tables. Related information will also be found in the text. Look at Table 2, Figure 1, and the accompanying text, and answer the following questions.

1 How many places of articulation are there for English consonants? _____

2 What are the three main manners of articulation?
   a _____
   b _____
   c _____

3 List the IPA symbols for the following classes of English sounds:
   a affricates _____ _____
   b voiceless stops _____ _____ _____
   c voiced fricatives _____ _____ _____ _____

4 Find and write down the technical names given to each place of articulation for sounds that are produced at the following positions in the mouth:
   a on the soft palate _____
   b with both lips _____
   c between the front teeth _____

5 Find and highlight definitions for the following terms:
   a articulatory phonetics
   b place of articulation
   c manner of articulation
   d voiced sounds

TABLE 2 Some Consonant Sounds of English: Showing place and manner of articulation, phonetic symbols, and examples

PLACE / MANNER		Bilabial	Labiodental	Interdental	Alveolar	Palatal	Velar
Stops	voiceless	p *p*in			t *t*en		k *c*an
	voiced	b *b*in			d *d*esk		g *g*one
Fricatives	voiceless		f *f*an	θ bo*th*	s *s*ee	ʃ *sh*e	
	voiced		v *v*an	ð *th*e	z *z*oo	ʒ plea*s*ure	
Affricates	voiceless					tʃ *ch*in	
	voiced					dʒ *j*ust	

Table 2 shows how *articulatory phonetics*, the scientific study of the way speech sounds are produced, describes some of the consonants of English. Vertically, the table classifies these consonants by their *manner of articulation* – i.e., **how** the flow of air from the lungs is modified to produce each of three classes of sounds – *stops, fricatives,* and *affricates*. Table 2 also classifies consonants as *voiceless* or *voiced*. During a voiced sound – for example, the [z] in "zip" – the vocal cords in your larynx are shut but loose and the flow of air from your lungs causes them to vibrate. During the voiceless [s] in "sip," on the other hand, the vocal cords are open and tight and the airflow passes between them without causing them to vibrate. As the table shows, English stops, fricatives, and affricates all have voiceless and voiced versions.

Horizontally, Table 2 organizes English consonants into six classes by their *place of articulation* – i.e., **where** the flow of air from the lungs is modified in the vocal tract. Figure 1 shows the relevant features of the vocal tract – the air passages above the larynx that are involved in speech production – and relates them to the six places of articulation listed in Table 2.

FIGURE 1 **The Vocal Tract: Showing the six places of articulation for English consonants**

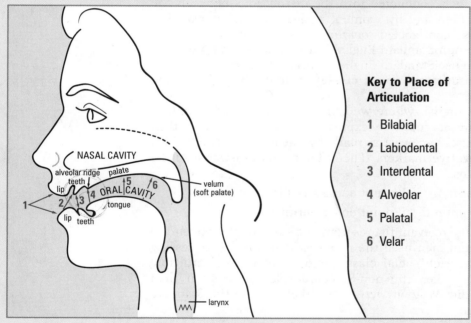

Key to Place of Articulation

1 Bilabial

2 Labiodental

3 Interdental

4 Alveolar

5 Palatal

6 Velar

SKILL PRACTICE 3

Answer as many of the following questions as you can from the information shown below in Table 3. Then answer the remaining questions from the text accompanying the table.

1 How does the behavior of males in this research differ from that of females?
2 How is the behavior of the middle class different from that of the working class?
3 On which variable – gender or social class – is the writer's main focus?
4 What are multiple negation markers?
5 Name and define the tendency that the writer illustrates in Table 3.

TABLE 3 Use of Multiple Negation Markers by Social Class and Gender

Social Class	Males	Females
Middle	19.3%	0.7%
Working	65.0%	47.2%

After research was conducted into the distinctions between the English used by men and by women, a clear pattern appeared, a tendency that has been labeled *sociolinguistic gender pattern*. Men tend to use more non-Standard English forms than women; women are more likely to use Standard English forms. The pattern seems to be maintained in different social classes, although the size of the difference may vary.

One aspect of English where we can observe male-female differences is the grammar used to express a negative idea. For this, Standard English uses one negative marker while non-Standard English uses multiple negative markers. The difference is illustrated in the following examples:

> *Standard:* I'm **not** doing anything.
>
> *Non-Standard:* I'm **not** doing **nothing**.

Table 3 shows the relevant figures from one study on the percentage of time women and men used the non-Standard rule for expressing negative ideas. In each social class, male speakers used multiple negative markers – i.e., the non-Standard rule, more often than female speakers did. Women were more likely to use the Standard English equivalent.

READING 3

CHILD LANGUAGE ACQUISITION: PHONOLOGY

GETTING INTO THE TOPIC

Discuss your answers to the following questions with a partner; if you can, provide examples of children's speech in your language.

1 At what age do children start to speak their native language and how good is their pronunciation when they begin to speak?
2 What sounds in your language do children usually have difficulty with?

GETTING A FIRST IDEA ABOUT THE ARTICLE

Tables or other graphic material can help you get an idea about an article before you start reading it. Look at Table 3.1 on page 134 and answer the following questions.

1 What is the topic of this table and what does it tell you about the topic of the article?
2 What do the four different columns show?
3 Which columns show how Michael's pronunciation differs from adult Standard English?
4 Which columns show how Michael's phonology progresses?
5 At age 24 months, which consonant sounds can Michael pronounce correctly at the beginning of words? How did you find the answer to this question?
6 At age 30 months, can Michael pronounce [p] and [t] at the beginning of words? If not, which consonants does he use instead of [p] and [t]? How did you find the answer to this question?
7 Which words in Table 3.1 begin with two consonant sounds in adult English? How does Michael change the pronunciation of words beginning with these sounds?

WHILE YOU READ

As you read the article, stop at the end of each sentence that contains boldface text and follow the instructions in the box in the margin.

Child Language Acquisition: Phonology

When language first emerges in young children (usually between 18 and 24 months), their pronunciation often bears little resemblance to that of mature users of the language. For example, English-speaking children are by no means able to produce the full range of English sounds. A child who says the word [da], for example, could be saying "car" or "star" or possibly something else. Despite any difficulties caused by imperfect pronunciation, however, family members are usually able to **interpret the child's utterances accurately.** [1]

If children's pronunciation is indeed imperfect, how can we account for the fact that it is comprehensible to those adults regularly exposed to it? One common sense possibility is that family members somehow adjust to the child's speech. Although this answer is vague, it is valuable because it suggests a question that can be empirically investigated: What properties in the child's pronunciation might help adults adjust to it? [2]

To answer **this question** adequately, we can use the knowledge we have acquired in the earlier chapter on articulatory phonetics. With this phonetic information, we are in a position to analyze children's early pronunciation of English and to identify those properties that make it comprehensible to adults. As we examine children's early speech, we find that their pronunciation is not random. On the contrary, even at this early stage, their imperfect utterances reveal regularities in the ways they differ from the Standard pronunciation of adult native speakers. Table 3.1 shows the English consonants in [3]

Read the first sentence of paragraph 2 and highlight the continuing idea. Use it to help you with the main idea of paragraph 1.

Check back and highlight the meaning of *this question*. As you continue to read, highlight the specific property of children's language identified by the writer in paragraph 3.

TABLE 3.1 Michael's Pronunciation at 24 and 30 Months

	Word	Adult Standard	At 24 months	At 30 months
1.	pig	pɪg	bɪ	bɪk
2.	pat	pæt	bæ	bæt
3.	big	bɪg	bɪ	bɪk
4.	bed	bed	be	bet
5.	tooth	tuθ	du	duf
6.	toe	to	do	do
7.	door	dor	do	do
8.	dig	dɪg	dɪ	dɪk
9.	cat	kæt	dæ	dæt
10.	goat	got	do	dot
11.	soap	sop	do	dop
12.	shoes	ʃuz	du	duf
13.	play	pleɪ	beɪ	beɪ
14.	star	stɑr	dɑ	dɑ
15.	spoon	spun	bun	bun

representative speech samples from the same child, Michael, recorded at the ages of 24 and 30 months.

Even at the earlier stage (24 months), **there are distinct patterns in Michael's pronunciation**. He can produce voiced consonants, like [b] and [d], but is not yet capable of uttering voiceless consonants like [p] and [t]. He can produce some stops, such as [b] and [d] but no fricatives such as [θ], [v], [s], [z], or [ʃ] and [ʒ]. (See also Table 3.2.) He can produce stops in the initial position in words but cannot yet produce them at the end of words.

Number each pattern as you find it.

A closer examination of the data reveals that these regular patterns fall into **two types**. The first can be termed *patterns of substitution*, in which certain sounds are replaced consistently by other sounds. For example, in word-initial position, the child is clearly substituting voiced stops for voiceless stops and fricatives: [b] for [p], [d] for [t], and [d] for [s]. Notice also that these substitutions are not random. Bilabial sounds are replaced by bilabials; alveolar sounds are replaced by alveolars. (See Table 3.2.) The second type consists of *patterns of simplification*, in which sounds are not replaced but omitted in specific circumstances. For example, in initial *consonant clusters* – that is, sequences of two consonant sounds – the child systematically omits one of the two consonants. (See items 13–15 in Table 3.1.) It is these regular patterns of substitution and simplification in Michael's English that enable his parents and other adults to understand his imperfect English.

Scan ahead and highlight the technical term for each of these types. Label them *Type 1* and *Type 2*. Then come back and continue reading.

The child's developing capacity to pronounce English sounds becomes evident **when we contrast the forms Michael produced** at 24 months with his later versions of the same words. At 30 months, he is able to produce the voiceless stops [p], [t], and [k], but only in word-final position and often as substitutes for voiced stops. Also at the end of words, we see the emergence of his first fricative, [f], which is being used as a substitute for the fricatives [s] and [z]. At this stage in his acquisition of English pronunciation, he seems to be applying the following rule: all word-initial consonants are voiced and all word-final consonants are voiceless.

Will this paragraph focus on (a) similarities or (b) differences between Michael's pronunciation at 24 and 30 months?

From the regular patterns and the original forms in the data, it is evident that the child is not merely imitating adults; he is constructing his own system for pronouncing English sounds. For many

TABLE 3.2 Place and Manner of Articulation of Selected Consonants in English

MANNER \ PLACE		Bilabial	Labiodental	Interdental	Alveolar	Palatal	Velar
Stops	voiceless	p			t		k
	voiced	b			d		g
Fricatives	voiceless		f	θ	s	ʃ	
	voiced		v	ð	z	ʒ	

Check back and highlight the words that *this* refers to.

researchers, the child's ability to do **this** is evidence that humans possess an innate ability to learn language. In other words, they are genetically programmed to listen to language and construct a simple system of pronunciation. This system becomes progressively more complex and more accurate until, by the age of five or six, a child's pronunciation is very much like that of the adults around them.

MAIN IDEA CHECK

Here are the main ideas of each paragraph in the article. Match each paragraph to its main idea. Write the number of the paragraph in the blank.

_____ A It is useful to investigate which qualities of children's imperfect speech enable adults to adjust to it and understand it.

_____ B Table 3.1 also shows that the child uses substitution and simplification in predictable ways.

_____ C If we use the science of articulatory phonetics to describe children's speech, we find that it differs from adult English in systematic ways.

_____ D Although the pronunciation of very young children differs a great deal from that of adults, it is easily understood by family members.

_____ E The data in Table 3.1 show that children develop their own systematic version of English pronunciation; for some researchers, this is evidence that humans are innately programmed to learn language.

_____ F The data in Table 3.1 show clear patterns in the types of consonants the child is capable and incapable of producing at these early stages.

_____ G The data in Table 3.1 show that, as children get older, they learn to produce sounds that they were incapable of saying at an earlier stage in their development.

A CLOSER LOOK

Look back at the article to answer the following questions.

1 Write definitions and provide examples for the following technical terms.
   a Consonant clusters
   b Simplification of consonant clusters
   c Patterns of substitution

2 Which generalization(s) describe Michael's pronunciation of English at the age of 24 months? Circle all that apply.
   a He can correctly pronounce all consonants at the beginning of words.
   b He can pronounce [b] and [d] at the beginning of words.
   c He can correctly produce [d] wherever it occurs.
   d He is better at pronouncing voiced sounds than voiceless sounds.
   e The consonants he can pronounce are unrelated and have nothing in common.

3 What has Michael learned about pronunciation between the ages of 24 and 30 months? Circle all that apply.

   a How to produce consonant clusters

   b How to produce his first fricative sound

   c How to produce more consonants at the end of words

   d How to produce some voiceless consonants

4 Children seem to learn pronunciation by creating their own simplified system of pronunciation and then gradually making it more complex. True or False?

5 From this article, you could conclude that the word [du] could have more than one meaning in Michael's earliest English. True or False?

6 The child's pronunciation differs from adult pronunciation in predictable ways. True or False?

VOCABULARY STUDY: SYNONYMS

Find words in the article that are similar in meaning to the following.

  1 to appear *(v)* Par. 1

  2 similarity *(n)* Par. 1

  3 correctly *(adv)* Par. 1

  4 to explain why *(v)* Par. 2

  5 possible to understand *(adj)* Par. 2

  6 unclear because of a lack of details *(adj)* Par. 2

  7 unsystematic and done by chance *(adj)* Par. 3

  8 things that a person says *(n)* Par. 3

  9 being an accurate example of something *(adj)* Par. 3

10 a point or period of time in a process *(n)* Par. 4

11 occurring at the start of something *(adj)* Par. 4

12 the replacement of one thing with another *(n)* Par. 5

13 items that follow each other in order *(n)* Par. 5

14 ability *(n)* Par. 6

15 to try to be the same as *(v)* Par. 7

VOCABULARY STUDY: WORDS IN CONTEXT

Complete the sentences with words from the list below. If necessary, review the words in the Key Vocabulary from the Readings on page 260.

properties	reveals	construct	samples	exposed to
innate	range	investigation	consistent with	mature

1 One of the most interesting _____ of children's early English is that it differs from adult English in systematic ways.

2 To study the development of a child's English, you first need to record _____ of his or her speech regularly over a period of a year or longer.

3 An examination of the data _____ regular patterns of substitution in a child's speech.

4 Young children automatically acquire the accent of the people whose speech they are most often _____.

5 Children's emerging language differs from mature English, but it is systematic. This is evidence that children _____ their own linguistic rules from the language in their environment.

6 All normal children acquire the language of their environment perfectly. This is evidence that the capacity to learn language is _____ in humans.

7 Children acquire the phonological rules of spoken English very early. Their vocabulary, however, continues to expand as they _____.

8 Although initial evidence suggests human error as a possible cause, the official _____ into the accident could take a year or more.

9 The data provided by this new study are _____ those from three other studies.

10 Although a U.S. undergraduate may major in English, he or she must take courses in a variety of other subjects, which can _____ from astronomy to sociology.

BEYOND THE READING

Research
Do some research into the pronunciation "mistakes" that children make as they are acquiring your language as their first language.

Discussion
Discuss the following situation with a partner.
- At 24 months, Michael has the same pronunciation for *star* and *car*, [da]. Does this mean that he doesn't hear and understand the difference between the two words? How could you determine if he knows the difference between the two words?

Writing
Write a short report on the results of your research or of your discussion.

READING 4

BRAIN DEVELOPMENT AND LEARNING A SECOND LANGUAGE

GETTING INTO THE TOPIC

Discuss the following questions with a partner.

1 Among immigrants, who finds it easier to learn the language of their new country: children or adults?
2 What most clearly tells native speakers of English that English is not your native language: your grammar, vocabulary, or pronunciation?

GETTING A FIRST IDEA ABOUT THE ARTICLE

Before doing the activity below, read the first paragraph of the article.

Read the first sentence of paragraph 2. Think of a question that you expect this paragraph to answer and match it to a question below. Continue in the same way for paragraphs 3–6. Write the number of the paragraph in the blank.

_____ A How do scientists explain why adults cannot attain native-speaker pronunciation in a second language?

_____ B What does aphasia research tell us about the link between language learning and cerebral lateralization?

_____ C What research provides evidence for the existence of the phenomenon described in Paragraph 1?

_____ D What is the connection between people suffering from aphasia and the critical period theory of second language learning?

_____ E What relevance does the critical period theory have for people learning a second language?

WHILE YOU READ

As you read the article, stop at the end of each sentence that contains boldface text and follow the instructions in the box in the margin.

Brain Development and Learning a Second Language

The question of how people learn a second language has received a great deal of scientific attention – **especially since the 1970s.** Research has offered evidence that has been used to support a number of conflicting claims about second language (SL) learning. However, one fundamental observation is less open to dispute than others. If success in adult second language learning is measured by how close the learner comes to the level of a native speaker, it is possible, and quite common, for adults to achieve a high degree of success in learning SL grammar and vocabulary. The same degree of success, though, is apparently unattainable in SL phonology; adult SL speakers who sound like native speakers are extremely rare.

Results obtained in a number of research studies offer evidence for the existence of **this phenomenon** and for its association with the age of the speaker. Scovel (1978) asked native speakers of Standard American English to distinguish between native and non-native American English in adult speech and writing. When they listened to recorded speech, Scovel's subjects were able to identify non-native speakers 97 percent of the time. In the task of identifying non-native writers, however, they attained an accuracy level of only 47 percent. In other words, they performed no better than a person completing the task by random guessing. Other studies (Asher and Garcia 1969; Oyama 1976) found that Cuban and Italian immigrants, provided that they had arrived in the United States before the age of ten, were much less likely to speak English with a foreign accent than those who had arrived at an older age. Among schoolchildren learning English in Germany, Fathman (1975) found that those in the six-to-ten age range had better pronunciation than their eleven- to fifteen-year-old peers.

How have scientists attempted to account for the remarkable inability of adult learners to acquire a native-like pronunciation in the second language? One attempt to explain this phenomenon is to be found in the *critical period theory*. Proponents of this theory argue that the acquisition of native-speaker pronunciation in any language is biologically possible only until about the age of twelve. This is the age at which *cerebral lateralization* is completed. Cerebral lateralization is the process by which the two hemispheres of the brain increasingly specialize in particular functions. At the end of this process, control of most language functions is permanently located in the left hemisphere, while the right hemisphere is responsible, among other things, for visual and spatial perception. When lateralization is complete, according to **the theory**, it closes the critical period of life during which humans can acquire native-speaker pronunciation in a language.

The critical period theory is consistent with a vast amount of data that has been accumulating for many years about patients suffering from *aphasia*, a loss of language abilities associated with brain damage from injury or disease. The data provide conclusive evidence

Use your experience with introductions to highlight two sentences that contain the specific ideas to be addressed in this article.

Check back and highlight the words that describe *this phenomenon.*

Check back to refresh your understanding of this theory. Highlight its name. Then draw brackets around the lines that explain the theory.

FIGURE 3.1 Functions of the Left and Right Hemispheres of the Human Brain

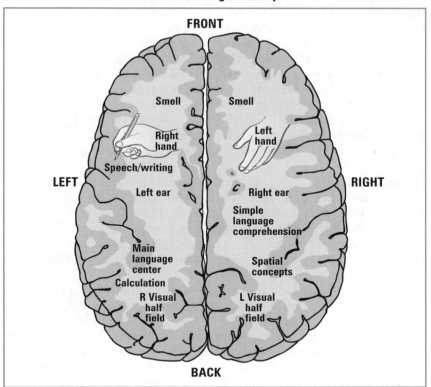

that language is localized in the brain's left hemisphere. Seventy percent of adult patients with an injury to the left hemisphere suffer from some language disability. However, patients with injuries to the right hemisphere retain the ability to speak and understand language perfectly. Their problems lie elsewhere, in activities such as recognizing faces and patterns or finding their way from one place to another.

Evidence for the effects of **cerebral lateralization** on language learning also comes mainly from research with patients suffering from aphasia after a *hemispherectomy*, surgery to remove one hemisphere of the brain. Lenneberg (1967), in his own research and in the relevant medical literature, found that 97 percent of children undergoing this operation before the age of ten recovered their language abilities after some temporary aphasia and continued to acquire their first language. In those rare cases where the same type of surgery was performed on adults, however, all the patients were left with complete and permanent aphasia. From this research, it seems that a child's brain has a degree of flexibility that allows the right hemisphere, when necessary, to take over the functions of the left. After lateralization, this flexibility declines significantly, and adults who lose language through brain injuries are unable to regain it. On the basis of these research findings, proponents of the critical period theory claim that it is this lack of flexibility in adults that limits their ability to acquire native-speaker pronunciation in a second language.

5

Scan back, find, and highlight the definition of *cerebral lateralization*. Then come back and continue reading.

As you continue reading, find two ways in which the theory is relevant for second language learning. Number them.

The critical period theory has certain, though limited, 6 **implications** for second language learners. It suggests strongly that learners who wish to acquire a native-speaker accent need to start on the task before their teens and that older learners are unlikely ever to achieve that goal. However, it must be emphasized that the theory does not justify bringing to a halt the teaching of SL pronunciation. There are too many counterexamples for such a conclusion to be valid – i.e., too many cases of adults who acquire adequate to very good pronunciation in a SL through instruction, hard work, and practice. While they may rarely be mistaken for native speakers, their efforts are rewarded by perfectly comprehensible speech.

References

Asher, J., and Garcia, R. 1969. The optimal age to learn a foreign language. *Modern Language Journal* 38, pp. 334–41.

Fathman, A. 1975. The relationship between age and second language productive ability. *Language Learning* 25, pp. 245–53.

Lenneberg, E. 1967. *Biological foundations of language.* New York: Wiley.

Oyama, S. 1976. A sensitive period for the acquisition of a nonnative phonological system. *Journal of Psycholinguistic Research* 5, pp. 261–83.

Scovel, T. 1978. The recognition of foreign accents in English and its implications for psycholinguistic theories of language acquisition. *Proceedings of the Fifth International Association of Applied Linguistics* (389–401). Montreal: Laval University Press.

MAIN IDEA CHECK

Here are the main ideas of each paragraph in the article. Match each paragraph to its main idea. Write the number of the paragraph in the blank.

_____ A Evidence from aphasia patients confirms that most language is processed in the left hemisphere of the brain.

_____ B Research studies have supported the claim that adults can rarely acquire native-speaker pronunciation in a second language.

_____ C Although native-speaker pronunciation in a second language may be unattainable, adults should not stop trying to improve their second language pronunciation.

_____ D Although adults can achieve a high level of competence in the grammar and vocabulary of a second language, they are generally less successful in mastering its pronunciation.

_____ E The critical period theory states that the ability to acquire native-speaker pronunciation disappears around the age of twelve, when, after lateralization, language functions permanently settle in the left hemisphere of the brain.

_____ F Evidence from brain surgery patients shows that lateralization causes the brain to lose some of its earlier capacity to acquire language.

A CLOSER LOOK

Look back at the article to answer the following questions.

1 Find and underline definitions of the following technical concepts:
   a Cerebral lateralization
   b Aphasia
   c Hemispherectomy

2 Adults learning a second language can come closer to native-speaker performance in pronunciation than they can in grammar and vocabulary. True or False?

3 What evidence do experts use to justify the claim that cerebral lateralization plays a role in our pronunciation of a second language? Circle all that apply.
   a The large majority of young children losing some or total use of their left hemisphere successfully acquire their native language.
   b When adults suffer the loss of their left cerebral hemisphere, the result is complete and permanent aphasia.
   c People who learn a second language as young children are less likely to speak that language with a foreign accent than those who learn a second language as adults.
   d Cerebral lateralization brings to an end the period when people can acquire native-speaker pronunciation in a second language.

4 What might the critical period theory have to say to those interested in second language learning and teaching? Circle all that apply.
   a It is a waste of time for adults to work to improve their pronunciation in a second language.
   b Adult second language learners should not expect perfect pronunciation in that language.
   c We can expect that people who start learning a second language as children will have better pronunciation than people who start as adults.
   d Adults have difficulty learning a second language because they do not practice enough.

5 Which conclusions can be drawn from observations of the behavior of patients, both children and adults, suffering from aphasia? Circle all that apply.
   a Aphasia is always a temporary condition.
   b Lateralization limits the brain's ability to acquire language.
   c The right hemisphere of the brain can take over the language functions from an injured left hemisphere in children but not in adults.
   d Language is usually processed in the left hemisphere of the brain.

6 Imagine that you are preparing for a test in which you expect to be asked to write a short description of the critical period theory. Identify the one paragraph that provides you with the information needed to prepare for the test.

VOCABULARY STUDY: SYNONYMS

Find words in the article that are similar in meaning to the following.

1 disagreeing *(adj)* Par. 1

2 doubt; disagreement *(n)* Par. 1

3 if and only if *(conj)* Par. 2

4 unusual and therefore worth examining *(adj)* Par. 3

5 extremely important *(adj)* Par. 3

6 supporters *(n)* Par. 3

7 for the rest of a person's life *(adv)* Par. 3

8 to be found in a small area *(v)* Par. 4

9 to experience a medical procedure as a patient *(v)* Par. 5

10 the quality of being able to adapt to and function in new situations *(n)* Par. 5

11 to recover something; to get something back *(v)* Par. 5

12 to prevent something from developing beyond a certain level or size *(v)* Par. 5

13 possible but unstated relevance *(n)* Par. 6

14 a stop; an end *(n)* Par. 6

15 to give something valuable for work that has been well done *(v)* Par. 6

VOCABULARY REVIEW: SAME OR DIFFERENT

The following pairs of sentences contain vocabulary from Readings 3 and 4. Write
S in the blank if the two sentences have the same meaning. Write *D* if the
meanings are different.

_____ 1 The data obtained in these investigations consistently reveal the same general properties in children's emerging English.

According to all these research studies, a number of qualities are shared by the early English of children.

_____ 2 In spite of all their efforts, researchers have not yet succeeded in accounting for the wide range in individual achievement in learning a second language.

Up to now, researchers have failed to explain why different people attain acceptable competence in a second language in spite of vastly different amounts of effort.

_____ 3 An examination of the early utterances of English-speaking children reveals consistent substitutions of certain categories of consonant sounds.

Observations of the early language of English-speaking children show that they randomly replace some consonant sounds with others.

_____ 4 The utterances of very young children are often incomprehensible to all except those people involved in taking care of them.

The emerging language of very young children can often be understood only by their peers.

_____ 5 One phenomenon that is apparently common to all young children's English is the temporary substitution of certain sounds by other, phonetically related sounds.

In their emerging English, it appears that, for a time, all young children replace certain sounds with other phonetically similar sounds.

_____ 6 Over the past ten years, the validity of Dr. Green's conclusions has been confirmed by an accumulation of evidence from a wide range of research studies.

Evidence provided by a wide variety of research investigations conducted over the past decade has exposed the flaws in Dr. Green's conclusions.

_____ 7 An investigation of a child's developing linguistic competence involves obtaining an initial speech sample and then, over a period of time, regularly gathering samples that can be compared with the original data.

To conduct a study of how a child's language progresses over time, you start by getting a sample of speech at an early stage and then continue, on a regular basis, to collect samples to compare with the initial data.

_____ 8 One fundamental requirement for a theory of language acquisition is that it must account for the fact that all children, by the age of six, have become fully competent in the phonology and grammar of their native dialect.

A basic necessity for a theory of language acquisition is that it must be able to explain how all children attain mastery of the phonology and grammar of their native dialect by the age of six.

BEYOND THE READING

Research

To show you differences between English and your own language, do the following research.

- Compare the consonant sounds in English with the consonant sounds in your language. Do some occur in English, but not in your language? Do some occur in your language, but not in English?
- Choose three consonant sounds that occur in both English and your language, and compare where they can occur in words – at the beginning, at the end, in the middle.
- Compare possible consonant clusters in both English and your language.

Discussion

Discuss the following question with a partner:
- Which features of English pronunciation give you the greatest difficulty?

Writing

Write a short report on the results of your research or your discussion.

SKILLS AND STRATEGIES 9
COMPARISON AND CONTRAST

Academic writing often contains texts in which ideas and information are compared and contrasted. There are different ways in which such texts may be organized. Being able to recognize and follow these different patterns of organization will help your reading.

EXAMPLES & EXPLANATIONS

Example

Sign languages, the communication systems developed by deaf people, **have** a great deal **in common** with spoken languages. Signers communicate at a speed **similar to** that of native speakers. Research has also shown that sign language and spoken language cause **the same** areas of the brain to become active.

Explanation

In this paragraph, the focus is on similarities. You can recognize the focus here by these phrases: *have . . . in common, similar to, the same.*

The backgrounds and experiences of today's immigrants to the United States are **different** from those of nineteenth-century immigrants. **Unlike** the earlier immigrants, who were almost all from Europe, the majority of contemporary immigrants come from Asia and Latin America. [A_1, B_1] **Instead of** moving into their own ethnic neighborhoods in the inner cities, as the nineteenth-century Europeans did, many of today's immigrants favor middle-class suburbs. [A_2, B_2]

In this paragraph, the focus is on differences. You can recognize this by the following words and phrases: *different, unlike, instead of.* Notice that the author contrasts the earlier and later immigrants point by point: [A_1, B_1; A_2, B_2]

The backgrounds and experiences of today's immigrants to the United States are **different** from those of 19th century immigrants. The earlier immigrants, who were almost all from Europe, settled in their own ethnic neighborhoods in the inner cities. [A_1, A_2] The majority of contemporary immigrants, **on the other hand**, come from Asia and Latin America and many of them favor American middle-class suburbs. [B_1, B_2]

In this paragraph, the focus is also on differences. Here, the author has used the same information as in the example paragraph above. However, instead of organizing the information point by point, the author has used contrasting blocks of points: [A_1, A_2; B_1, B_2].

THE LANGUAGE OF COMPARISON AND CONTRAST

In texts with comparison and contrast organization, you will see Comparison Markers, (words that mark similarities) and Contrast Markers (words that mark differences).

COMPARISON MARKERS

NOUNS	VERBS	ADJECTIVES	CONNECTORS
comparison	to compare	both	in common (with)
equivalence	to resemble	common	like
resemblance		comparable	similarly
similarity		equivalent	
		similar	
		universal	

CONTRAST MARKERS

NOUNS	VERBS	ADJECTIVES	CONNECTORS
change	to change	changing	but
contrast	to contrast	contrasting	however
difference	to differ	different	in contrast to
distinction	to distinguish		instead of
variety	to vary	+ comparative adjectives or adverbs – e.g., *rarer, more appropriate, less effectively*	in theory
+ nouns describing changes – e.g., *decline, fall, increase, rise*	+ verbs describing changes – e.g., *decline, fall, increase, rise, used to*		in practice
			on the one hand
			on the other hand
			rather than
			unlike
			whereas
			while

STRATEGIES

These four strategies will help you understand texts with comparison and contrast organization.

- While you are reading, look for Comparison Markers and Contrast Markers.
- Identify the general subject of the comparison or contrast.
- As you read the details, identify the organization used by the writer. Is it [A_1, A_2; B_1, B_2] or [A_1, B_1; A_2, B_2]?
- In your notes, make charts that clearly show the points of contrast and/or similarity.

SKILL PRACTICE 1

In the following sentences, circle the Comparison Markers and the Contrast Markers. Then indicate whether the sentence deals with similarities (S) or differences (D). The first sentence has been done for you as an example.

__D__ 1 (Unlike) his older brother, Jim, who is completing a degree in mathematics, Matthew intends to study music at college.

_____ 2 A characteristic that is common to the health care systems of both developed and developing countries is that they tend to give priority to the treatment of disease.

_____ 3 While affordable health care is available in Canada to everyone, about 41 million Americans do not have easy access to care because they have no health insurance.

_____ 4 Some of the problems facing privately funded health care systems resemble those confronting publicly funded systems.

_____ 5 It is possible to distinguish two main types of linguistic variation: between-group variation and variation within the individual.

_____ 6 How you address a person varies depending on your relationship with that person and the setting in which you are speaking.

_____ 7 Speech acts such as thanking, apologizing, accepting or refusing offers are probably universal behaviors that are common to all cultures.

_____ 8 Children can acquire perfect pronunciation in a second language, whereas most adults learning a second language never achieve perfect pronunciation in it.

SKILL PRACTICE 2

In the following paragraphs, highlight the sentence that contains the main idea. Circle any Comparison Markers and Contrast Markers, and indicate whether the paragraph focuses on similarities (S) or differences (D). Paragraph 1 has been done for you as an example.

__D__ 1 Questions that may be perfectly appropriate and polite in one culture may be considered impolite in another culture. In some cultures, for example, the question "How is your wife?" is an acceptable one to ask a friend or a colleague. In some other cultures, (however,) the same question would be unacceptable.

_____ 2 Appropriate classroom behavior may vary from culture to culture. In some countries, students are expected to sit quietly in class and absorb the information and ideas presented by the professor. Rarely, if ever, do students ask questions. In the United States, on the other hand, teachers encourage students to ask questions. In fact, if a student never asks questions in class, the professor may get the impression that the student is inattentive or uninterested in the work.

_____ 3 There are only a few similarities between the traditional behavior of language teachers and that of adults caring for young children up to the age of four or five. These caregivers resemble second language teachers in correcting children when they use a wrong vocabulary item – e.g., "We don't call that a fork. We call it a spoon." They are also acting like teachers in attempting to develop in children an awareness of socially appropriate and inappropriate speech, with comments like "Don't say that! It's not polite!"

_____ 4 The language used by parents with two-year-olds has qualities that distinguish it from the speech used with older children and adults. Research has found, for example, that adults make their pronunciation more precise and distinct when they are talking with children of around two. It has also been established that adults often repeat nouns rather than use pronouns. In addition, they talk about actions occurring in the here and now; for example, "Now Daddy is going to the bedroom to get your shoes."

SKILL PRACTICE 3

The following text contrasts the American family of the 1960s with that of the 1990s. The writer contrasts blocks of points. Complete the chart to show the same information contrasted point by point.

AREA OF CONTRAST	FAMILIES IN THE 1960s	FAMILIES IN THE 1990s
Working mothers with children under one year		
Children living with two parents		
Children living with one parent		
Divorce rate		

The typical American family experienced considerable changes in the second half of the twentieth century. In 1960, 31 percent of mothers with children under one year were working outside the home. In the same year, a large majority (88 percent) of children were living with both their parents; only 9 percent were living in single-parent households. The number of divorced people stood at a low 2 percent of the adult population.

By the twenty-first century, however, the American family looked very different. By 2001, 58 percent of mothers with children younger than one had jobs outside the home. The proportion of two-parent families had fallen to 74 percent, while kids living in single-parent households had risen to 25 percent. Americans appeared to have become more willing to solve marriage problems by divorce. By 2001, the divorce rate, as measured by the number of divorced adults in the total adult population, had risen to 9.4 percent.

MAIN READING
LANGUAGE ACQUISITION: THE EARLY YEARS

GETTING INTO THE TOPIC

Discuss the following questions with a partner.

1 How is the speech of young children (up to age four) who are acquiring your native language as their first language different from adult speech?
2 What do you know about your own speech when you were that age?

GETTING A FIRST IDEA ABOUT THE ARTICLE

For information about the organization and topics of this article, read the section headings, look at the illustrations, and scan the introduction. Then complete the chart by matching each topic with the section that deals with it. Some sections may have more than one topic. Write the number of the section (I–V) in the blank.

SECTION	TOPIC
	An examination of grammar in the speech of young children
	How researchers approach the study of language acquisition
	Two types of scientific theory of first language acquisition
	An outline of the topics discussed in the article
	The speech that adults use when they interact with young children
	An evaluation of language acquisition theories
	Data in the form of utterances produced by young children

WHILE YOU READ

Read the article section by section. Stop after each sentence that contains boldface text and follow the instructions in the box in the margin. After you read each section, answer the Main Idea Check and A Closer Look questions, which can be found on pages 160–166.

Language Acquisition: The Early Years

I. INTRODUCTION

By the time children have reached the age of about five, they have accomplished something we all take for granted. They have learned how to speak their native language. In the years that follow, of course, they will continue to learn vocabulary; they will also acquire a few additional grammar patterns and new styles of speaking for new situations. Many, but by no means all, will learn to read and write – if they are given favorable opportunities to do so. However, what remains true for all children is the enormous achievement during those first five years of life. The children have acquired perfect pronunciation of their language, a goal most adults learning a second language fail to achieve. They have acquired most of the grammatical knowledge necessary to speak and understand their language. Yet the systems of grammar and sounds they have learned, apparently with ease, are so complex that highly trained **linguists still have difficulty giving an adequate description of them.**

This remarkable achievement takes place with little or no formal teaching. Parents generally do not correct their children's utterances even when their speech contains pronunciation and grammatical errors. Nor do they offer explanations of grammatical and pronunciation rules; in fact, most parents have no conscious knowledge of the vast majority of rules governing their language. Parents and others who look after children, known in the research as *caregivers*, simply allow and encourage infants and young children to take part in conversations. They speak to the children and wait for responses; they interpret the responses and react naturally to what a child has said or to what they think a child has said. This linguistic interaction between children and their caregivers, and, later, their peers is the only language to which children are exposed. In a sense, it is a language "class," but it is one that bears no resemblance to traditional school classes.

Another characteristic of first language acquisition is its universal 100-percent success rate. All normal children brought up in a normal social environment acquire the language of that environment. Language acquisition takes place regardless of whether the caregivers are educated, prosperous citizens of a so-called advanced society or are uneducated, even illiterate, impoverished members of a developing country. It occurs regardless of the differences in individual children's intellectual abilities; during those first five years or so, a future dish-washer will be as successful in language learning as a future Nobel Prize winner in physics. Deaf children will also successfully acquire their own first language – provided that the language of their environment is accessible to them. If caregivers know and use sign language, deaf children will acquire a native competence in sign language and will use it just as naturally as a hearing child uses speech.

How do children acquire their native language? This question has fascinated people for centuries. However, only since the 1960s has the question been a subject of extensive investigation. In this article,

> Read the first sentence of paragraph 2 and highlight the continuing idea. Use it to help you identify the main idea of paragraph 1.

> Check back and highlight one sentence in paragraph 2 that mentions the first two characteristics. Then note each characteristic in the margin of the paragraph that discusses it.

The word *first* indicates the beginning of a list of items. Find and circle the other words in the paragraph that will help you find the order of ideas in this article.

we **first** briefly outline the goals and methods of *developmental psycholinguistics*, the scientific study of language acquisition. Then we examine some data. We look at what English-speaking children actually say during the first three or four years of the language acquisition process, and then we turn our attention to the speech and behavior of their caregivers. Finally, we examine two types of theory that attempt to account for child language acquisition and assess the adequacy of each.

II. GOALS AND METHODS

Like all sciences, the study of language acquisition seeks to 5 describe and then explain a natural phenomenon – in this case, how children approach the task of learning their native language. To advance toward these goals, language acquisition researchers, like other scientists, construct hypotheses on the basis of theories. These hypotheses are then empirically tested against data obtained from experiments and observation. If hypotheses are not confirmed by experimental or observational data, they are revised and tested again or rejected, and the theories are modified.

Scan forward to identify and mark the place where the writer finishes discussing *goals* and begins discussing *methods*. Then come back and begin reading the section.

In developmental psycholinguistics, observing language in natural 6 or experimental settings and recording data are fundamental steps in the process of investigation. For the most part, the basic data will consist of the utterances produced by children. In recording this data, researchers must maintain a high degree of accuracy. An additional requirement is to obtain representative data samples. In other words, the samples must come from a wide range of children so that scientists can feel confident that they are observing how children in general learn their first language. If scientists do not observe widely, their conclusions will be of limited validity; and if they fail to ensure accuracy, the validity of the entire scientific investigation will be in doubt.

Scan forward and highlight three major components of language that can help to narrow the focus of research. Then come back and continue reading.

Because of the complexity of their subject, language acquisition 7 researchers typically focus on a narrow range of **linguistic phenomena**. In vocabulary, for example, they may look at how a child's comprehension of certain words develops. In phonology, researchers may examine the development of a small number of sounds in children's emerging English. In grammar, investigators may focus on how a small number of children first begin to ask questions and how their formulation of questions changes over time. Alternatively, they may conduct experiments that measure a child's ability to produce certain word-endings (e.g., plural *-S* or past tense *-ED*) at a given stage in the child's development.

III. CHILDREN'S ENGLISH AND THE DEVELOPMENT OF GRAMMAR

A comprehensive treatment of child language acquisition would 8 involve looking at data on the development of a child's phonology, grammar, and vocabulary. Here, however, we will limit ourselves to examining data on children's acquisition of English grammar. This narrower focus is justifiable because the general properties of children's

TABLE 3.3 Utterances of Two Children at 24 Months (Pakenham, 1991)

Child's English	Adult Equivalent
1. Dada wet	Daddy's wet. (father after running)
2. Dada dry	Daddy's dry. (father after shower)
3. Bye-bye car	Are we going out in the car?
4. Mama help	Mommy, help me!
5. Katie do	Let me do it!
6. Katie cry	Katie is crying.
7. Michael night-night	I want to go to bed.
8. Michael sleep	Michael is sleeping.
9. Michael book	This is my book.
10. More juice	Can I have more juice?

emerging grammar are very similar to those visible in their developing phonology and vocabulary.

The grammar of children's English becomes evident when they are 9 able to produce utterances consisting of two words. Consider the examples in Table 3.3. For clarity, the examples are in normal English spelling. This gives a false impression of their phonological competence; readers should remember that the children's pronunciation is far from perfect and is itself still developing. For example, "Katie cry" is pronounced [didi dɑɪ] and "Michael sleep" is pronounced [mɑɪbəl dip].

From these examples, which are similar to the two-word utterances 10 documented by other researchers, **a number of the typical characteristics** of child grammar are evident. First, the utterances are clearly and significantly different from what the children could have heard. In other words, the children are producing new utterances. It is in this sense that we use the term *creative* to describe child language.

Systematic simplification by omission is another characteristic of 11 child language. The utterances recorded in Table 3.3 are all simpler than their adult equivalents because elements of the adult English utterances have been omitted. Consider the types of words the children are using in Table 3.3. They are all nouns, verbs, and adjectives, or *content words*, which refer to persons, animals, objects, actions, quantities, and qualities. Now consider the types of words that are absent. Notice that the utterances do not contain the words *the, to, in, I, me, we, is,* and *are.* These articles, prepositions, pronouns and auxiliary verbs are *function words.* Function words are part of the grammatical system of English and are usually predictable for adult native speakers of English. Since function words like these are among the most frequently used words in English, they are certain to have been present in the caregiver language to which the children were exposed. Yet they are completely absent from the children's English at this stage of linguistic development.

When we consider what children do *not* say, we notice a third 12 important property of child language – children use correct word

Scan this paragraph and the first sentences of paragraphs 11–14. Highlight the words that show you the writer is introducing another characteristic. Then come back and continue reading this paragraph.

order. For example, neither of the children were ever heard to say the following:

- Wet Dada
- Help Mama
- Do Katie
- Night-night Michael
- Sleep Michael
- Book Michael
- Juice more

The total absence of such examples, in which the word order is reversed, draws our attention to the consistent word order used by children at this stage and to the fact that their English, even at this early stage, is rule-governed and not random. Their correct use of basic word order suggests that they have learned two fundamental facts about English grammar: word order is crucial for communication in English, and the basic word-order pattern is a sequence of subject and verb.

Another characteristic of children's English becomes evident when 13 children leave the two-word-utterance stage. They begin to add more words or parts of words and to combine utterances they have produced at an earlier stage. **Consider the examples listed in Table 3.4.** By comparing the children's earlier and later utterances, we see the increasing complexity of their English. At the age of thirty months, they are obviously producing grammatically more advanced patterns of English than they were initially.

Children's errors are further evidence of the rule-governed and 14 creative nature of their utterances. These mistakes show that children construct grammatical rules for themselves without direct teaching. By beginning to use incorrect plural forms like *mens, foots, feets,* and *mouses,* children between two and three show they have learned the rules for regular plurals. Over the next three or four years, errors of the same type become more frequent and persist in children's English. The following conversation (Cazden, 1972, p. 92) shows a child of four extending the rule for regular past tense verbs to an irregular verb.

Child: My teacher holded the baby rabbits and we patted them.
Adult: Did you say your teacher held the baby rabbits?
Child: Yes.
Adult: What did you say she did?
Child: She holded the baby rabbits and we patted them.
Adult: Did you say she held them tightly?
Child: No, she holded them loosely.

Study Table 3.4. Highlight the elements in the child's English at 30 months that distinguish it from the earlier version.

Scan forward and highlight seven examples of *errors.* Then, as you continue reading, identify and highlight both the term for these types of errors and its definition.

TABLE 3.4 Utterances of Two Children at 30 Months (Pakenham, 1991)

Child's English (24 months)	Child's English (30 months)	Adult Equivalent
1. Bye-bye car?	Bye-bye white car?	Are we going out in the white car?
2. Dada work?	Dada work white car?	Is Daddy going to work in the white car?
3. Katie cry	Katie crying	Katie is crying.
4. Michael night-night	Michael no night-night	I don't want to go to bed.

"No, Jimmy, it's not 'I sawed a chair'—
it's 'I have seen a chair' or 'I saw a chair'."

These and many other examples documented in the literature show the phenomenon of *overgeneralization*, in which a child clearly applies a rule he or she has constructed to a case where it is not applicable. It is also significant that the child persists in the overgeneralization, even when the adult's speech to the child contains the correct form.

IV. CAREGIVER LANGUAGE

A number of researchers have investigated *child-directed speech* 15 (CDS), the language used by caregivers, especially mothers, in their interactions with infants and young children. The empirical evidence provided by this research has clearly established that CDS is generally similar to speech used in adult-to-adult speech. When children are around age two, however, and only for a short time, CDS has properties that make it significantly different from the language that caretakers use with infants, children thirty months or older, or adults.

With children of this age, caregivers seem to use **a number of** 16 **strategies** to make their CDS more comprehensible. One strategy is to pronounce sounds more clearly. Malsheen (1980) found that caregivers made their pronunciation of vowels and consonants more accurate and distinct when they were talking with children in the one-word stage of language learning. Caregivers also repeat words they might not normally repeat with adults or older children. Newport (1975), for example, found that caregivers tended to repeat important

Scan forward and highlight the general description of each strategy. Number them. Then come back and continue reading the paragraph.

nouns rather than replace them with pronouns. They also speak
about topics directly related to the physical setting of the interaction.
Studies (e.g., Cross, 1977; Snow, 1972) have documented the tendency
of the caregiver to focus on the here and now in conversations with
young children and to label relevant objects (Tomasello & Farrar,
1986) while they are performing a task, such as dressing or washing
the child. Caregivers also avoid vocabulary and grammatical forms
perceived to be beyond the child's capacity to comprehend (Anglin,
1977; Mervis & Mervis, 1982; Sachs, 1983).

After this short stage, however, the vast majority of CDS is speech 17
whose general properties are typical of adult-adult interaction. First
and foremost, caregivers almost invariably treat the child's utterance
as one component of a genuine conversation and respond naturally to
its perceived meaning. The following example illustrates this property.

> *Child:* Water, Dada. [wawa dada]
> *Adult:* Okay, I'll get you some. You know, I'm thirsty too!

CDS is also similar to speech directed toward adults in its absence 18
of correction. In responding to children's utterances, caregivers do
not correct the phonological or grammatical errors. When such corrections do occur, as in the following example (Braine, 1971, p. 161),
they are usually an informal experiment, an attempt by the caregiver
to observe the child's reactions. As language lessons using correction,
imitation, and repetition, however, **these attempts invariably end in
frustration and failure**. Children seem unwilling or unable to imitate
the caregiver's model.

> *Child:* Want other one spoon, Daddy.
> *Father:* You mean you want "the other spoon."
> *Child:* Yes, I want other one spoon, please, Daddy.

Father: Can you say "The other spoon"?
Child: Other . . . one . . . spoon.
Father: Say "other."
Child: Other.
Father: "Spoon."
Child: Spoon.
Father: "Other . . . spoon."
Child: Other . . . spoon. Now give me other one spoon?

V. THEORIES OF LANGUAGE ACQUISITION

The preceding description has identified some of the clear proper- 19 ties of child language and caregiver speech during the acquisition process. The discussion enables us to list some of the phenomena that an adequate theory of language acquisition must account for.

- Children are not good conscious imitators of grammar or phonology.
- Children create original linguistic forms that are not present in their linguistic environment.
- Children's utterances are rule-governed.
- Children's speech grows in phonological and grammatical complexity until it matches the speech of their community.
- Caregivers generally do not correct phonological and grammatical errors in children's developing English.
- Caregivers respond positively to children's attempts to communicate even though the utterances are often linguistically incorrect.

For the purpose of this introduction to early child language 20 acquisition, we will distinguish **two theories** that seek to account for language acquisition. The first of these is the *behaviorist theory*, often referred to as the *imitation-reinforcement theory*, or *I-R theory*. It claims that children imitate what they hear; when they say something that is correct, they receive a reward from the caregiver (e.g., they are understood and perhaps praised, and the caregiver may do what they want). By reinforcing the connection in the child's mind between the utterance and the situation for which it was appropriate, the reward increases the likelihood that the child will use this correct example of language again. Similarly, when children make a linguistic error, according to the theory, they receive a correction from their caregivers. This makes it more likely that the child will use the correct form in future utterances.

Scan this paragraph, and as many other paragraphs as needed, to find and highlight the names of these theories. Then come back and continue reading.

It seems clear that imitation and reinforcement are factors in 21 language acquisition. Imitation explains why children brought up in an English-speaking environment learn English as their native language, why Japanese children acquire Japanese, and so on. Reinforcement also plays a role, but probably a different one than behaviorist researchers once thought. If caregivers signal that they do not understand an utterance, for example, studies have established that children will attempt to change that utterance.

Will the paragraph focus on (a) the strengths of the I-R theory or (b) its weaknesses? Use your answer as your main idea hypothesis.

There are, however, a number of major flaws in the I-R theory, 22 shortcomings that are serious enough to invalidate its claim to be an adequate account of how a native language is acquired. First, many examples of early child language, including data presented in the preceding sections, show that children are not good imitators. They are, on the other hand, wonderful creators of original language forms, forms they could never have heard in their linguistic environment. An insistence on imitation as the major acquisition strategy makes the theory **incapable of accounting for this obvious property of child language**.

A second problem for the theory is the fact that the creativity, or 23 originality, evident in child language is not random. In fact, as we established earlier, it is systematic and rule-governed. However, there is nothing in the imitation-reinforcement theory that can account for this rule-governed creativity.

Third, empirical research has not confirmed the assumption that 24 reinforcement plays the central role in language acquisition that behaviorist theories claim. From observing child-caregiver interaction, it is clear that caregivers rarely attempt to correct children's pronunciation and grammar. When such corrections do occur, as in the spoon conversation cited earlier, children appear unable or reluctant to repeat the model they are given.

The I-R theory, because it relies heavily on reinforcement, also has 25 a problem accounting for the fact that children's grammar and phonology continue to develop. **The example of the caregiver replying to the thirsty child** shows that caregivers understand children's English and react positively to it even though it is far from perfect. According to the theory, successful outcomes like these provide positive reinforcement, which should cause children to stop trying to perfect their pronunciation and grammar. In actual practice, however, the halt in linguistic development predicted by the I-R theory does not occur. Instead, children continue developing their language and, as they do, their English increasingly resembles the English of their environment.

A more recent theory offers a very different approach to language 26 acquisition. The *creative construction theory*, or *CC theory*, focuses on the central and crucial role of the child in the language acquisition process. It argues that humans are born with an innate capacity for language, which begins to operate when children are exposed to meaningful language in their environment. The *innateness hypothesis*, as it is called, explains why language, under normal circumstances, emerges at more or less the same time in all children. It also explains why all children, apparently with no special effort, attain a uniformly high level of ability in the spoken language of their environment during the first five years, in spite of a wide range of living conditions and intellectual abilities. **Neither of these aspects of child language acquisition** is addressed by the I-R theory.

Because of the innateness hypothesis, the CC theory can argue 27 that children themselves make a massive contribution to the language acquisition process. Their innate capacity for language acquisition first enables them unconsciously to look for patterns in the language they hear. Then it enables them, again unconsciously, to formulate rules, which they apply to the production of utterances. Finally it

This is one flaw of the I-R theory! Scan paragraphs 23–25 and highlight words that show you where to expect more of these weaknesses. Then come back and continue reading.

Scan back for this example and note the number of the page and paragraph where you found it.

What are these two aspects of *child language acquisition*? Check back and number them.

permits them gradually to add complexity to these rules so that they increasingly resemble the rules of the adult speech in their environment.

By arguing that children use **this innate ability** to acquire language, the CC theory can account for much of the data left unexplained by the I-R theory. It explains children's creativity – i.e., their use of forms they have never heard in mature English. It explains the rule-governed nature of children's language, which is revealed, for example, in the errors of overgeneralization we have already seen – namely, the use of the *-s* and *-d* endings for irregular plurals and for the past tense of irregular verbs. It is also consistent with the fact that children continue to develop their language in spite of frequent feedback from caregivers that their imperfect English has been understood.

28

Check back and highlight the words that introduce three specific components of *this innate ability*. Then number the components.

The CC theory, therefore, is generally a much more complete account of language acquisition than the I-R theory. **However**, there are many crucial questions still to be answered before a fully adequate theory of language acquisition can be developed. Some of the questions focus on the child's contribution to the acquisition process. For example, what does the innate capacity of the human mind to learn language consist of? To what extent is it an ability that is designed exclusively to process language data? Other questions focus on the contribution of the environment. For example, are there any normal caregiver behaviors that can help or hinder language acquisition?

29

Will this paragraph focus on (a) the shortcomings of the CC theory or (b) its strengths?

At present, language acquisition researchers are offering sometimes conflicting answers to such questions. At the same time, as more research is conducted all over the world, evidence is accumulating that the language produced by children during the acquisition process contains a great deal of individual variation. To what extent does such variation reflect differences in children's acquisition processes? These and other unanswered questions make it clear that much of the process of first language acquisition remains to be explained.

30

References

Anglin, J. 1977. *Word, object, and conceptual development.* New York: Norton.

Braine, M. D. S. 1971. The acquisition of language in infant and child. In C. E. Reed (Ed.), *The learning of language.* New York: Appleton-Century-Crofts.

Cazden, C. 1972. *Child language and education.* New York: Holt, Rinehart and Winston.

Cross, T. G. 1977. Mothers' speech adjustments: The contributions of selected child listener variables. In C. Ferguson and C. Snow (Eds.), *Talking to children: Language input and acquisition.* Cambridge, U.K.: Cambridge University Press.

Malsheen, B. 1980. Two hypotheses for phonetic clarification in the speech of mothers to children. In G. Yeni-Komshian, J. S. Kavanagh, and C. A. Ferguson (Eds.), *Child phonology: vol 2. Perception.* New York: Academic Press.

Mervis, C. B., and Mervis, C. A. 1982. Leopards are kitty-cats: Object labelling by mothers for their thirteen-month-olds. *Child Development* 53, pp. 258–66.

Newport, E. L. 1975. *Motherese: The speech of mothers to young children.* Technical Report no. 52. San Diego: Center for Human Information Processing, University of California.

Pakenham, K. J. 1991. Personal data collection.

Sachs, J. 1983. Talking about then and there: The emergence of displaced reference in parent-child discourse. In K. Nelson (Ed.), *Children's language.* New York: Gardner Press.

Snow, C. 1972. Mother's speech to children learning language. *Child Development* 43, pp. 549–65.

Tomasello, M., and Farrar, M. J. 1986. Joint attention and early language. *Child Development* 57, pp. 1454–63.

SECTION I: Introduction

MAIN IDEA CHECK

Here are the main ideas of each paragraph in this section of the article. Match each paragraph to its main idea. Write the number of the paragraph in the blank.

Paragraphs 1–4

_____ A Provided they have access to the language spoken in their environment, all children successfully learn that language, regardless of their intellectual or socioeconomic differences.

_____ B Children's acquisition of their native language, during the first five years of life, is an impressive achievement.

_____ C This article examines psycholinguistic research into how children acquire their native language.

_____ D The language acquisition process is completed successfully without the help of formal teaching.

A CLOSER LOOK

Look back at Section I of the article to answer the following questions.

1 Children have learned the sounds of their native language by about the age of five. True or False?

2 Acquiring the spoken language will ensure that people also learn to read and write that language. True or False?

3 Which fact(s) does the writer report about the linguistic interaction between children and caregivers? Circle all that apply.

  a Caregivers do not need to correct children's language because it contains no errors.

  b Caregivers generally ignore grammar and pronunciation errors in children's language.

  c Caregivers involve children in natural communication.

  d Caregivers go to classes so that they can learn how to correct children's language.

4 In the United States, a deaf child is born to deaf parents who communicate with American Sign Language. Which language(s) will the child learn as his or her native language?

  a American Sign Language

  b English

  c No language

  d Both English and American Sign Language

5 Find and highlight a definition for *developmental psycholinguistics*.

SECTION II: Goals and Methods

MAIN IDEA CHECK

Here are the main ideas of each paragraph in this section of the article. Match each paragraph to its main idea. Write the number of the paragraph in the blank.

Paragraphs 5–7

_____ A Ensuring that the data are accurate and representative is essential in child language acquisition research.

_____ B Because of the complexity of language and human behavior, research projects in developmental psycholinguistics usually have a narrow focus on small aspects of language acquisition.

_____ C Developmental psycholinguistics seeks to account for language acquisition by developing hypotheses from theories and testing them empirically.

A CLOSER LOOK

Look back at Section II of the article to answer the following questions.

1 This diagram describes the scientific process as it applies to language acquisition research. Reread paragraphs 5–6. Then complete the diagram with sentences A–F. Write the correct letter in each box.

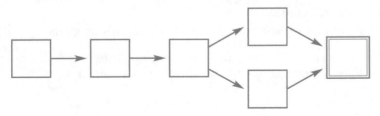

A A hypothesis may not be confirmed by the data.

B Language acquisition theories suggest hypotheses to researchers.

C The hypothesis is revised and tested again.

D Researchers test hypotheses against data obtained by observation and experiments.

E The hypothesis is rejected.

F The theory is modified.

2 Identify the two basic requirements, outlined in paragraph 6, that research data must meet in order to maintain the validity of the research.

3 According to information in paragraph 7, the following could be the title of a typical research project in child language acquisition: "The Acquisition of Regular English Plural Markers in Two Children Aged 2–4." True or False?

SECTION III: Children's English and the Development of Grammar

MAIN IDEA CHECK

Here are the main ideas of each paragraph in this section of the article. Match each paragraph to its main idea. Write the number of the paragraph in the blank.

Paragraphs 8–14

_____ A The word-order patterns found in children's English show that their language is rule-governed.

_____ B The utterances of very young children are simpler than those of adults because children systematically omit function words.

_____ C Children's developing grammar is first visible when they start producing two-word utterances.

_____ D In addition to reflecting the rule-governed creativity of their language, children's errors of overgeneralization show that they construct their own grammatical rules.

_____ E This article focuses on one component of children's early English, its grammar.

_____ F As children's utterances become longer, it becomes clear that their grammar increases in complexity.

_____ G The data shows that the language produced by children is creative.

A CLOSER LOOK

Look back at Section III of the article to answer the following questions.

1 Write out definitions and provide examples for the following technical concepts:

a creativity in child language

b systematic simplification

c content words

d function words

e overgeneralization

2 What properties of children's English does the writer exemplify in this article? Circle all that apply.

a Children use linguistic forms they could not have heard in the speech of their caregivers.

b As children grow older, their English utterances increase in complexity.

c Children randomly omit words that occur in the adult equivalents of their utterances.

d Children's early utterances show that they have acquired basic patterns of word order.

e Children tend to produce errors through a process of overgeneralization.

f In the earliest stages of the acquisition process, children use some of the commonest function words of adult English.

SECTION IV: Caregiver Language

MAIN IDEA CHECK

Here are the main ideas of each paragraph in this section of the article. Match each paragraph to its main idea. Write the number of the paragraph in the blank.

Paragraphs 15–18

_____ A Caregivers normally do not correct errors in grammar or pronunciation in children's English; when they do so, children are unable to use the correction.

_____ B Child-directed speech (CDS) is generally similar to speech used with adults, except during a short period when the child is about two years of age.

_____ C Caregivers almost always react to children's speech as a natural attempt to communicate; they respond to its perceived meaning.

_____ D For a short time, caregivers change their speech in a number of ways in order to make it easier for children to understand.

A CLOSER LOOK

Look back at Section IV of the article to answer the following questions.

1 What changes do caregivers make to the speech they use with children around the age of two? Circle all that apply.
   a They tend to talk about objects and actions in their immediate environment.
   b They pronounce their words more clearly.
   c They begin to correct their children's mistakes in grammar and pronunciation.
   d They avoid vocabulary and grammar that they think might be difficult for the child to understand.

2 How is child-directed speech similar to the speech used by adults in conversation with other adults? Circle all that apply.
   a Caregivers focus on what the child is trying to communicate.
   b Caregivers correct any phonological or grammatical errors they hear in the child's utterance.
   c Caregivers treat the child's utterance as part of a natural conversation.
   d Caregivers tend to ignore mistakes in grammar or pronunciation that may occur in the child's speech.

SECTION V: Theories of Language Acquisition

MAIN IDEA CHECK

Here are the main ideas of each paragraph in this section of the article. Match each paragraph to its main idea. Write the number of the paragraph in the blank.

Paragraphs 19–25

_____ A The imitation-reinforcement (I-R) theory cannot explain how children continue developing their grammar and pronunciation without any correction from their caregivers.

_____ B A theory of language acquisition must account for these properties of child and caregiver language, which were identified in Section III.

_____ C By relying on imitation, the I-R theory cannot explain data that show children are not good imitators but excellent creators of language.

_____ D The first of two theories argues that language is acquired through a process of imitation and reinforcement.

_____ E The imitation-reinforcement theory also cannot explain the rule-governed nature of children's original utterances.

_____ F Imitation and reinforcement play some role in language acquisition.

_____ G Reinforcement cannot be a major component of child language acquisition because caregivers rarely correct children's errors in grammar and pronunciation.

_____ H By arguing that the ability to acquire language is innate in humans, the creative construction theory can explain two general aspects of the process left unexplained by the I-R theory.

_____ I There still remains a great deal to be understood about the process of language acquisition.

_____ J By arguing that children are innately equipped to learn language, the creative construction theory is able to explain much that the I-R theory cannot.

_____ K Although it is more adequate than the imitation-reinforcement theory, the creative construction theory leaves many important questions unanswered.

_____ L The creative construction theory argues that children themselves play a very significant role in their acquisition of language.

A CLOSER LOOK

Look back at Section V of the article to answer the following questions.

1 This diagram describes how proponents of the reinforcement-imitation theory view the process of language acquisition. Reread paragraph 20. Then complete the diagram with sentences A–G. Write the correct letter in each box.

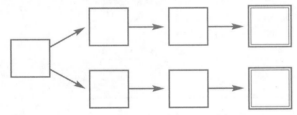

A The caregiver corrects the child or does not reward the child.

B The child produces an utterance by imitating adult language.

C The utterance is incorrect.

D The reward increases the likelihood that the child will produce similar correct utterances.

E The child is rewarded when the caregiver understands and perhaps praises the child or does what the child wants.

F The utterance is correct.

G The lack of reward reduces the probability that the child will use the incorrect utterance again.

2 This diagram describes how proponents of the creative construction theory
   view the process of language acquisition. Reread paragraphs 26–27. Then
   complete the diagram with sentences A–E. Write the correct letter in each box.

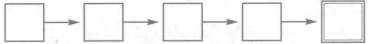

   A The language capacity operates as soon as children hear language being used
      naturally.
   B Children make the rules more complex and more like the rules of mature English.
   C Children are born with an innate capacity for language.
   D Children unconsciously formulate rules and use them to produce utterances.
   E Children are able unconsciously to search for patterns in language.

3 In Section V, the author contrasts two theories of language acquisition, using
   the block method of contrast [A_1, A_2, A_3; B_1, B_2, B_3]. Complete the chart below
   with the paragraph number(s) in which you find the relevant information. By
   doing this, you will be displaying the same information point by point [A_1, B_1;
   A_2, B_2; A_3, B_3].

	I-R THEORY	CC THEORY
Description of the theory		
Evidence supporting the theory		
Weaknesses in the theory		

BEYOND THE READING

Research

Do Internet or library research on the acquisition of your native language. Look for examples of children's grammar and identify some of its general properties. Are they similar to or different from the properties you have read about in this article?

Discussion

With a partner, discuss what you would say to the parents in the following situation.

- Friends who have a three-year-old child come to you. They are very concerned about the child's speech. Here are some of their concerns:

    "He makes a lot of mistakes in grammar. He says things like "My feets hurt" and "We readed it yesterday." We try to correct him, but we don't always have the time for that. Also, neither of us was very good in grammar in school. What should we do?"

Writing

Look at the chart you completed on page 166. Here you have identified the ideas that you could use to assess the two competing theories of language acquisition. Use this chart to help you write an answer to the following question, which might be given as an exam question in a linguistics class.

- Give a brief description of the two theories of language acquisition. Identify three phenomena in the child language data that you have studied and assess which theory better explains the data.

MAKING CONNECTIONS

The vocabulary in these two exercises comes from all the readings in Unit 3. The exercises will help you see how writers make connections across sentences in a text.

EXERCISE 1: CONNECTIONS BETWEEN SENTENCES

Read the numbered sentence. Then choose and circle the sentence, a or b, that logically follows it. Then, from the box, decide how the sentence you chose connects to the first. Write *A*, *B*, or *C* to identify the connection.

> A It provides research results to support the general statement in the first sentence.
>
> B It develops a contrast to what is described in the first sentence.
>
> C It continues, in greater detail, the topic described in the first sentence.

_____ 1 Results obtained in a number of studies support the claim that adult learners of a second language rarely attain the same level of success in pronunciation that they can apparently achieve in its grammar and vocabulary.

    a One fundamental weakness of this claim is that it is too vague and thus cannot undergo the empirical testing that is necessary in scientific investigations.

    b Scovel (1978) found that English native speakers were consistently able to distinguish between native and non-native speakers by their speech but not by their writing.

_____ 2 Earlier investigations of language acquisition contained a number of critical flaws.

    a Later studies avoided some of these fundamental weaknesses by basing their analyses on samples of genuine utterances produced by children.

    b The researchers were able to develop a theory that accounted for a wide range of data obtained by expert observers.

_____ 3 Investigators have gained a better understanding of language acquisition from an apparently unusual source: the linguistic errors produced by children, which have been documented extensively in the literature.

    a Mistakes such as "I eated everything," for example, reveal that children have an innate capacity to seek and identify rules in the language they are exposed to.

    b In spite of their efforts to account for these mistakes, researchers have been unable to develop a valid explanation for them.

_____ 4 If we define linguistic competence in English as the capacity of the native speaker to comprehend and produce new utterances in English, what specifically might that linguistic competence involve?

    a Conducting research in English involves collecting data, ensuring that the data is correct and representative, and developing the competence to analyze the data.

    b One of its components is phonological competence – i.e., knowing the sounds of English and the rules for combining them into sequences and for modifying them in ways that are appropriate for the speech situation.

_____ 5 As children, we all attain a uniform level of competence in our first language, apparently with little conscious effort, merely by interacting with mature speakers in our environment.

    a To a great extent, this process resembles our experience in school, where our individual differences quickly emerge and are revealed in achievement ranging from poor to excellent.

    b For most adults, however, learning a second language seems to be a fundamentally different process that involves much conscious effort and produces widely varying degrees of success.

EXERCISE 2: CONNECTIONS WITHIN PARAGRAPHS

Make a clear paragraph by putting sentences A, B, and C into the best order after the numbered sentence. Write the letters in the correct order. The boldface words help you identify continuing ideas.

1 Ironically, it is the language errors made by children that often provide evidence for how children acquire their native language. ____ ____ ____

A	B	C
Such overgeneralization errors, which are extremely rare in adult English but are typical of children's speech, reveal that children do not merely imitate the English of their linguistic environment.	In the literature, for example, we consistently find utterances like "I seed Santa Claus," "I holded the bunny," and "We readed a story."	**They** also demonstrate that children have the innate capacity to construct grammatical rules for the language they are exposed to and to apply these rules as they create novel utterances.

2 There is a widespread assumption that the rules and conventions for polite linguistic interaction are universal. ____ ____ ____

A	B	C
The research, for example, documents a tendency for Americans to say thanks in situations where such an expression would be inappropriate, perhaps even offensive, in some South Asian cultures.	However, data collected in investigations of thanking in different cultures are inconsistent with this popular notion.	**Such evidence** reinforces the position of researchers who argue that the rules for appropriate speech often vary from culture to culture.

3 In linguistics, *style* is defined as that version of our speech that is appropriate to a specific social situation; *style shifting* refers to our ability to modify our speech, so that it fits a number of situations, ranging from formal to casual. ___ ___ ___

| **A** **Style shifting** produces variation in each of the three major components of language: grammar, vocabulary, and pronunciation. | **B** Despite the differences in the linguistic properties of **these examples**, native speakers will have no difficulty accurately judging which utterances are formal and which are informal. | **C** Compare, for example, the English used by the same person in these two utterances: "Are you participating in tomorrow's race?" and "You runnin' tomorrow?" |

4 Although most people agree that regional varieties, or dialects, exist in English, what might surprise some people is the claim by linguists that there are also gender varieties – i.e., that there are distinctions between the English used by men and by women. ___ ___ ___

| **A** Investigators have also found, for example, that men tend to use informal or casual grammar and pronunciation more often than women, who tend to prefer the Standard equivalent. | **B** The **differences** are not limited to vocabulary, where they might be expected because of differences in the conventional interests that males and females are socialized to have. | **C** Data obtained by a number of researchers, however, confirm that **such differences** exist. |

5 A fundamental challenge for psycholinguistic researchers has been to account for children's remarkable capacity to acquire their native language merely through exposure to it in meaningful interaction with competent native speakers. ___ ___ ___

| **A** For example, changes in newborns' rate of sucking reveal that infants can distinguish between speech sounds and other sounds in their environment. | **B** Empirical evidence is emerging, from the earliest stages of child development, to support the view that **this ability** is innate. | **C** By six months, babies are focusing on the crucial meaning-carrying sounds of their native language. |

Looking After Planet Earth

SKILLS AND STRATEGIES 10-12
- Problem-Solution Texts
- *-ing* Words That Express Results
- Nominalization

READINGS
- The Aral Sea: An Environmental Crisis
- Ecology, Overpopulation, and Economic Development
- Unsustainable Development and the Mayan Civilization
- Biological Diversity Under Attack
- Climate Change: Managing the Global Greenhouse

SKILLS AND STRATEGIES 10

PROBLEM-SOLUTION TEXTS

Writers use problem-solution organization for paragraphs, for sections, and for entire articles. Becoming familiar with this type of organization will help your academic reading.

EXAMPLES & EXPLANATIONS

Example

The cheapest, most effective solution to the problem of heart disease is for people to start taking more responsibility for maintaining their own health.[1] They can do this by developing healthier eating habits, by getting adequate exercise, by reducing stress in their lives, and by avoiding activities that increase the risk of a heart attack.[2]

Explanation

In sentence 1, the writer clearly identifies a problem (heart disease) and describes a general solution to the problem (people taking more responsibility for staying healthy).

In sentence 2, the writer describes four specific ways to achieve the general solution in sentence 1.

THE LANGUAGE OF PROBLEM-SOLUTION

Here's a list of problem-solution markers that you will find in your academic reading. These words may differ in meaning to some extent, but you can learn the differences by studying the words in context.

PROBLEM MARKERS			
NOUNS			
burden	*danger*	*hardship*	*puzzle*
challenge	*deficiency*	*issue*	*risk*
complication	*difficulty*	*lack*	*setback*
concern	*dilemma*	*mystery*	*shortage*
conflict	*dispute*	*obstacle*	*threat*
crisis	*excess*	*problem*	*trouble*

SOLUTION MARKERS

VERBS			NOUNS
to address	to ease	to resolve	relief
to alleviate	to improve	to respond	remedy
to answer	to overcome	to settle	resolution
to cope with	to relieve	to solve	response
to deal with	to remedy	to tackle	solution

STRATEGIES

These strategies will help you recognize and understand texts that have problem-solution organization.

- Look for Problem Markers and Solution Markers while you preview or read an article.
- When you see a Problem Marker, scan forward through the text to identify if and where the writer starts dealing with solutions.
- After identifying a Problem or a Solution Marker, read closely to determine the specific problem or solution.
- Expect some cause and effect analysis of problems. Then look for the logical connection between the cause of a problem and the suggested solution.

SKILL PRACTICE 1

In the following sentences, circle the Problem Markers and underline the problem. The first one has been done for you as an example.

1 A dangerous global (crisis) arose in 1962 when the United States determined that the <u>Soviet Union was placing nuclear missiles in Cuba</u>, only ninety miles off the coast of Florida.

2 The threat of possible nuclear war between the two superpowers – the United States and Russia – lessened considerably in the 1990s.

3 How to strengthen their economies and at the same time protect the environment is a dilemma that all countries will have to recognize.

4 When people move to another country, one obstacle they may face is their inability to speak and understand the language of their new home.

5 The project to land an American astronaut on the moon experienced a serious setback when three astronauts were killed in a training exercise in 1967.

6 Many Americans, even college students, live with the burden of heavy debt because they have easy access to credit cards, but little or no experience in using them wisely.

7 Differences in sociolinguistic rules of speaking can give rise to complications when people from two different cultures try to communicate.

8 The difficulty of learning technical vocabulary is one that both native and non-native speakers of English have in common in their university classes.

9 In spite of major advances toward a color-blind society, the United States still faces challenges associated with its racially oppressive past.

10 Another issue that the government has ignored is the tendency of new immigrants to settle in high numbers in a few parts of the country.

SKILL PRACTICE 2

In the following sentences, circle any Problem Markers, highlight the Solution Markers, and underline any actual solutions. The first one has been done for you as an example.

1 The Cuban missile (crisis) of 1962 was settled when each side agreed to move its weapons from the other's borders.

2 One way to alleviate the burden of having large numbers of immigrants settle in one area of the country is to offer immigrants incentives to live elsewhere.

3 Increased support from the federal government would relieve some of the difficulty of providing services to large numbers of immigrants.

4 Ethnic communities have been a source of support for new immigrants as they learn to cope with the challenges and hardships of life in the United States.

5 The United Nations is attempting to persuade the two countries to begin talking about a resolution of the conflict between them.

6 For more than a century, the United States has tended to deal with labor shortages by encouraging suitably qualified workers to immigrate.

7 For decades, no British government attempted to address the fundamental issue in health care in the United Kingdom, namely, its chronic underfunding.

8 The U.S. government uses a number of strategies to remedy the injustices that remain from the nation's racist past.

9 Debt relief must be a component of any comprehensive international effort to tackle the problems of underdevelopment and poverty.

10 In 2003, the major obstacle to organizing a fully effective response to the AIDS crisis was the lack of a vaccine.

SKILL PRACTICE 3

In the following texts, circle the Problem Markers and highlight the Solution Markers. Then write either *Problem* or *Solution* in the margin next to the relevant information. The first one has been done for you as an example.

1   As more and more women take jobs outside the home, the (lack) of high quality, affordable child care not only puts working parents in a (dilemma) but creates a (challenge) for organizations who wish to hire the best-qualified workers. Some employers have addressed the (problem) by establishing their own child-care centers.

Problem

Solution

2   Culture shock has been described as a problem afflicting people who live in a culture that is not their own. Its symptoms can range from mild homesickness to severe depression and disorientation, which can leave a person incapable of coping with even the minor demands of life. The two basic ways to overcome culture shock are spending some time in the new culture and maintaining an interest in it.

3   Many societies today face the challenge of dealing with an increase in violent crime. A frequent response is to focus on law enforcement by, for example, hiring more police, increasing punishment for violent criminals, and building more prisons. A very different approach to the problem is to attempt to prevent people from developing into violent criminals in the first place, for example, by identifying and changing social conditions that are likely to produce such criminals.

4   According to some experts, the irresponsible behavior of insurance companies was a major contributor to the rapidly rising costs of U.S. health care in the 1980s and early 1990s, costs that were of concern to businesses and the public alike. To increase their profits, some companies refused to pay for any preexisting medical conditions and denied insurance to people with a higher risk of developing a disease. These people, however, could often obtain treatment from hospitals, which covered their losses by raising the costs for insured patients.

For the experts, therefore, one way to respond to rising health care costs was for the government to force insurance companies to provide coverage to all who need it and for all conditions, preexisting and new. An alternative was for the government to follow the example of Sweden, Canada, and other countries and adopt a system of national health insurance funded by a federal health tax.

5   In the early 1990s, the number of unmarried teenage girls becoming pregnant and having babies reached crisis level in the United States. The majority of these young mothers failed to complete school and find employment. Within two years, many became pregnant again.

In an attempt to address the problem of teenage pregnancy and motherhood, some school districts established special schools that provided regular health clinics for the expectant mothers and free day care for the children while the new mothers attended classes until graduation. The success of such programs was visible in their high graduation rates and in their low rates of repeat pregnancies. In one such program, 80 percent of the girls finished high school while only 9 percent of them became pregnant again within two years. Outside such programs, the rate was a depressing 80 percent.

READING 1

THE ARAL SEA: AN ENVIRONMENTAL CRISIS

GETTING INTO THE TOPIC

Study the map on the opposite page. Then discuss the following questions with a partner.

1 What changes can you identify in the Aral Sea between 1960 and 1989?
2 What might have caused these changes?

GETTING A FIRST IDEA ABOUT THE ARTICLE

To prepare you for the content of a paragraph, you should read its opening sentence and formulate a question that you expect the paragraph to answer.

In the chart below, formulate a question for each paragraph that is missing one. Read the first sentence of the paragraph and formulate a question that you think the paragraph will answer. Write the question in the chart.

PARAGRAPH	QUESTION
1	Which region's ecology has been damaged by economic development?
2	Where exactly is the Aral Sea?
3	
4	How could the decision to expand agriculture affect the Aral Sea so much?
5	
6	
7	What are the results of the contamination of local drinking water?
8	
9	So why is the story of the Aral Sea important?

Now read through the questions in the completed chart to anticipate the information you will encounter in the article.

WHILE YOU READ

As you read the article, stop at the end of each sentence that contains boldface text and follow the instructions in the box in the margin.

The Aral Sea: An Environmental Crisis

For many decades, environmental scientists have been warning us
that enormous damage can be done to the ecology of a region by pressure for economic development and by apparently reasonable, but in
reality short-sighted, responses to this pressure. The damage will not
only negate any economic progress the region experiences but also has
the potential to make the region unlivable. The recent history of the
Aral Sea, described in an article in *Environment* magazine by V. M.
Kotlyakov, a Russian geographer, is a clear example of **the damage
that poorly planned economic activity can have on the environment**.

1

The Aral Sea is located in a semiarid region of south-central Asia,
in the recently independent states of Kazakhstan and Uzbekistan. Its
basin extends into three other independent republics: Turkmenistan,
Tajikistan, and Kyrgyzstan. (See Figure 4.1.) As recently as the 1950s,

2

Which of the following
paragraphs deal with the
causes and which deal with
the effects? Scan the first
sentence of paragraphs 2–7
and look for Cause and
Effect Markers to help you
answer this question. Label
the paragraphs *Cause* or
Effect.

FIGURE 4.1 Map of the Aral Sea Basin

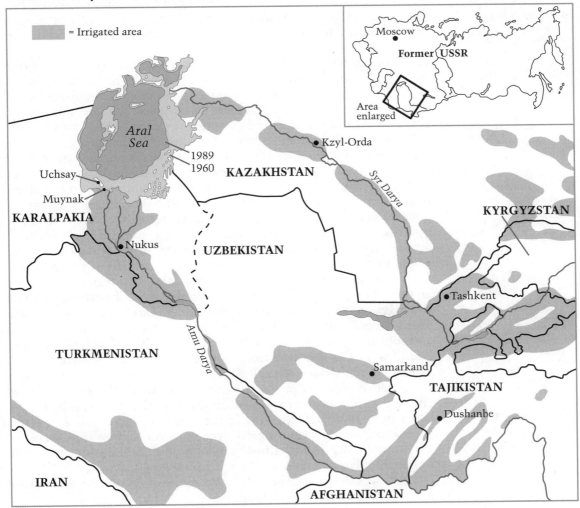

the sea covered an area of 66,000 square kilometers, with a mean depth of 16 meters. Its waters were fresh, with a mean salt content of 1 percent to 1.1 percent. Two large rivers, the Amu Darya and the Syr Darya, flowed into the sea. The water from the two rivers, plus the annual rainfall, maintained the volume of water in the sea.

By 1990, however, the Aral Sea had shrunk to about 55 percent of its original area and had become two separate lakes. Its total water volume had dropped to less than one third of its 1950s volume. The sea's salt content, on the other hand, had increased by almost 300 percent. **3**

The root cause of **these massive changes** in the physical character of the Aral Sea was the decision, made in the late 1950s, to develop agriculture by using water from the Amu Darya and the Syr Darya rivers for irrigation. From the early 1960s, the area of irrigated agricultural land expanded rapidly, an expansion that reduced the flow of water into the Aral Sea to approximately 13 percent of its pre-1960 total. **4**

The consequences of the reduction in water flow and the increase in the Aral Sea's salt content have been **catastrophic for the area surrounding the sea**. Whole species of fish have died out, and commercial fishing, which used to be a productive economic activity, has practically stopped. Without the moderating influence of the vast expanse of the original sea, the climate of the territory within one hundred to two hundred kilometers of the sea has become more extreme. Rainfall has decreased, while summers have become shorter and warmer. As a result, there are no longer enough frost-free days in the year for growing cotton, once the main crop of the Amu Darya delta. In addition, as the water level has dropped, the forests on either side of the Amu Darya river have dried up, causing the loss of about half the region's bird and mammal species. Another problem is that salt from the exposed sea bed is spread by storms on the surrounding land, increasing its salt content and **reducing its fertility**. **5**

The impact of attempts at economic development on the ecology of the Aral Sea region, however, goes beyond the immediate consequences of falling water levels. Inefficient methods of irrigation allow much of the water to evaporate, causing *soil salinization*, the accumulation of crop-damaging salts in the soil. Farmers use more water to wash these salts out of the soil; the salts then enter the rivers, ultimately increasing the salinization of areas downstream and the Aral Sea itself. **Other short-sighted agricultural practices in the irrigated land include** the extensive use of artificial fertilizers and chemical pesticides to support production of the two main crops, rice and cotton. As a result, the water that ultimately drains back into the Amu Darya and the Syr Darya from the fields carries high concentrations of phosphates and nitrates, as well as chemical pesticides. **6**

The accumulation of these toxic chemicals in the rivers is now contaminating local supplies of drinking water. As a result, in the years since 1975, people living in the area have increasingly suffered from a number of serious health problems. As is often the case with environmentally linked illness, infants and children are the most vulnerable. For example, in Karakalpakia, now the region of Uzbekistan closest to the Aral Sea, the 1989 mortality rate for children was among the highest in the world. **7**

Check back to identify *these massive changes*. Number each change.

As you continue reading, find and number at least six catastrophic consequences of the changes in the Aral Sea.

Read the first sentence of paragraph 6 and underline the continuing ideas. Use this information to help you identify the main idea of paragraph 5.

Other tells you that the writer has already mentioned some practices. Check back and highlight two.

In 1990, a conference of international scientists met to consider 8
the Aral Sea crisis. The scientists concluded that the Aral Sea region
was already an ecological disaster area and that massive changes in
agricultural policy and practices were urgently needed to reverse the
process of environmental destruction. If **such measures** were not
taken without delay, the Aral Sea basin would become a wasteland,
incapable of supporting human settlements and activities.

Check back and highlight the meaning of *such measures*.

The case of the Aral Sea and its basin is not unique; it is a powerful 9
example of *anthropogenic desertification*, the conversion of agricultural land to desert by environmentally destructive human activities.
This is a global problem. Indeed, the United Nations Environment
Program estimates that about 60 percent of all agricultural land in
drier regions may be affected to some degree by desertification.
Salinization, for example, threatens 20 percent of all irrigated land in
the United States. The Aral Sea crisis, therefore, offers a clear
warning of the dangers of poorly planned economic development. It
also, however, offers an opportunity to gather information needed to
find solutions to desertification and to create alternative models of
economic development.

MAIN IDEA CHECK

Here are the main ideas of each paragraph in the article. Match each paragraph to
its main idea. Write the number of the paragraph in the blank.

Paragraphs 1–4

_____ A The basic cause of the damage to the Aral Sea was the use of irrigation to
expand agriculture.

_____ B This paragraph gives physical details of the Aral Sea in 1950.

_____ C This paragraph gives details of how the Aral Sea changed between 1950 and
1990.

_____ D The Aral Sea illustrates the massive ecological damage that can be caused by
the careless economic development of a region.

Paragraphs 5–9

_____ E As a result of the chemical contamination of drinking water, there has been
an increase in human health problems.

_____ F The reduced flow of water into the Aral Sea has had disastrous
environmental and economic consequences for the sea and its basin.

_____ G In 1990, a scientific conference decided that the Aral Sea region was an
ecological disaster area in need of urgent action to prevent its complete
destruction.

_____ H The story of the Aral Sea is one example of the global problem of desertification through human activities.

_____ I Short-sighted agricultural practices have increased the levels of salts, pesticides, and other damaging chemicals in the environment.

A CLOSER LOOK

Look back at the article to answer the following questions.

1 The following diagram represents the general process exemplified by the history of the Aral Sea. Complete the diagram with sentences A–E. Write the correct letter in each box.

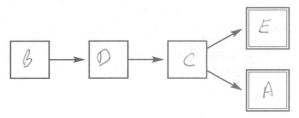

A Humans may no longer be able to make a living, or even live, in the region.

B The people and government of a region feel that economic development is a major priority.

C The economic development policies cause great damage to the region's ecology.

D In the pressure for economic development, short-sighted decisions are taken.

E The ecological damage will negate the economic advances that the region may have made.

2 What change(s) did the Aral Sea itself undergo between 1960 and 1990? Circle all that apply.

a It became much saltier.

b It expanded rapidly because of irrigation.

c It experienced no changes. The water from two large rivers and the annual rainfall maintained the volume of water in the sea.

d It decreased in area and volume.

3 Find and highlight two technical terms, and underline their definitions.

4 The article outlines a clear solution to the problems affecting the Aral Sea region. True or False?

5 The following diagram represents the process of environmental decline in the Aral Sea region. For each section of the diagram, reread the relevant part of the article. Then complete the diagram with sentences A–J. Write the correct letter in each box.

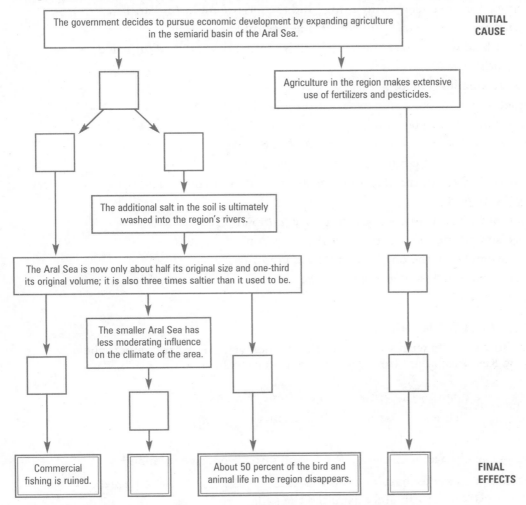

A The region's human population, especially the young, suffer severe and widespread health problems.

B The volume of water flowing into the Aral Sea from its two main rivers is considerably reduced.

C The area experiences less rainfall and more frost.

D Entire species of fish in the sea die out.

E Agriculture uses large amounts of water from the Aral Sea's two main rivers for irrigation purposes.

F Toxic chemicals drain into the region's rivers.

G Traditional cotton growing is no longer possible.

H Because irrigation methods are inefficient, a large proportion of the water evaporates and leaves salt in the soil of the agricultural fields.

I The riverside forests dry up.

J The region's drinking water is contaminated by toxic chemicals.

VOCABULARY STUDY: SYNONYMS

Find words in the article that are similar in meaning to the following.

1 the connections between living things and the environment *(n)* Par. 1
2 to destroy the positive effect of something else *(v)* Par. 1
3 an area of land whose water ultimately flows into a river or lake *(n)* Par. 2
4 average *(adj)* Par. 2
5 to become smaller *(v)* Par. 3
6 the process of bringing water to agricultural land *(n)* Par. 4
7 causing something to become less extreme *(adj)* Par. 5
8 the dirt or earth in which plants grow *(n)* Par. 6
9 not occurring in nature but made by humans *(adj)* Par. 6
10 chemicals used to control harmful insects or small animals *(n)* Par. 6
11 to flow away *(v)* Par. 6
12 not well protected against danger or injury *(adj)* Par. 7
13 to cause something to go in the opposite direction *(v)* Par. 8
14 very unusual; being the only one of its kind *(adj)* Par. 9
15 the process in which something is changed from one form to another *(n)* Par. 9

VOCABULARY STUDY: WORDS IN CONTEXT

Complete the sentences with words from the list below. If necessary, review the words in the Key Vocabulary from the Readings on page 263.

fertile	climate	arid	efficient	roots
evaporate	measures	species	mortality	crop

1 Irrigation can change _____ land into productive farmland.

2 In an attempt to make their land more _____, Aral Sea farmers used chemicals that ultimately damaged the soil.

3 Our new air-conditioning system is much more _____ than the one it replaced. It cools faster and uses 25 percent less energy.

4 The _____ in some areas of the United States is quite extreme, with hot summers and very cold winters.

5 The _____ of this plant do not reach deep into the soil. That's why it will not grow in regions with little rainfall.

6 The lesson of the Aral Sea is this: Apparently reasonable _____ taken to develop an economy can have disastrous ecological consequences.

7 In the Aral Sea region, the high _____ rate in young children has been linked to chemical pesticides that have contaminated the drinking water.

8 It is very risky when people come to depend on one _____ for their daily nutrition. If it fails, they could face starvation.

9 It's wasteful to water your garden at noon on a sunny day in the summer because a lot of the water will simply _____.

10 After a century of being hunted, the blue whale, the largest animal on Earth, is clearly an endangered _____.

BEYOND THE READING

Research

Do Internet or library research to find additional, up-to-date information on one or more of these questions.

- What changes have occurred in the Aral Sea since 1990?
- What has happened to the city of Muynak?
- How has the political breakup of the former Soviet Union affected the situation in the Aral Sea basin?
- What international assistance is the Aral Sea region receiving?

Discussion

Discuss the following question with a partner.

- How could the Aral Sea region have achieved economic development without causing the ecological damage you have read about?

Writing

Write a short report on the results of your research or your discussion.

READING 2
ECOLOGY, OVERPOPULATION, AND ECONOMIC DEVELOPMENT

GETTING INTO THE TOPIC

Read the title of this article. Then discuss the following questions with a partner.

1. Why is overpopulation a problem, especially with regard to a country's ecology?
2. What is the connection between a country's population growth and its economic development?

GETTING A FIRST IDEA ABOUT THE ARTICLE

In the chart below, formulate a question for each paragraph that is missing one. Read the first sentence of the paragraph and formulate a question that you think the paragraph will answer. Write the question in the chart.

PARAGRAPH	QUESTION
1	How quickly did the world's population grow in the past 10,000 years?
2	
3	What evidence is there that population growth is a danger to the environment locally?
4	What evidence is there that population growth is a danger to the environment at the national level?
5	
6	
7	Why are birth-control programs not enough to solve the problem of overpopulation?
8	
9	What complicates the process of finding an effective solution to the problem?
10	

Now read through the questions in the completed chart to anticipate the information that you will encounter in the article.

WHILE YOU READ

As you read the article, stop at the end of each sentence that contains boldface text and follow the instructions in the box in the margin.

Ecology, Overpopulation, and Economic Development

Approximately ten thousand years ago, when the first permanent human settlements emerged after about 2 million years of hunter-gatherer society, the total population of the earth was only about 5 million people. Not until the beginning of the nineteenth century did the population exceed 1 billion. During that time, the human species had a negligible influence on the ecology of the planet as a whole.

By the beginning of the twentieth century, however, the population stood at 2 billion. By 1950, it was 2.5 billion. Then, in the next fifty years, it more than doubled, to 6.1 billion. According to United Nations' projections, although the rate of population growth will stabilize and may fall in the future, the total population will continue to increase significantly and will reach 9.3 billion by 2050. All of this growth will be in less-developed countries, which will be home to more than 85 percent of the world's people in 2050. Today, as a direct result of population growth, the impact of human activities on the world's ecology is already substantial. In the future, it may be catastrophic.

Studies have shown that runaway population growth represents a massive **threat to the environment on the local, national, and global levels**. In areas of Nepal, for example, the pressure of overpopulation and poverty forces farmers into the hills, where they cut down the vegetation to provide wood for heating and construction, food for their animals, and land to raise crops. In a short time, the fertile topsoil is eroded by rain because it is now without the protection offered by the natural vegetation. The hillside fields then become unproductive, incapable of supporting the people who have settled there.

Elsewhere, in the world's tropical zones, to provide employment and earn money from exports, nations like Indonesia, Malaysia, and Thailand have been cutting down their hardwood forests faster than they can replace these valuable resources. Brazil, in a desperate attempt to relieve poverty and create economic growth, has permitted the destruction of vast areas of its Amazon rain forest for agricultural use. The sad irony is that much of the cleared land proves unsuitable for traditional farming after a few years because the destruction of the forest has interrupted the recycling of natural nutrients to the soil.

By 2000, at least half the world's tropical forests had disappeared. Their destruction has **consequences** that cross national borders and are felt globally. First, the burning of the forests releases large amounts of carbon dioxide into the atmosphere – emissions that are contributing to potentially disastrous changes in global climate patterns. Second, as the forest vanishes, so too does its diverse plant and animal life. Thus, the human race may be losing, along with the tropical forests, a vast potential source of scientific knowledge.

Clearly, if action is not taken soon, the ecological damage caused by overpopulation and unwise development threatens to run out of control. **A partial solution to the crisis may lie in the family-planning**

Treat the first two paragraphs as the introduction. Highlight two sentences that give you the clearest idea about the topic of the article.

Scan forward and highlight words that mark where the article begins to deal with each of the three levels of threat. Then come back and continue reading.

Scan forward and highlight words that show you how many *consequences*. Then come back and continue reading.

Every few years, poor rural farmers clear a new area of tropical rain forest for farmland because the land quickly loses its fertility.

Family planning is only a partial solution. Scan ahead and highlight a phrase marking where another solution begins. Then come back and finish reading paragraph 6.

programs that have been operating in a number of developing countries for some time. In Indonesia, for example, the family-planning program established a large number of village centers that distribute free contraceptives and information about birth control. The program has had considerable success. Between 1972 and 1988, the fertility rate fell by almost 40 percent, and the number of couples practicing birth control increased fifty-fold. A reduction in the birthrate has also been experienced by other countries with family-planning programs, including South Korea, Thailand, Mexico, and Tunisia. And there is clear evidence, too, that lower birthrates can bring economic benefits to developing nations. According to a 2002 U.N. report, declines in the birthrate accounted for 33 percent of the economic growth in East Asia between 1960 and 1995.

As a response to the problem, birth-control programs are necessary 7 but, for at least one good reason, not sufficient. Since a large proportion of the population of developing countries consists of children below reproductive age, the world's population is certain to grow when these children reach adulthood and begin having children. Even if birth control becomes widely accessible and acceptable, therefore, a fifty percent increase in the world's population is inevitable by 2050.

According to most experts, the second essential component of a 8 solution to the overpopulation-environment problem is social and economic development. The history of the industrial world clearly shows that birthrates fall and stabilize at a significantly lower level when a society offers the majority of its people an acceptably high standard of living. Prosperity, better educational and career opportunities, especially for women, adequate health care, and relative financial security for people in their old age are probably all factors that have contributed to the low, stable birthrates of the affluent nations. For this reason, most experts believe that the birthrates of the less-developed nations will decline as their populations experience the benefits of **economic development**.

The situation today, however, is more complex than this apparently simple solution would suggest. A first major complication is that one essential component of the solution – namely, economic development – is also one cause of the problem. Birthrates will not fall without economic development. However, most of the danger to the world's ecological systems comes directly from the attempts of nations to pursue economic development. A second complication is that the industrial world must now ask poorer nations to give up the same strategy for economic development that brought it prosperity – the exploitation of natural resources with little thought for the future. Let us remind ourselves of one historical cost of this strategy. In the course of their history, Europeans have destroyed almost 80 percent of the forests that originally covered their continent; and North Americans have destroyed 75 percent of the forests covering North America. Today, Europeans and North Americans are asking the people of developing nations to cease doing what they themselves have been doing for centuries.

Because all countries have the right to pursue the goal of economic development for their people, **two conclusions** are unavoidable. First, the traditional development policies pursued by the poorer countries must be fundamentally revised. The policies now in operation will both exhaust those nations' ecological resources and cause serious, perhaps irreversible, damage to the world's ecology. They are, in a word, *unsustainable*. Second, because unsustainable economic development is a clear characteristic of the industrial world, it is the obligation of the most prosperous nations to lead the way. They can do so by modifying many of their unsustainable policies and practices and by offering economic and technical assistance to the poorer countries that are willing to **do the same**. In this way, they will be supporting, and not undermining, global efforts to encourage sustainable development.

Read the first sentence of paragraph 9 and highlight the continuing ideas. Use this information to help you identify the main idea of paragraph 8.

Scan forward and highlight the words that mark where the writer introduces each conclusion. Then come back and continue reading.

Check back and highlight the meaning of *do the same*.

MAIN IDEA CHECK

Here are the main ideas of each paragraph in the article. Match each paragraph to its main idea. Write the number of the paragraph in the blank.

Paragraphs 1–5

_____ A The disappearance of tropical forests – a result of countries' attempts at economic development – is causing great damage to the natural resources and the ecology of those nations.

_____ B The destruction of the world's tropical forests will have negative consequences for the entire globe.

_____ C Up until two hundred years ago, humans did not have a significant effect on the ecology of planet Earth.

_____ D Locally, people respond to the pressures of overpopulation in ways that destroy the ecology of the areas they live in.

_____ E Because of the massive increase in population in the last two centuries, damage to the ecology from human activities is considerable and may become much worse.

Paragraphs 6–10

_____ F Social and economic development is also an essential part of a solution to the environmental damage caused by overpopulation.

_____ G In both developing and developed countries, traditional economic development must be replaced by policies and practices that are sustainable.

_____ H Family-planning programs, which have proved successful in some developing countries, could contribute to the solution of the overpopulation problem.

_____ I Economic development, which is the answer to the problem of overpopulation, is also the cause of massive damage to the environment.

_____ J The number of children currently in the world's population means that birth control cannot be the sole solution to the problem of overpopulation.

A CLOSER LOOK

Look back at the article to answer the following questions.

1 This diagram represents the process of environmental destruction occurring in Nepal. Reread paragraph 3. Then complete the cause and effect diagram with sentences A–D. Write the correct letter in each box.

| Nepal is poor, and some areas are overpopulated. | → | D | → | C | → | A | → | B |

A The fertile topsoil is eroded by rain.
B The hill areas can no longer support the new settlers.
C The soil's natural protection is removed.
D For a better life, farmers move into the hill country, where they cut down the natural vegetation.

2 What reason does the writer give for the claim that birth-control programs are only a partial solution to the overpopulation problem?

a It is unrealistic to imagine that birth control will be acceptable at present to all societies and cultures.
b It is unrealistic to expect that we can quickly make birth control freely available everywhere it is needed.
c The large proportion of children in the world's population guarantees a massive population increase in the future.
d Developing nations are becoming more prosperous and, as their people become wealthier, they can afford to have larger families.

3 What factor(s) does the writer identify as contributing to a decline in a nation's birthrate? Circle all that apply.

a Increasing prosperity
b Poverty
c Adequate health care
d Financial security for the elderly
e Economic development

4 This diagram represents the process of environmental decline described in this article. Complete the diagram with sentences A–C. Write the correct letter in each box.

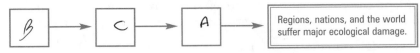

| B | → | C | → | A | → | Regions, nations, and the world suffer major ecological damage. |

A Governments pursue traditional economic development, which tends to be environmentally unsustainable.
B The population is poor and is growing rapidly.
C Governments are under pressure to meet the needs of the expanding population.

5 Scan for details that would help you explain the term *unsustainable development.* Then write your own brief definition of this idea.

VOCABULARY STUDY: SYNONYMS

Find words in the article that are similar in meaning to the following.

1 very small and therefore unimportant *(adj)* Par. 1

2 numbers calculated now but expected in the future *(n)* Par. 2

3 large and therefore important *(adj)* Par. 2

4 the plants growing in a specific region *(n)* Par. 3

5 to damage something by gradually taking away parts of it *(v)* Par. 3

6 regions or areas *(n)* Par. 4

7 a situation that has the opposite result of what was intended or expected *(n)* Par. 4

8 to allow something to flow out into the environment *(v)* Par. 5

9 to give things out to a number of people *(v)* Par. 6

10 items that are intended to prevent pregnancy *(n)* Par. 6

11 related to the ability of living things to produce young *(adj)* Par. 7

12 to stop changing *(v)* Par. 8

13 the use of something in order to make a profit *(n)* Par. 9

14 to use up something completely *(v)* Par. 10

15 impossible to continue doing *(adj)* Par. 10

VOCABULARY REVIEW: SAME OR DIFFERENT

The following pairs of sentences contain vocabulary from Readings 1 and 2. Write *S* in the blank if the two sentences have the same meaning. Write *D* if the meanings are different.

__D__ 1 DDT, an artificial pesticide that causes serious reproductive problems in birds and animals, is still used in some countries.

Some countries still use the artificial pesticide DDT to control reproduction in bird and animal populations.

__D__ 2 As a result of the shrinking Aral Sea, the climate of the region has undergone substantial changes.

The decrease in size of the Aral Sea has had a negligible effect on the weather patterns of the region.

__D__ 3 Often measures taken to convert arid land to fertile farmland can cause serious ecological damage.

Pressure on natural ecosystems can be relieved if we take steps to develop agriculture on arid, unproductive land.

__S__ 4 After an area has been deforested, its soil is more vulnerable to being washed away by heavy rain because it is no longer protected by the native vegetation.

Deforestation increases the likelihood of erosion by removing the trees and smaller plants that offer the soil shelter from heavy rain.

_S_ 5 In some countries, the efforts of birth-control programs were undermined by the failure of these programs to take measures against the poverty that was the root cause of high birthrates.

Family-planning programs in some countries had negligible success because they did not attempt to relieve poverty, which is the basic reason why people feel obliged to have large families.

_S_ 6 Because we have the obligation not to waste the world's water resources, we should discontinue the use of inefficient irrigation systems that allow up to 70 percent of their water to evaporate.

Our duty to protect global water resources requires us to stop using wasteful irrigation systems that lose a large proportion of their water through evaporation.

_D_ 7 By 1990, commercial fishing in the Aral Sea had practically ceased because the sea's ecosystems could no longer sustain large numbers of fish, whole species of which had disappeared.

In the period up to 1990, ecological damage to the Aral Sea had undermined the sea's capacity to support life, and entire varieties of fish had vanished; these developments stabilized the commercial fishing industry.

_S_ 8 Removing the vegetation of the tropical forests provides land for crops, but it also interrupts the natural process by which nutrients are recycled back into the soil, which loses its fertility.

Although tropical deforestation makes land available for agriculture, it ultimately causes that land to become unproductive by preventing the recycling of natural fertilizing material back into the soil.

BEYOND THE READING

Research
Do Internet or library research to find additional, up-to-date information on global population growth today.

Discussion
Discuss the following question with a partner.
- Most experts believe that birth control is a necessary part of a solution to the problem of overpopulation. What obstacles stand in the way of organizing effective birth-control programs in countries with overpopulation problems?

Writing
Write a short report on the results of your research or your discussion.

SKILLS AND STRATEGIES 11
-ING WORDS THAT EXPRESS RESULTS

In special circumstances, *-ing* words can express the result of an action described earlier in the sentence. Being able to identify these circumstances will add to your understanding of academic English.

EXAMPLES & EXPLANATIONS

Examples

Inefficient methods of irrigation allow much of the water to evaporate, **leaving** crop-damaging salts to accumulate in the soil.

Storms spread salt on the surrounding land, **increasing** its salt content and **reducing** its fertility.

Explanation

Clause + comma + verb *-ing*. In this pattern, the verb *-ing* marks a direct effect of the action described in the part of the sentence that ends with a comma. A simpler-to-read version of this sentence is:

Inefficient methods of irrigation allow much of the water to evaporate. This leaves crop-damaging salts to accumulate in the soil.

The result of the sentence may have more than one verb *-ing*. Here you see two effects of the action described earlier in the sentence. A simpler-to-read version of this sentence is:

Storms spread salt on the surrounding land. This increases its salt content and reduces fertility.

STRATEGIES

Use the following three strategies to help you recognize and understand results expressed by verb *-ing*:

- Look for the following sentence pattern: clause + comma + verb *-ing*.
- Find the verb *-ing* and interpret it as the direct result of the action described in the part of the sentence before the comma.
- When necessary, simplify the sentence for yourself by starting a new sentence after the original comma. Begin the second sentence with *This*.

SKILL PRACTICE 1

Circle the verbs with *-ing* endings that express a result. Then highlight the complete result. The first sentence has been done for you as an example. But be careful because not every verb *-ing* expresses a result. Three sentences in this exercise contain reduced relative clauses (see Skills and Strategies 6 on page 91).

1 Unemployment and poverty have greatly increased in the last few years, (forcing) more and more people to move into the cities.

2 The forests on either side of the Amu Darya river have dried up, leading to the loss of about half the region's bird and mammal species.

3 Water containing dangerous levels of chemicals drains into the rivers, making the region's fish unfit to eat and undermining its fishing industry.

4 In 1984, toxic gas escaped from a chemical plant in Bhopal, India, killing approximately 2,000 people and leaving tens of thousands with long-term, often fatal, health problems.

5 People living in the area have organized powerful resistance to the planned nuclear power plant, forcing the government to look elsewhere for a more acceptable site.

6 Winters in the region surrounding the Aral Sea have become colder and longer, making cotton growing impossible in many areas.

7 Poorly planned economic development can frequently damage the ecology of a region, negating any benefits that the development might have promised.

8 International organizations have provided funding for family-planning programs, enabling a number of countries to lower their birthrates significantly.

SKILL PRACTICE 2

Rewrite each sentence by making two simpler sentences, with the second sentence expressing the result of the first. The first one has been done for you as an example.

1 Unemployment and poverty have greatly increased in the last few years, forcing more and more people to move into the cities.
   Unemployment and poverty have greatly increased in the last few years. This has forced more and more people to move into the cities.

2 In 1965, the immigration laws were changed, making it easier for people from Asia and Latin America to settle in the United States.

3 To expand agriculture in the Aral Sea basin, the government diverted enormous quantities of water from the region's two main rivers, reducing the flow of water into the sea by almost 90 percent.

4 In the 1980s and 1990s, the British government did not maintain adequate funding for the National Health Service, causing hospitals to reduce the number of doctors and nurses they employed.

5 Poor people move into the country, where they cut down the trees and other vegetation on hillsides, leaving the soil without its natural protection against erosion by wind and rain.

6 Whole species of fish disappeared from the Aral Sea, bringing a halt to commercial fishing there.

7 Employers reduced the level of benefits in their health insurance programs, forcing employees to pay more for health care expenses out of their own pockets.

8 In nineteenth century Europe, the old agricultural system was disintegrating, putting unskilled laborers out of work and persuading many to emigrate.

SKILL PRACTICE 3

Read the following sentences and then write answers to the questions that follow. The first one has been done for you as an example.

1 Old electrical power plants release large quantities of carbon dioxide into the air, contributing significantly to the problem of global warming.
   Question: How do old power plants contribute to global warming?
   Answer: They release large quantities of carbon dioxide into the air.

2 Rice growing on artificial wetlands and cattle farming have expanded rapidly, producing much greater amounts of methane, a gas that retains heat twenty times more efficiently than carbon dioxide does.
   Question: What is the immediate reason for an increase in methane in the atmosphere?

3 Establishing forest reserves, areas in which all economic exploitation of the tropical rain forests is illegal, will preserve millions of unknown and probably unique natural species, giving scientists the opportunity to study them and the ecosystems that support them.
   Question: What will be the ultimate result of establishing reserves in the tropical rain forests?

4 Ethnic neighborhoods provide social and economic opportunities for new immigrants, helping them make the transition to life in their new society.
   Question: What makes it easier for new immigrants to adjust to life in their new country?

5 As humans clear forested areas to provide fields for crops and farm animals, the native vegetation disappears, interrupting the process by which natural nutrients are recycled back into the soil.
   Question: What happens after an area of forest is cut down?

6 In the earthquake, most of the area's bridges were destroyed, making the task of distributing food to the needy extremely slow and difficult.
   Question: Why was it so difficult to distribute food to the victims of the earthquake?

7 Often economic development proves to be unsustainable, leaving the resources of a region exhausted and its people without the means to support themselves.
   Question: What effects can unsustainable economic activity have on a region?

8 Inefficient methods of irrigation allow much of the water to evaporate, causing crop-damaging salts to accumulate in the soil. These salts are then washed out of the fields and into the rivers, ultimately increasing the salt content of the Aral Sea itself.
   Question: What is the first step in the cause and effect process described here? What is the final result in the process?

READING 3
UNSUSTAINABLE DEVELOPMENT AND THE MAYAN CIVILIZATION

GETTING INTO THE TOPIC

Read the title of this article and study the illustrations. Then discuss the following questions with a partner.

1 Who are the Mayas and what do you know about their history?
2 Why might the issue of unsustainable development be important in Mayan history?

GETTING A FIRST IDEA ABOUT THE ARTICLE

In the chart below, formulate a question for each paragraph that is missing one. Read the first sentence of the paragraph and formulate a question that you think the paragraph will answer. Write the question in the chart.

PARAGRAPH	QUESTION
1	Have earlier cultures suffered from environmental problems?
2	
3	
4	What ecosystems were open to damage?
5	How developed was the Mayan culture?
6	
7	
8	What were the results of this decrease in food production?
9	

Now read through the questions in the completed chart to anticipate the information that you will encounter in the article.

WHILE YOU READ

As you read the article, stop at the end of each sentence that contains boldface text and follow the instructions in the box in the margin.

Unsustainable Development and the Mayan Civilization

As you continue reading, answer this question: "Was agriculture good or bad for the environment?" Highlight two words that help you decide on your answer.

Scan forward to identify this *major social development*. Highlight it. Then draw a simple three-part arrow diagram of the general cause and effect process.

In most discussions of environmental issues, it is generally assumed that environmental problems have affected only contemporary societies. Consider, for example, the damage to the ecology and to human health from the use of toxic pesticides, which emerged as an issue during the later decades of the twentieth century. Similarly, acid rain and air pollution are, to a great extent, the result of the burning of fossil fuel, which has characterized economic development since the early nineteenth century. However, an examination of history reveals that the negative impact of human activities on the environment goes back much further than the last two hundred years.

One of the most **environmentally significant** events in history was the development of agriculture approximately ten thousand years ago. Agriculture involved a massive disruption of natural ecosystems. As humans cleared areas to provide fields for crops and domesticated animals, they eliminated the native vegetation, disturbing the process by which natural nutrients were recycled back into the soil. As a result, humans had to intervene in order to sustain the new system, usually by providing water and fertilizing material.

Agriculture also **brought about a major social development** that caused additional strain on natural ecosystems. It led to the first settled societies. These could come about because the extra food produced by efficient farmers was able to support growing numbers of non-producing consumers – rulers, priests, soldiers, and bureaucrats. Once they became established, these settled societies created further environmental pressure. They required space for fields, construction materials for houses, and fuel for cooking and heating, demands that inevitably led to greater deforestation.

Historically, the spread of agriculture and the rise of settled societies placed immense strain on those ecosystems that were particularly susceptible to disruption. Such was the situation in Mesopotamia, where the world's first literate societies developed and where the most extensive alterations to the natural environment were made. Similar situations arose in the Mediterranean basin and in the rain forests of Central America, where the Mayan civilization flourished for a time. It is the ecological history of this latter culture that we will now examine in some detail.

Over many centuries, the Mayan culture developed in the tropical rain forests of what is now part of Mexico, Honduras, Belize, and Guatemala. By the seventh century, the Mayas had built a number of cities with magnificent temples, palaces, and public buildings and with large permanent populations. The cities appear to have been in competition with one another, and war among them was frequent. It is estimated that the largest of these cities, Tikal, had a permanent population of between thirty thousand and fifty thousand and that the total Mayan population was 5 million. (See Figure 4.2.)

To support such a population, the Mayas developed **a complex agricultural system**. They cleared the tropical vegetation from the hillsides, thereby destroying the soil's natural protection against erosion. To control the inevitable soil erosion on the new hillside farmland, they made extensive use of terracing. In addition, in the

6

As you continue reading, number three features that made this system a complex one.

FIGURE 4.2 **The Mayan Civilization**

The Temple of the Grand Jaguar in Tikal is one of the magnificent buildings constructed by the Mayas at the height of their civilization.

Check back and highlight the meaning of *The process*.

Now highlight two consequences of this rise in water levels.

wet lowlands, they constructed extensive systems of drainage ditches and used the material from the ditches to form raised fields protected from flooding, where cotton and food crops could be grown. This vast system of intensive agriculture was the basis for all the achievements of the Mayan civilization.

When the Mayas demanded too much of their complex agricultural system, however, the system could not withstand the strain. In the end, it began to collapse. **The process** seems to have begun after the year 600, at a time when the population was increasing rapidly to meet the rulers' growing demands for construction workers and soldiers. To satisfy the growing population's need for food, fuel, and land, the Mayas cut down more and more of the tropical forests on hillsides. Although the soil in the forest areas is fertile, much of it was, and still is, extremely vulnerable to erosion by wind and rain. Probably soil erosion caused by the extensive deforestation began to reduce the crop harvests from the hillside fields. The soil that had been washed down from the hills increased the amount of silt in the lowland rivers and drainage ditches. As a result, **water levels rose**, flooding the raised fields and thereby reducing the harvests still further.

Because of the deterioration of the artificial environment created by the Mayas, food production dropped dangerously low. The consequences were disastrous. The first signs of a decline can been seen in human skeletons from the years leading up to the year 800. They show increased mortality among infants and mothers, and increasing levels of nutritional deficiency. After this, conflicts probably intensified among the Mayan cities over the declining resources of the region. Wars among them became more common and widespread. The wars, together with the loss of food production, brought about very high death rates and a catastrophic fall in population, which ended the Mayan civilization. Within a few decades, the cities and fields were abandoned. Today the region supports a population consisting of only a few tens of thousands.

What happened to the Mayas is one example of the **unsustainable development** that destroyed many of the world's earliest settled societies. By using the natural resources available, by finding ways to exploit them fully, by creating artificial environments, the Mayas were able to build a complex society capable of great cultural and intellectual achievements. For a considerable time, their society continued to develop and flourish. However, the demands of this ever-expanding society outgrew the ability of the altered environment to support it. Actions to ensure the food supply, which at first must have looked like creative solutions to environmental limitations, proved to have disastrous long-term effects. Ultimately, the Mayas destroyed the environment on which they relied for food, the environment that was the basis for their survival.

9

As you continue reading, highlight the sentence that begins to describe why Mayan development can be described as unsustainable.

MAIN IDEA CHECK

Here are the main ideas of each paragraph in the article. Match each paragraph to its main idea. Write the number of the paragraph in the blank.

Paragraphs 1–4

_____ A The settled societies that agriculture made possible also placed considerable strain on the environment.

_____ B Clearing fields for agricultural use, which began ten thousand years ago, had a very disruptive effect on the environment.

_____ C Mesopotamia, the Mediterranean basin, and the Central America rain forests were areas where the ecology was disrupted by early human activities.

_____ D Humans have been damaging the environment for much longer than the last century.

Paragraphs 5–9

_____ E The loss of food production caused increased fighting for the available resources; this destroyed the Mayan civilization.

_____ F The Mayas' expanding system of agriculture collapsed when the ecology of the region could no longer sustain it.

_____ G This paragraph describes the cities and population of the Mayan civilization.

_____ H Like many other cases, the expansion of the Mayan civilization was unsustainable; it ultimately destroyed the environment that supported it.

_____ I To grow the crops needed to support their large population, the Mayas replaced the forest with a complex artificial environment consisting of raised fields and terraces with a drainage system.

A CLOSER LOOK

Look back at the article to answer the following questions.

1 This diagram represents the cause and effect relationship that has historically existed between agriculture and environmental change. Reread paragraph 2. Then complete the diagram with sentences A–D. Write the correct letter in each box.

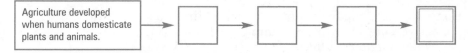

Agriculture developed when humans domesticate plants and animals.

A To provide fields, humans removed the natural vegetation.
B Humans themselves had to provide water and fertilizer.
C The natural recycling of nutrients back into the soil was disturbed.
D Agriculture needed fields for crops and domesticated animals.

2 This diagram shows another aspect of the relationship between agriculture and environmental damage. Reread paragraph 3. Then complete the diagram with sentences A–E. Write the correct letter in each box.

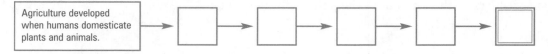

Agriculture developed when humans domesticate plants and animals.

A Farmers were able to feed settled societies in which increasing numbers of food consumers could live.
B People cut down increasing numbers of trees.
C There was an increased need for space, fuel, and construction materials.
D Natural ecosystems come under additional pressure.
E Food production became much more efficient.

3 What modification(s) did the Mayas make to the natural ecology of the region where they lived? Circle all that apply.
a They constructed drainage systems for naturally wet areas.
b They planted large numbers of trees.
c They built fields on the sides of hills.
d They converted forest to farmland.

4 This diagram represents the process that ended with the collapse of the Mayan civilization. Reread paragraphs 7 and 8. Then complete the diagram with sentences A–H. Write the correct letter in each box.

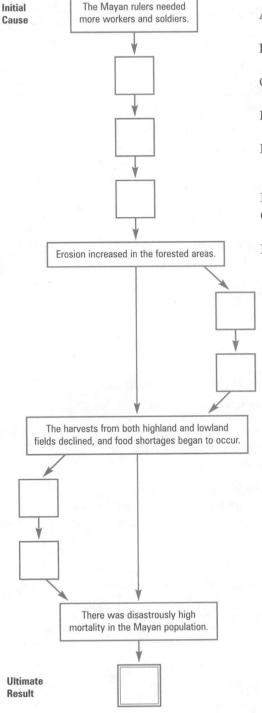

Initial Cause

The Mayan rulers needed more workers and soldiers.

⬇

⬇

⬇

Erosion increased in the forested areas.

⬇

The harvests from both highland and lowland fields declined, and food shortages began to occur.

⬇

There was disastrously high mortality in the Mayan population.

⬇

Ultimate Result

A The population increased to meet the demand for more soldiers and workers.

B Silt accumulated in the lowland rivers and drainage ditches.

C Wars became more widespread and common.

D The Mayas cut down more and more of the forest.

E Competition intensified between Mayan cities for the declining resources of the region.

F The Mayan civilization collapsed.

G There was an increased need for food, fuel, and land.

H Water levels rose, and the agricultural fields of the lowland began to suffer from flooding.

VOCABULARY STUDY: SYNONYMS

Find words in the article that are similar in meaning to the following.

1   no longer wild; used by humans for work or food production *(adj)* Par. 2
2   to take action in a situation when not originally involved in it *(v)* Par. 2
3   people who buy and use what others produce *(n)* Par. 3
4   enormous *(adj)* Par. 4
5   changes *(n)* Par. 4
6   flat areas of land created by humans on the side of a hill *(n)* Par. 6
7   channels in the ground to take water away *(n)* Par. 6
8   a large amount of water that covers a usually dry place *(n)* Par. 6
9   pressure that causes a system to work harder than it should *(n)* Par. 7
10   because of this *(adv)* Par. 7
11   the bones in a human or an animal body *(n)* Par. 8
12   to leave a place forever, often because it is impossible to stay there *(v)* Par. 8
13   to become too large for something *(v)* Par. 9
14   show after some time that something has a certain quality *(v)* Par. 9
15   needing many years to develop *(adj)* Par. 9

VOCABULARY STUDY: WORDS IN CONTEXT

Complete the sentences with words from the list below. If necessary, review the words in the Key Vocabulary from the Readings on page 266.

flourished	collapsed	perspective	deteriorated	intensified
withstand	fossil fuels	harvests	disrupt	susceptible to

1   Even though the earthquake was not very strong, some older buildings
    _____, and many others were badly damaged.

2   Weather forecasters are advising motorists not to drive today because
    conditions on the roads have _____ rapidly in the last two hours.

3   Mayan society developed and _____ for a number of centuries
    before it went into a decline.

4   From the _____ of the Mayas, the modifications they made to
    their environment must have seemed like reasonable efforts to feed their
    families.

5   As the pressure to feed their people _____, wars broke out among
    the Mayas over the declining resources of the region.

6   Mayan history shows how the pressure of human populations can
    _____ the natural ecology of a region and make it unlivable.

7 The increasing use of _____, which releases additional carbon dioxide into the atmosphere, is one possible cause of long-term climate change.

8 This piece of land is lower than the land around it and does not drain very well, so in wet weather it is _____ flooding.

9 A number of ancient civilizations collapsed when their environment could not _____ the strain of supporting their growing populations.

10 Because the fertile soil of the Mayan hillside fields was eroded by wind and rain, the _____ declined disastrously.

BEYOND THE READING

Research
Do Internet or library research to find additional, up-to-date information on the Mayas and their culture, or on other reasons why their civilization collapsed.

Discussion
Discuss the following question with a partner.
- In what ways is the story of the Mayas similar to or different from the more recent history of the Aral Sea?

Writing
Write a short report on the results of your research or your discussion.

READING 4
BIOLOGICAL DIVERSITY UNDER ATTACK

GETTING INTO THE TOPIC

Discuss the following questions with a partner.

1. You have already read about ethnic and cultural diversity. So what could biological diversity be?
2. What might be attacking biological diversity, and why is this a problem?

GETTING A FIRST IDEA ABOUT THE ARTICLE

In the chart below, formulate a question for each paragraph that is missing one. Read the first sentence of the paragraph and formulate a question that you think the paragraph will answer. Write the question in the chart.

PARAGRAPH	QUESTION
1	How many species are there on earth?
2	
3	How does tropical deforestation affect the species living in the forests?
4	
5	Which rain forest species could be domesticated?
6	
7	What can we do to save the great variety of species in the rain forest?
8	Why are forest reserves an answer to the loss of biodiversity in the rain forests?
9	
10	

Now read through the questions in the completed chart to anticipate the information that you will encounter in the article.

WHILE YOU READ

As you read the article, stop at the end of each sentence that contains boldface text and follow the instructions in the box in the margin.

Biological Diversity Under Attack

To date, biologists have described **fewer than one million of the earth's natural species**. With estimates ranging from a conservative 3 million to 30 million, scientists are far from unanimous on how many species exist (Solbrig, 1991). Yet, despite disagreement about the total number of species, there is a consensus among scientists that at least half of the world's species live in the rain forests of the earth's tropical zones. To appreciate the immense biodiversity in these forests, consider the following figures: There are only thirty-two native species of trees in the United Kingdom today (Hart, 1973). However, in each of two small plots of rain forest in Peru (roughly one-millionth the area of the United Kingdom), a U.S. researcher identified approximately three hundred tree species (Wilson, 1989).

For some years, however, the moist forests of the earth's tropical regions have been the scene of massive destruction, as humans cut down or burn the trees to provide hardwood or land for agriculture and settlements. By 2000, for example, deforestation in Brazil's Amazon region totaled 64 million hectares, the equivalent of an area as large as Sweden. Between 1980 and 2000, Malaysia destroyed an estimated 6 million hectares of its tropical forests. During the same two decades, Indonesia lost 23 million hectares, an area more than double the size of Portugal (WRI, 1993; UN, 2003). Nor were early figures from the twenty-first century more encouraging. In the year ending August 2002, the Brazilian rain forest retreated at a rate in excess of **2.3 million hectares**.

It is difficult to exaggerate the impact of such massive deforestation on tropical species. It destroys natural habitats, causing species to become extinct on a scale unprecedented in human history. One study, which assumed a conservative total of 2 million species living exclusively in the tropical rain forests, estimates that between 4,000 and 6,000 species a year are currently being driven to extinction (Wilson, 1989). Even these conservative estimates, the study points

From the title, we expect biological diversity to be in danger. Scan ahead and mark where the writer begins to discuss the danger.

Read the first sentence of paragraph 3 and highlight the continuing idea. Use this information to help you identify the main idea of paragraph 2.

FIGURE 4.3 Tropical Forest Loss in the 12 Leading Countries, 1990–2000

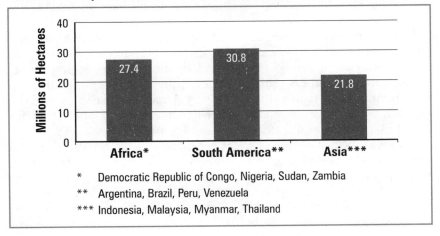

Millions of Hectares

Africa* — 27.4
South America** — 30.8
Asia*** — 21.8

*   Democratic Republic of Congo, Nigeria, Sudan, Zambia
** Argentina, Brazil, Peru, Venezuela
*** Indonesia, Malaysia, Myanmar, Thailand

Human destruction of tropical forests is driving unknown numbers of natural species to extinction.

Scan forward for words that show you where to find each of these reasons. Highlight and number them. Then come back and continue reading paragraph 4.

out, represent a rate of extinction that is approximately ten thousand times greater than the extinction rate that existed prior to the appearance of humans on the earth. Other studies suggest that the extinction rate could rise to between 7,000 and 27,000 species a year (WRI, 1993).

For a number of reasons, the threatened species of the rain forests are an immense, irreplaceable resource. First, because of their genetic diversity, they are a source of information and material that can be utilized to strengthen domesticated varieties that become susceptible to pests or disease. For example, the wild American oil palm has a natural resistance to *spear rot*, a disease that is destroying the domesticated African oil palm. Researchers are using genes from the American plant to develop resistance to the disease in its African cousin (Smith et al., 1991).

Second, tropical species are a potentially vast source of tree and plant species that could be domesticated for human use. Twenty-four crop species have been domesticated in the Amazon region alone, and countless numbers remain. For example, *Caryocar villosum* is a tree that produces fruit valued highly by Amazonian peoples, and the *Copaifera* tree species produces substances that can substitute for diesel fuel (Smith et al., 1991).

Tropical species also have great potential as a source of medicinal drugs. Wilson (1989) cites the example of *Catharanthus roseus*, a small plant native to Madagascar that has medicinal properties. It produces *vinblastine* and *vincristine,* which are extremely effective in the treatment of two forms of cancer. The income generated by these two substances exceeds $100 million a year. None of the five other species of *Catharanthus* had been carefully studied by 1989, but one of the five was close to extinction because its habitat was threatened by deforestation.

7 What can be done to preserve the biological diversity of the tropical rain forests, with their wealth of scientific information and unrealized potential as a source of material benefits? The prospects are poor that the extinctions can be completely halted (Holdgate, 1991). However, some authorities are cautiously optimistic that today's rate of extinction can be slowed if we address **both the immediate and the root causes of the crisis** (McNeely et al., 1990).

Scan paragraphs 8–10 and find each of these causes and number them.

8 We can establish forest reserves – areas where all economic exploitation of the forest is forbidden. This will preserve the habitats of tropical species, thus protecting them and slowing the pace of extinction. Conservation measures such as these are necessary steps in the fight against deforestation, the immediate cause of biodiversity loss. By themselves, however, they are insufficient responses to the problem.

9 At the same time, we need to accelerate the pace of scientific research into the species of the tropical rain forests. Such research is our only means of identifying areas that should be given priority in conservation decisions. It will also provide necessary information about the value of as-yet-unstudied species, **helping us to address another cause of the problem**: human ignorance about the value of the natural world and about our dependence on it. Such information will be essential if we are eventually to convince people that the biological resources of the rain forests are worth preserving.

Highlight what will help address the cause of this problem.

10 A third essential step is to address the root cause of biodiversity loss – the economic pressures that cause people to destroy the forests for short-term gain. Accomplishing **this**, however, is the greatest challenge facing the international community, because it involves tackling the complex and related problems of international debt, poverty, and overpopulation in the developing world. Just how we might tackle these problems will be the subject for a later article.

Check back and highlight the meaning of *this*.

References

Hart, C. 1973. *British trees in colour.* London: Michael Joseph.

Holdgate, M. W. 1991. The environment of tomorrow. *Environment* 33.6, pp. 14–42.

McNeely, J. A., Miller, K. R., Reid, W. V., Mittermeier, R. A., and Werner, T. B. 1990. Strategies for conserving biodiversity. *Environment* 32.3, pp. 16–40.

Smith, N. J. H., Williams, J. T., and Pluckett, D. L. 1991. Conserving the tropical cornucopia. *Environment* 33.6, pp. 6–32.

Solbrig, O. T. 1991. The origin and function of biodiversity. *Environment* 33.5, pp. 16–38.

United Nations. 2003. *The state of the world's forests* 2003. Information Division, United Nations Food and Agriculture Organization. New York: United Nations.

Wilson, E. O. 1989. Threats to biodiversity. *Scientific American,* 261 (3).

World Research Institute. 1993. *World resources* 1992–1993. New York: Oxford University Press.

MAIN IDEA CHECK

Here are the main ideas of each paragraph in the article. Match each paragraph to its main idea. Write the number of the paragraph in the blank.

Paragraphs 1–6

_6_ A The endangered species of the tropical rain forests could be a source of important new medications.

_2_ B Tropical forests are rapidly being destroyed by humans.

_5_ C The wild species of the tropical forests are an underused, valuable source of wild plants that could be domesticated.

_3_ D The destruction of tropical forests is causing the rapid extinction of the natural species that are native there.

_4_ E Rain forest species are a valuable resource because their genes may enable scientists to strengthen domesticated species.

_1_ F More than half of the world's natural species have their home in tropical forests.

Paragraphs 7–10

_____ G We need to reduce the economic pressures that force people to destroy the rain forests.

_____ H The rapid loss of tropical species can be slowed if we address all its causes.

_____ I To provide the information needed for conservation and education, we need to speed up research into the species of the tropical rain forests.

_____ J Conservation is a necessary component of a solution to the biodiversity crisis.

A CLOSER LOOK

Look back at the article to answer the following questions.

1 Why does the writer include the two examples, Peru and the United Kingdom in paragraph 1?

   a To show how many tree species there are in the world

   b To support the idea that biodiversity is under attack in the United Kingdom

   c To support the idea that a large proportion of the world's biodiversity is to be found in the tropical rain forests

   d To show how few of the world's natural species have been studied and described by scientists

2 How fast are tropical species now becoming extinct? Circle all that apply.

a At a rate similar to the rate that existed before the appearance of humans on the earth   *4-6 Th.*

b At a pace much faster than the rate that existed before the emergence of humans   *2 M*

c At the rate of exactly six thousand species per year   *4-6   7- 27,000*

d Faster now than at any other time since humans appeared on the earth   *none of the above*

3 What does the writer point out as justification for the claim that wild species in tropical forests are extremely valuable resources for humans? Circle all that apply.

a Their potential as domesticated species

b Their potential as suppliers of genetic material

c Their potential medicinal value

d Their role in maintaining the ecological balance of the forests

e) a,b, d c   f.   a d c

4 Write the names of the tropical species that the writer uses to illustrate each potential benefit listed in question 3 above.

5 What, according to the article, is a contributing factor to the biodiversity crisis? Circle all that apply.

a Sustainable economic development

b Poverty

c Overpopulation

d Lack of appreciation of the value of biological resources

6 In the table below, describe the solution proposed by the author for each cause of biodiversity loss.

CAUSE OF BIODIVERSITY LOSS	SOLUTION
Deforestation	
Lack of knowledge about the species of the rain forests and their potential value	
The economic pressures that lead to deforestation	

VOCABULARY STUDY: SYNONYMS

Find words in the article that are similar in meaning to the following.

1 slightly wet *(adj)* Par. 2
2 to move backward *(v)* Par. 2
3 to overstate *(v)* Par. 3
4 the natural home of a plant or animal *(n)* Par. 3
5 new, never experienced in the past *(adj)* Par. 3
6 to use *(v)* Par. 4
7 to produce *(v)* Par. 6
8 to be more than; to do more than *(v)* Par. 6
9 not yet achieved *(adj)* Par. 7
10 to cause something to move faster *(v)* Par. 9
11 the protection of natural resources *(n)* Par. 9
12 finally *(adv)* Par. 9
13 important and useful enough *(adj)* Par. 9
14 profit *(n)* Par. 10
15 borrowed money that needs to be repaid *(n)* Par. 10

VOCABULARY REVIEW: SAME OR DIFFERENT

The following pairs of sentences contain vocabulary from Readings 3 and 4. Write
S if the two sentences have the same meaning. Write *D* if the meanings are
different.

_____ 1 Today, natural species are vanishing at a faster pace than at any other time in history.

Natural species today are becoming extinct at an unprecedented rate.

_____ 2 The Mayas were obliged to alter their natural environment in order to sustain their society.

The environmental alterations that the Mayas were forced to make caused their society to collapse.

_____ 3 Evidence for disruptions in the Mayan food supply is visible in skeletons that show malnutrition in adults.

We know that Mayan society had little difficulty producing sufficient food because skeletons reveal no signs of adult malnutrition.

_____ 4 The deterioration in weather conditions in the region caused a failure of the harvest on an unprecedented scale.

Because of the worsening weather conditions, the harvest in the region was the worst in history.

_____ 5 There is no consensus among scientific authorities about measures to slow the current pace of deforestation in the dense tropical rain forests.

Scientific experts agree unanimously that the prospects are good that we can stabilize the rate of deforestation in the dense tropical rain forests.

_____ 6 To slow the pace of climate change, the world needs to reduce its consumption of fossil fuels.

Reducing the rate of climate change will require a global cutback in the burning of fossil fuels.

_____ 7 It is difficult for people to appreciate the enormous scale of the threat represented by global warming because its effects are gradual and long-term.

Convincing people that global warming is an immense danger is not easy because its effects are neither sudden nor immediate.

_____ 8 To appreciate the seriousness of the ecological threat represented by global climate change, today's generations can utilize computer models to view the problem from the point of view of future generations.

By allowing them to see the problem from the perspective of future generations, computer models help current generations to comprehend the scale of the danger that global warming represents to the world's ecosystems.

BEYOND THE READING

Research
Do your own Internet research to find up-to-date information on tropical deforestation or the loss of biodiversity elsewhere in the world.

Discussion
Discuss this question with a partner.
- You are working for the government of a developing country that is losing large areas of rain forest every year. What government actions would help to slow, or even stop, the destruction of your forests?

Writing
Write a short report on the results of your research or your discussion.

SKILLS AND STRATEGIES 12
NOMINALIZATION

To concentrate a substantial amount of information in one sentence, academic writers use a grammar technique we call *nominalization.* For example, instead of a one- or two-word subject, they sometimes create complex noun phrases as subjects. These longer subjects make sentences more challenging to read. Learning to recognize and understand nominalization, therefore, will help you become a more efficient reader. Although nominalization can occur in other parts of a sentence, the focus here is on nominalization in subjects only.

EXAMPLES & EXPLANATIONS

Examples

The emergence of drug-resistant bacteria is worrying health experts.

Explanations

Noun + *of* + noun phrase + verb. To understand a nominalized subject with this pattern, follow the steps below to make two simpler sentences.

1. Change the first noun (*emergence*) into the verb from the same word-family (*are emerging*)

2. For the subject of the new verb, use the noun phrase that follows the preposition *of* (*drug-resistant kinds of bacteria*).

3. Start a new, second sentence by inserting *This* before the verb of the original sentence (*is worrying*).

Drug-resistant kinds of bacteria are emerging. This is worrying health experts.

The company's decision to open a new plant in Southport was welcomed by the town's residents.

Noun + *'s* + noun phrase + verb. To understand this pattern of nominalization, follow the steps below to make two simpler sentences.

1. Change the second noun (*decision*) into a verb (*decided*).

2. For the subject of the new verb, use the first noun (*company* – without apostrophe -*s*).

3. For the second sentence, insert *This* before the verb of the original sentence.

The company decided to open a new plant in Southport. This was welcomed by the town's residents.

The careless use of pesticides by farmers in the Aral Sea basin contaminated local supplies of drinking water.

Noun + *of* + noun phrase + *by* + noun phrase + verb. To understand this pattern of nominalized subject, follow the steps below to make two simpler sentences.

1. Change the first noun (*use*) into a verb (*used*). Change any adjectives with this noun (*careless*) into adverbs (*carelessly*).

2. For the subject of the new verb, use the noun phrase after *by*.

3. For the object of the new verb, use the noun phrase after *of*.

4. Start the second sentence by inserting *This* before the verb of the original sentence (*contaminated*).

Farmers in the Aral Sea basin used pesticides carelessly. This contaminated local supplies of drinking water.

THE LANGUAGE OF NOMINALIZATION

The noun markers in the chart will help you recognize many nouns that may be used to form nominalized subjects.

MARKERS OF NOMINALIZATION					
ENDINGS FOR ACTION/STATE NOUNS					
-ness	-ety	-ance	-ism	-ion	-ing
-ment	-ity	-ence	-asm	-tion	-th
-hood	-ty	-ency		-sion	

Note, however, that many nouns do not contain special noun markers – e.g., *attack, collapse, damage, increase, release, spread, use.*

STRATEGIES

Experience will enable you to understand nominalized English without mentally changing the text as you read. However, until you have enough experience, you can learn to deal with such texts by using the following three strategies:

- Identify the noun that shows an action or a state.
- Identify any phrases and noun clauses that belong with this noun.
- Change the original sentence into two simpler sentences by following the steps outlined under Examples & Explanations on the opposite page.

SKILL PRACTICE 1

In the following sentences, highlight the main verb and underline the entire nominalized subject. The first one has been done for you as an example.

1 The researcher's claim that he had discovered a cure for the common cold was received with disbelief by the scientific community.

2 The government's decision to raise income taxes has angered a lot of people.

3 The allegation by some people that immigrants take more out of the U.S. economy than they contribute to it is rejected by most economists.

4 The student's slow and painful adjustment to life overseas was to be expected.

5 The tendency of new immigrants to settle in their ethnic communities is sometimes wrongly cited as evidence that they do not wish to become integrated into American society.

6 The public's perception of immigrants as unwilling to learn English may arise because few Americans understand how difficult it is for an adult to learn a second language.

SKILL PRACTICE 2

In the following sentences, highlight the main verb and underline the entire nominalized subject. Then rewrite the sentence as two simpler sentences. The first one has been done for you as an example.

1 The researcher's claim that he had discovered a cure for the common cold was received with disbelief by the scientific community.
   The researcher claimed that he had discovered a cure for the common cold. This was received with disbelief by the scientific community.

2 The retention by immigrant families of parts of their native culture has added variety to U.S. society.

3 The use by first-generation immigrants of their native languages is interpreted by some Americans as a refusal to become part of the mainstream society.

4 The public's lack of appreciation of the ecological and scientific value of rain forest species is an obstacle to solving the problem of biodiversity loss.

5 The accumulation of carbon dioxide in the atmosphere over the last century has convinced most scientists that climate change is a major threat.

6 The resentment among female workers that their male peers receive higher wages for doing the same work is an issue that the company has not addressed.

SKILL PRACTICE 3

Underline the nominalized part of each sentence. Then answer the question that follows. The first one has been done for you as an example.

1 The clearing of forests by early human settlers to provide fuel, wood for construction, and fields for farming probably caused the first major threats to the natural environment.
   Question: What caused the first major threat to the natural environment?
   Answer: *Early human settlers cleared forests to provide fuel, wood for construction, and fields for farming.*

2 The attempts by nations to pursue economic development are the source of the greatest danger to the world's ecology.
   Question: Why is the global ecology in danger?

3 The destruction of vast areas of the Amazon rain forest by wealthy cattle-farming businesses is driving large numbers of tropical species to extinction.
   Question: Why are large numbers of tropical species dying out in the Amazon basin?

4 The government's decision to expand agriculture by using enormous amounts of water from the region's two main rivers for irrigation was the root cause of the environmental catastrophe in the Aral Sea basin.

Question: Why did this environmental disaster happen?

5 The collapse of the Mayan civilization began when soil erosion reduced the productivity of the hillside fields.

Question: What happened when soil erosion made the hillside fields less productive?

6 The establishment of forest reserves – areas in which any economic exploitation of the rain forest is forbidden – will protect tropical species by preserving their habitats.

Question: How can we preserve the habitats of tropical species?

7 The presence of large amounts of toxic chemicals in the environment has produced one of the highest rates of infant mortality in the world in the region of Karalpak in Uzbekistan.

Question: Why have so many infants died in Karalpak?

8 An acceleration of the pace of research into the species of the tropical rain forests will provide the scientific community with the information it needs in order to convince people that the rain forests are worth preserving.

Question: How can scientists acquire the information needed to convince the public that rain forest species are worth preserving?

MAIN READING
CLIMATE CHANGE: MANAGING THE GLOBAL GREENHOUSE

GETTING INTO THE TOPIC

Read the title of the article and discuss the following questions with a partner.

1 According to many scientists, what is happening to the world's climate at the present time?
2 What are the immediate causes of this development?
3 When and in which ways might this development become dangerous for people?

GETTING A FIRST IDEA ABOUT THE ARTICLE

For information about the organization and topics of this article, read the section headings, look at the illustrations, and scan the introduction. Then complete the chart below by matching each topic with the section that deals with it. Some sections may have more than one topic. Write the number of the section (I–V) in the blank.

SECTION	TOPIC
	Greenhouse gases and how they produce a warming effect
	Reasons why global warming is a problem
	Possible ways to address the problem of climate change
	The political and scientific controversy caused by global warming
	The process by which carbon dioxide accumulates in the atmosphere
	What we know and don't know about global warming
	The need to change our attitudes and behavior

WHILE YOU READ

Read the article section by section. Stop after each sentence that contains boldface text and follow the instructions in the box in the margin. After you read each section, answer the Main Idea Check and A Closer Look questions, which can be found on pages 227–234.

Climate Change: Managing the Global Greenhouse

I. INTRODUCTION

In the late 1980s, warnings began to come from leading authorities in the scientific community.

> "The world is warming. Climatic zones are shifting. Glaciers are melting. Sea level is rising. These are not hypothetical events from a science-fiction movie; these changes and others are already taking place, and we expect them to accelerate over the next years as the amounts of . . . gases accumulating in the atmosphere through human activities increase. . . . A rapid and continuous warming will not only be destructive to agriculture but also lead to the widespread death of forest trees, uncertainty in water supplies and the flooding of coastal areas" (Houghton & Woodwell, 1989, p. 36).

According to experts, we are leaving our children and grandchildren a frightening inheritance: an increased accumulation of so-called greenhouse gases in the atmosphere and the potentially disastrous climate changes that this increase may bring about. However, the scientific community is not speaking with one voice. Other scientists claim that the evidence for global warming is inconclusive and argue that predictions based on it are questionable. The scientific debate has been intense. It has also fueled a political controversy about what measures, if any, should be taken to address the possible problem of climate change.

In the presence of scientific debate and political controversy, what should a concerned public think about global warming? For an adequate assessment of the issue, **an essential first step is to identify what we know** and what we do not yet know about the phenomenon.

II. GLOBAL WARMING: FACTS AND UNCERTAINTIES

First, there is unanimous scientific agreement that gases like carbon dioxide (CO_2), chlorofluorocarbons (CFCs), and methane (CH_4) produce a greenhouse effect in the earth's atmosphere. These gases allow sunlight to pass through and warm the earth. Then, when the earth releases that heat in the form of infrared radiation, the same gases retain the heat very efficiently, not allowing it to escape out into space. (See Figure 4.4.)

There is also little doubt among atmospheric scientists that an increase in the greenhouse gases will have a warming effect on the earth's climate. Evidence for a connection between these gases and climate changes has been provided by a team of scientists who analyzed the gases trapped in a 2,000-meter core of Antarctic ice (Lorius et al., 1990). The ice comes from snow that accumulated over the previous 160,000 years. It contains a record of the earth's atmosphere and climate during that time. The analysis shows that between or after the Ice

Scan the first sentences in paragraphs 3–6. Highlight the words that tell you that the paragraph deals with facts not uncertainties. Then come back and continue reading Section II.

FIGURE 4.4 The Greenhouse Effect

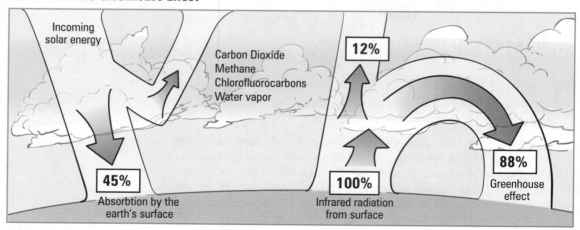

Ages, Antarctic temperatures were ten degrees Celsius higher and the atmosphere contained 25 percent more carbon dioxide and 100 percent more methane than during the Ice Ages.

Also undisputed is the fact that any potential effects of greenhouse 5 gases will be both long-term and global. Unlike other pollutants that remain in the atmosphere only for days or weeks, carbon dioxide, methane, and CFCs will accumulate and remain there between ten and one hundred years. It is also clear that they do not remain localized in the areas in which they are originally released. They spread throughout the global atmosphere. Thus, their effects will be felt by future generations all around the world.

Another well-established fact is that the concentration of greenhouse 6 gases in the atmosphere has been increasing. Analysis of the air contained in glacier ice shows that, over the last two centuries, there has been a 31-percent increase in carbon dioxide and a 150-percent increase in methane. A large proportion (60 percent) of the carbon dioxide increase occurred between 1959 and 2000. CFCs, which have only been in widespread use since the mid-twentieth century, are a relatively recent addition to the traditional greenhouse gases. (See Table 4.1.)

What has caused this significant increase in greenhouse gases? We 7 know that carbon dioxide is released into the atmosphere by processes occurring in nature. (See Table 4.2.) However, it is clear that the main reason for the increased presence of these gases in the atmosphere is the growth of industry within the last century. During this time, many countries experienced some degree of industrializa-

> After you read this paragraph, draw a three-part cause and effect diagram to help you remember the main idea.

TABLE 4.1 Increases in Greenhouse Gases 1800–2000

Date	CO_2	CH_4	CFCs
1800	280 ppm*	0.70 ppm	0
2000	368 ppm (+31%)	1.75 ppm (+150%)	995 ppt**
*ppm: parts per million; **ppt: parts per trillion			

tion, a process that has depended on the burning of coal, oil, and gas to produce energy. The burning of these fossil fuels is known to be the chief human source of carbon dioxide emissions. Industrial expansion also brought about the development of CFCs, gases that for decades were widely used in refrigeration, air-conditioning, aerosols, and other applications. These gases, although they are present in the atmosphere in much smaller quantities than carbon dioxide, retain radiated heat much more efficiently.

Just as industrialization has contributed to increased emissions of greenhouse gases, so too have the responses to **the problem of feeding the world's rapidly growing population**. Two of these responses have been a massive expansion of rice growing and cattle farming. Both activities have become significant sources of additional methane, a gas whose heat-retaining properties are approximately twenty times greater than those of carbon dioxide. **8**

As you read paragraph 8, look for a connection between this idea and global warming. Then draw a three-part cause and effect diagram.

Deforestation has become a common policy in developing countries, particularly those in the tropical zones of South America, Africa, and Asia. By 1988, according to MacNeill (1989), Ethiopia had lost about 97 percent of the forests that existed forty years before. India had lost 72 percent of its forests since the turn of the century. In Africa, the proportion of trees being destroyed to those being planted was 29 to 1. As well as causing massive soil erosion and the extinction of thousands of species, such deforestation releases significant amounts of carbon dioxide into the air. In 1987, for example, the burning of the dense rain forest in the Amazon basin of Brazil produced emissions of carbon dioxide larger than those of the entire United States for that year. In addition, as these enormous forests shrink, so does the earth's natural capacity to absorb carbon dioxide from the air. **9**

As you read, look for two links between deforestation and global warming. Then highlight the words that explain the links.

There is clear evidence, too, that during the last one hundred years of industrialization and rapid population growth the earth has **10**

TABLE 4.2 Sources and Amounts of Annual Atmospheric CO_2 Gain and Loss in Billions of Metric Tons

		Gain	Loss
Natural	Oceanic absorption		−92.0
	Oceanic releases	+90.0	
	Photosnythesis		−61.4
	Vegetation and soil releases	+60.0	
Anthropogenic (of human origin)	Fossil fuel use and cement production	+5.5	
	Land-use changes, such as deforestation	+1.6	
	Reforestation		−0.5
	Total gain and loss	+157.1	−153.9
	Net annual gain	+3.2	

Natural processes maintain the atmospheric balance on which life depends. Today, however, human activities are causing a significant increase in atmospheric CO_2.

become warmer. From their review of the relevant research, international scientists concluded that the mean global-surface temperature rose between 0.4 and 0.8 degrees Celsius during the twentieth century, and that 1998 was the warmest year in the Northern Hemisphere since instrumental records began in 1861. Other evidence to confirm the existence of a warming trend includes a 40 percent reduction in the thickness of sea ice in the North Polar region in recent decades, the retreat of nonpolar inland glaciers, and an annual increase in global sea level of ten to twenty centimeters during the twentieth century (IPCC, 2001).

Scan this paragraph and circle any assessment markers. Use these to help you identify the two reasons why scientists are uncertain. Highlight them. Then come back and continue reading.

However, **some scientists are still reluctant** to attribute the 11 obvious global warming trend of the last one hundred years to the buildup of greenhouse gases in the atmosphere. Such a conclusion, they argue, is not justified by the present evidence, which merely shows that a slight global warming trend has occurred at the same time as concentrations of greenhouse gases in the atmosphere have been climbing. Another reason for treating the causal link as unproven is that the warming trend has not been consistent. It was interrupted between 1945 and 1970, a period when global temperatures dropped so significantly that some contemporary scientists were speculating on the approach of a new Ice Age! Such an interruption is not consistent with the global warming theory, which predicts that average temperatures should gradually rise as the concentration of greenhouse gases in the atmosphere increases. The lack of consistency suggests to some scientists that, at the very least, the effects of the greenhouse gases on global climate have been overstated.

Highlight the new ideas in this sentence. Use these ideas to form your first hypothesis for the main idea of this paragraph.

In addition to some scientific disagreement about how to interpret 12 the warming trend of the last one hundred years, there is also a degree of uncertainty in predicting future climatic developments. To make such predictions, teams of scientists use computer models based on assumptions about the rate of increase in carbon dioxide in the atmosphere. For example, by projecting CO_2 concentrations ranging from 540 to 970 ppm, the 2001 report by the Intergovernmental Panel on Climate Change (IPCC) calculated an average global-temperature increase of 1.4 to 5.8 degrees Celsius by 2100. Although it may seem narrow, the range in the predicted temperature increases is wide enough to be problematic. A projected increase of one degree might cause little disruption to human activities and might justify taking little action against global warming. The effects of a 6-degree increase, on the other hand, would be catastrophic and would demand immediate, far-reaching measures.

III. POTENTIAL EFFECTS OF CLIMATE CHANGE

Some politicians and governments have used the lack of absolute 13 scientific certainty on global warming as a justification for not taking immediate action to control it. Their attitude is that we can't afford to worry about something that may not be a significant problem. The majority of scientists, however, argue that recent investigations have produced much more reliable evidence of warming. They argue that if we take effective measures now, we can slow the rate at which greenhouse gases accumulate in the atmosphere. If we do nothing, however, the impact of the warming and the ultimate costs of dealing with it will be much greater.

If the warming that occurs is in the middle or upper part of the 14 predicted range, there will be **extremely serious consequences for natural ecosystems, agriculture, and human settlements**. In the past, ecosystems have successfully adapted to slow and gradual temperature changes. For example, the belt of forest that runs across Canada and the northern United States has shifted slowly north from its original location in the past ten thousand years, in response to a slow increase (about 0.002 degrees Celsius annually) in temperature. Yet, the increase of 2 to 6 degrees Celsius, which could occur in the next one hundred years, is approximately fifty times more rapid than the "natural" increase. In such circumstances, the forest belt would be under immense strain and would probably not be able to adapt. The likely result of global warming, in this case, would be the destruction, on a massive scale, of the North American forests and of other ecosystems worldwide.

Agriculture will also be seriously damaged by unchecked global 15 **warming.** Higher temperatures are likely to be accompanied in some regions by a significant reduction in rainfall. The resulting demand for irrigation might well exceed the supply of water available. One study, cited by Schneider (1989), predicted that a 3-degree Celsius climb in temperatures in the western and the Great Plains states would bring with it a 33 percent reduction in the land available for crop production. The impact on the supply of domestically produced food in the United States would be disastrous. Similar catastrophic effects on agriculture could be expected elsewhere around the globe.

At the same time as climbing temperatures interfere with agriculture 16 and disrupt ecosystems as large as the North American forests, settlements, especially those in coastal areas, will face **a different threat**. The higher global temperatures that are expected, especially in the higher latitudes, will bring about a rise in sea level. The IPCC projections range from 9 to 88 centimeters by the year 2100. A rise in ocean level at the lower end of this range would have negligible effects. A rise of almost one meter, however, would flood densely populated coastal areas of the world – for example, Bangladesh (Holdgate, 1991) and the small, vulnerable, low-lying island nations of the Pacific and Caribbean, forcing millions of people to abandon their homes and creating economic and social disruption on a massive scale.

IV. RESPONDING TO THE THREAT

The enormous, widespread damage that anthropogenic climate 17 change could cause by the end of the twenty-first century would inevitably have large-scale economic, social, and political consequences. Most environmental scientists and an increasing number of politicians, therefore, believe that we should slow global warming by taking immediate measures to reduce greenhouse gas emissions. This, they argue, would be a form of insurance against catastrophe.

How could an adequate reduction of greenhouse gas emissions be 18 accomplished? Most experts agree that the industrial countries of the world must take the lead, thus ensuring a fast start to a fair solution

Scan paragraphs 14–16 and highlight the word that marks where the writer begins to deal with the consequences for each area. Then come back and continue reading paragraph 14.

Identify the initial cause and ultimate effect of the process in this paragraph. Use this information to draw a two-part cause and effect diagram in the margin.

As you read, draw a simple three-part cause and effect diagram in the margin to help you remember this threat.

Rising sea levels due to global warming could have a devastating impact on many low-lying densely populated areas of the world.

of the problem. After all, it is the long-established industrial nations that are to blame for most of the greenhouse gases that accumulated in the atmosphere before the 1990s. In addition, their economic resources, scientific knowledge, and technological expertise place them in a better position to introduce measures to reduce greenhouse gas emissions.

A general, short-term strategy must be energy conservation – a 19 reduction in the use of energy produced by fossil fuel burning. One specific measure is to encourage recycling. Another is to introduce incentives both for manufacturers to develop products with greater energy efficiency and for consumers to buy these energy-efficient products. The incentives could include tax credits for manufacturers' costs of research and development and for consumers' costs of replacing old, inefficient appliances with the new higher-efficiency versions.

A second, longer-term strategy must be to replace fossil fuels with 20 environmentally safe, alternative sources of energy that will be sustainable and will not exhaust a region's natural resources. To accomplish **this**, governments will again need to introduce incentives for research into alternative energy sources and for the development of affordable technology to exploit these sources. Expanding our use of wind power to generate electricity, for example, is a possibility for the near future. A longer-term, even revolutionary possibility, is to develop the technology to use hydrogen to generate and store electricity.

Conservation policies like those mentioned above are attractive 21 because they have been effective in the past. For example, in the 1970s and 1980s, the U.S. government introduced fuel-economy standards for cars, causing automobile manufacturers to make their products considerably more efficient without a loss in performance or safety. During the same period of drastic increases in the price of oil, industrial production in Japan, Sweden, and West Germany

Check back and highlight the meaning of *this*.

Check back and highlight two specific examples of *Conservation policies*. Draw an arrow from paragraph 21 back to these examples.

became 40 percent more energy-efficient. The prospects are good that such policies will also work in the future.

More good news for conservation is that technologies already exist 22 that are capable of significantly reducing energy consumption and greenhouse gas emissions – provided that the right incentives are offered. For example, the use of coal-generated electricity accounts for a significant proportion of carbon dioxide emissions in the United States. However, substantial energy savings are possible if full use is made of the most energy-efficient appliances, materials, and building design. If the most efficient energy-saving technologies were utilized in new buildings and, where possible, in existing buildings, it is estimated that a 40 percent reduction in energy consumption would be possible (Norberg-Blohm 1991).

There is also bad news, though. First, the direct costs of conservation 23 measures will be high. Governments must finance the incentives described earlier. In addition, to discourage consumers from simply using the same amount of energy to drive their energy-efficient vehicles further and to keep their energy-efficient homes warmer or cooler, governments will need to increase the price of energy to all consumers through user fees or higher taxes. Second, the conversion from fossil fuels to sustainable methods of generating electricity will also be enormously expensive. Research and development will be extremely costly in themselves. Additional costs will result from the need to support people whose lives will be disrupted by the transition to the carbon-free generation of energy – that is, those whose livelihoods depend on the coal and oil industries.

In the course of this century, the total costs of measures to address 24 global warming will be huge. Stabilizing atmospheric carbon dioxide at a safe level (350 ppm) would cost the world up to $18,000 billion (IPCC, 2001). Some economists have argued that spending at this level would endanger economies across the globe. However, a recent study (Azar and Schneider, 2002), which considered the effects of such spending on projected global income, provided a more encouraging perspective. Even with these expenditures, global income in the twenty-first century would grow at a mean annual rate of 9.9 percent – only 0.2 percent lower than the growth rate that had been widely projected without the expenditures.

The obligation to take action against global warming, however, 25 **does not lie exclusively with the industrial world**. In their attempts at rapid economic development, the developing countries are beginning to produce greenhouse gas emissions equaling those in the wealthier nations. In the 1990s, for example, their carbon dioxide emissions increased by 37 percent, more than double the rate in the United States and in the European Community (World Resources Institute, 2003). The beneficial effects of conservation programs in the industrial world are likely to be undermined or completely negated if the emission of greenhouse gases by developing nations continues to increase at this rate. And emissions will surely increase if developing countries continue to respond to the pressure to feed, house, and employ its growing populations by pursuing economic development regardless of the cost to the environment.

Scan forward and highlight words that mark where the writer introduces each problem. Then continue reading paragraph 23.

Scan ahead and highlight who else must act. Then continue reading paragraph 26.

People from different parts of the world view environmental issues — and each other's role in environmental problems — from different perspectives.

Now go back and underline the root cause of the problems that this paragraph has identified.

Highlight the continuing idea here. Use it to confirm your main idea of paragraph 27.

Under these circumstances, the only realistic strategy for the industrial world is to ensure that developing nations are in a position to pursue climate-friendly policies for development. To achieve this, the wealthy nations must effectively address the problem of the massive external debt carried by developing countries. Because of the need to repay this debt, developing countries have little choice but to base their economic development on an increased use of fossil fuels. Because of the same need, these countries are also destroying the immense forests that for millennia have helped to maintain the carbon dioxide balance in the atmosphere. Significantly, of the fifteen countries suffering the greatest deforestation between 1990 and 2000, ten were classified by the World Bank (2001) as **"severely indebted."** 26

Many experts consider debt forgiveness an essential, inevitable component of any program of debt relief. Debt forgiveness, however, need not be unconditional. It could take the form of an agreement between developing, debtor nations and their wealthy creditors. It could be offered, for example, in return for commitments by the developing nations to cease or severely restrict deforestation, to pass strict environmental protection laws, to enforce these laws rigorously, and to pursue environmentally safe development policies. 27

In addition to resolving the debt crisis, however, the industrial world must provide increased aid to developing countries. This aid should take the form of direct economic assistance, technical assistance, and better access to the newest technologies for reducing greenhouse gas emissions. Such assistance will be needed if developing countries are to attain their goals of economic development and a better standard of living for their people. Together with debt relief, it will permit these countries to pursue policies of sustainable development, thus enabling them to make their essential contribution to resolving the problem of global warming. 28

V. RETHINKING OUR PRIORITIES

In conclusion, then, this article is arguing that the problem of 29 global climate change cannot be effectively addressed without the decision, especially by the wealthier countries, to spend vast amounts of money. As we have seen, studies in 2001 and 2002 estimated that dealing with the crisis would require total expenditures of up to $18,000 billion by 2100.

To raise spending to these levels, some people have argued that **a** 30 **global revolution in public and political thinking will be necessary** – the development of a global ecological perspective that will change our traditional attitudes, policies, and behavior. The revolution will require both the public and the politicians to be convinced that the greatest danger to their long-term security comes from the fossil fuel economies that are the root cause of global warming. In addition, the global nature of the threat means that any solution will require unprecedented cooperation among nations.

Scan paragraphs 30–31. Find where the author describes this revolution and label it *Revolution* in the margin. Then highlight words that show the author's opinion about how likely the revolution is to happen.

Just how likely is such a revolution? There may be cause for cau- 31 tious optimism in evidence that public thinking on the environment began to change in the last decades of the twentieth century. By 2003, opinion polls reflected a willingness in leading industrial nations to give priority to protecting the environment even if it caused slower economic growth and some loss of jobs. (See Figure 4.5.) There is also evidence of a growing public appreciation of the need to think globally in environmental matters. In 2002, for instance, polls showed that 92 percent of Europeans and 79 percent of Americans considered global warming either an extremely important or an important threat to their countries.

Some government action has accompanied **the changes in public** 32 **opinion** – for example, the Montreal Protocol of 1990, by which 59 nations agreed to halt the use of CFCs by the year 2000. The Framework Convention on Climate Change (FCCC) was signed by 153 nations at the 1992 Earth Summit in Rio de Janeiro. This agreement committed the wealthier countries to stabilizing their greenhouse gas emissions by the year 2000 at 1990 levels and to taking the lead in reducing emissions of greenhouse gases. In the 1997 agreement referred to as

Check back and number two examples of *the changes in public opinion.*

FIGURE 4.5 2003 Public Support for Protecting the Environment in Spite of Costs

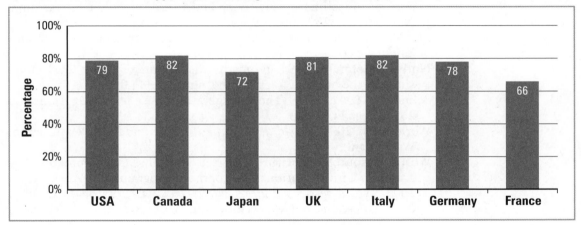

the Kyoto Protocol, the industrialized nations accepted an outline of a plan that would oblige them to reduce greenhouse gas emissions by between 6 and 8 percent.

Will this paragraph focus on progress or problems in addressing global warming? Highlight words in this sentence that help you answer the question.

However, developments between 1997 and 2002 showed that there 33 were still major obstacles to a workable international agreement on **climate change**. In 2000, negotiations on the details of the Kyoto Protocol ended in failure. Developing countries refused to consider limiting their greenhouse gas emissions. In addition, deep differences emerged between the domestic, political, and economic priorities of the European Union and those of a group of nations headed by the United States and Japan. In 2001, the new government in Washington refused to restart the Kyoto negotiations and seemed interested in slowing down efforts to address climate change. At the same time, **economies across the globe were in decline**, making it easier for politicians to argue against expensive measures to reduce emissions of greenhouse gases.

Highlight the effect of this economic decline.

By 2004, therefore, the necessary revolution in environmental 34 thinking was far from completed. But who would have predicted the 1989–91 political revolutions that ended the Cold War and altered the political map of the globe? Given this precedent and the growing capacity of science to provide reliable information on climate change, perhaps we can still hope that politicians will act to meet their obligations to future generations.

References

Azar, C., and Schneider, C. H. 2002. Are the economic costs of stabilizing the atmosphere prohibitive? *Ecological Economics*, 42, pp. 73–80.

Holdgate, M. 1991. The environment of tomorrow. *Environment* 33 (6), pp. 14–42.

Houghton, R. A., and Woodwell, G. M. 1989. Global climatic change. *Scientific American*, 260 (4), pp. 36–44.

IPCC. 2001. *Climate change 2001: Synthesis report. A contribution of working groups I, II, and III to the Third Assessment Report of the Intergovernmental Panel on Climate Change* [Watson, R.T., and the Core Writing Team (Eds.)]. Cambridge, U.K., and New York: Cambridge University Press.

Lorius, C. J., Raynaud, D., Hansen, J., and Le Treut, H. 1990. The ice-core record climate sensitivity and future greenhouse warming. *Nature* 347 (6289), pp. 139–145.

MacNeill, J. 1989. Strategies for sustainable economic development. *Scientific American*, 261 (3), pp. 155–165

Norberg-Blohm, V. 1991. From the inside out: reducing CO2 emissions in the building sector. *Environment* 33 (3), pp. 16–44.

Schneider, S. H. 1989. The changing climate. *Scientific American* 261 (3), pp. 70–79.

World Bank. 2001. *World development indicators 2001.* Washington: World Bank.

World Resources Institute, United Nations Development Programme, United Nations Environment Program, and World Bank. 2003. *World resources 2002–2004: Decisions for the earth. Balance, voice, and power.* Washington: World Resources Institute.

SECTION I: Introduction

MAIN IDEA CHECK

Here are the main ideas of each paragraph in this section of the article. Match each paragraph to its main idea. Write the number of the paragraph in the blank.

Paragraphs 1–2

_____ A There has been an intense debate among both scientists and politicians about global warming and about the appropriate response to it.

_____ B The article will try to help the public understand the issue of global warming.

A CLOSER LOOK

Look back at Section I of the article to answer the following questions.

1 There is agreement among scientists that global warming is a serious problem. True or False?

2 There is agreement among politicians on what should be done about global warming. True or False?

3 What words and phrases in the text helped you answer questions 1 and 2?

SECTION II: Global Warming: Facts and Uncertainties

MAIN IDEA CHECK

Here are the main ideas of each paragraph in this section of the article. Match each paragraph to its main idea. Write the number of the paragraph in the blank.

Paragraphs 3–6

_____ A There is historical evidence linking increases in the earth's temperature to increased carbon dioxide and methane in the atmosphere.

_____ B Scientists have shown that the amount of greenhouse gases in the atmosphere has been increasing since 1800.

_____ C Any effects of greenhouse gases on climate will be felt worldwide and by future generations.

_____ D Gases like carbon dioxide, methane, and CFCs clearly produce a greenhouse effect because they prevent heat released by the earth from escaping into space.

Paragraphs 7–12

_____ E Scientists have established that the earth has become warmer in the last one hundred years.

_____ F Predicting the size of future temperature increases involves some uncertainty.

_____ G A substantial increase in cattle rearing and rice production are major factors in the increase of methane in the atmosphere.

_____ H The burning of tropical forests in developing countries is a major contributor of carbon dioxide in the atmosphere.

_____ I Industrialization, not processes occurring in nature, accounts for much of the increase in greenhouse gases over the last one hundred years.

_____ J Some scientists are not prepared to conclude that the warming trend of the last one hundred years is due to increased greenhouse gases in the atmosphere.

A CLOSER LOOK

Look back at Section II of the article to answer the following questions.

1 Here are ideas from this section. Choose the idea(s) about which there is agreement. Circle all that apply.

  a Industry and agriculture are large contributors to greenhouse gases in the atmosphere.

  b The earth has become warmer during the past one hundred years or so.

  c Computer predictions of global climate change have convinced everyone that immediate action is necessary.

  d Over the past two centuries, the amount of greenhouse gases in the atmosphere has been increasing.

  e If greenhouse gases have an effect, it will be felt globally.

  f The warming trend of the last century has been caused by the accumulation of greenhouse gases in the atmosphere.

2 This diagram represents the connections between human activities and climate
   change. Reread paragraphs 6–10. Then complete the diagram with items A–F.
   Write the correct letter in each box.

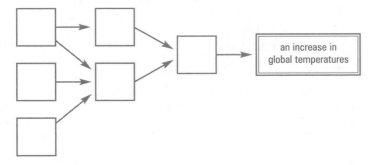

A an increase in emissions of CO_2 and other greenhouse gases
B reduction in the earth's natural ability to absorb CO_2
C deforestation by burning
D the expansion of intensive agriculture
E a significant increase in greenhouse gases in the atmosphere
F the expansion of fossil fuel-based industry

SECTION III: Potential Effects of Climate Change

MAIN IDEA CHECK

Here are the main ideas of each paragraph in this section of the article. Match
each paragraph to its main idea. Write the number of the paragraph in the blank.

Paragraphs 13–16

_____ A Higher temperatures will also probably have a destructive impact on
          agriculture.

_____ B The consequences for ecosystems will be extremely serious if temperature
          increases are between 2 and 6 degrees Celsius.

_____ C Higher temperatures will lead to a rise in ocean level, which may endanger
          vast areas of densely populated, low-lying land.

_____ D Despite some political opposition, most scientists argue that the evidence
          justifies our taking immediate steps to cut the emission of global gases.

A CLOSER LOOK

Look back at Section III of the article to answer the following questions.

1 Some people believe that we should not do anything about global warming
   until we are certain about its effects. True or False?

2 Why does the writer use the example of the North American forest belt in paragraph 14?

   a To show the potential destructive effects of global warming on natural ecosystems

   b To show that natural ecosystems have the ability to adapt to the expected temperature changes associated with global warming

   c To show how global warming would affect agriculture

   d To show how global warming would affect human settlements

3 This diagram represents the possible relationship between global warming and agriculture. Reread paragraph 15. Then complete the diagram with sentences A–C. Write the correct letter in each box.

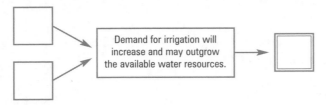

   A Rainfall will decline in certain areas.

   B There could be a disastrous reduction in the amount of land available for growing crops.

   C Temperatures will increase in certain areas.

4 Coastal areas of the world will escape the possibly catastrophic effects of global warming. True or False?

SECTION IV: Responding to the Threat

MAIN IDEA CHECK

Here are the main ideas of each paragraph in this section of the article. Match each paragraph to its main idea. Write the number of the paragraph in the blank.

Paragraphs 17–20

_____ A Governments must also develop alternative, sustainable sources of energy to replace fossil fuels.

_____ B The industrial nations should be the first to start programs to reduce greenhouse gas emissions.

_____ C The majority of environmental scientists believe that we should take immediate measures to cut greenhouse gas emissions and avoid a future catastrophe.

_____ D Governments must develop energy conservation policies that will reduce the demand for energy produced by burning fossil fuels.

Paragraphs 21–24

_____ E A major disadvantage of programs designed to reduce greenhouse gas emissions is their enormous costs.

_____ F Policies to increase energy efficiency were successful in the past.

_____ G The good news is that measures to stabilize atmospheric carbon dioxide at a safe level, though expensive, will not significantly slow the expected increase in global income.

_____ H We could reduce energy consumption and greenhouse gas emissions substantially with technology that exists today.

Paragraphs 25–28

_____ I Debt forgiveness could be offered to developing countries who commit themselves to protecting the world ecology.

_____ J Developing countries will also require increased economic and technical assistance if they are to help solve the problem of greenhouse gases.

_____ K Actions by the wealthier countries to reduce greenhouse gas emissions will not solve the problem of global warming if we ignore emissions in developing nations.

_____ L The industrialized world must ease the burden of debt carried by the poorer countries so that these nations can pursue ecologically responsible economic development.

A CLOSER LOOK

Look back at Section IV of the article to answer the following questions.

1 The writer believes that the world's leading industrial nations have a responsibility to start the process of reducing greenhouse gas emissions.
True or False?

2 Scan paragraphs 19–22 to identify why the writer believes that incentives such as tax credits are necessary to help solve the problem of global warming. Circle all that apply.
a They encourage the use of existing energy-efficient technologies.
b They encourage the development of more energy-efficient products.
c They encourage consumers to purchase more energy-efficient products.
d They encourage research into alternative sources of energy to replace fossil fuels.

3 This diagram represents the writer's ideas for a process that would reduce the contribution by industrial countries, especially the United States, to global warming. Reread paragraphs 19–22. Then complete the diagram with sentences A–F. Write the correct letter in each box.

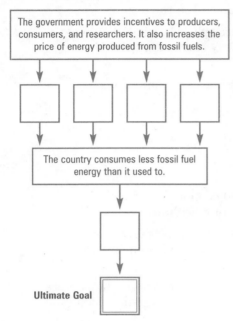

The government provides incentives to producers, consumers, and researchers. It also increases the price of energy produced from fossil fuels.

The country consumes less fossil fuel energy than it used to.

Ultimate Goal

A Greenhouse gas emissions are reduced.

B Industry and consumers have financial reasons to recycle.

C The global warming trend is slowed.

D Consumers have a reason to buy products that are energy-efficient.

E Alternative sources of energy and technologies to exploit them are developed.

F Industry is encouraged to develop products that are energy-efficient.

4 The diagram in question 3 does not show the negative sides of the solutions described in this section of the article. List two negative aspects of the solutions.

5 This diagram represents how developing countries contribute to the buildup of greenhouse gases in the atmosphere. Reread paragraphs 25–26. Then complete the diagram with sentences A–D. Write the correct letter in each box.

Initial Cause

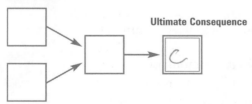

Ultimate Consequence

C

A The top priority for developing countries is economic development, regardless of its cost to the environment.

B Developing countries have growing populations that need food, housing, education, and jobs.

C Emissions of greenhouse gases increase.

D Developing countries have enormous external debts that they must pay off.

6 This diagram represents the writer's idea of how the problem discussed in this section should be solved. Reread paragraphs 26–28. Then complete the diagram with sentences A–D. Write the correct letter in each box.

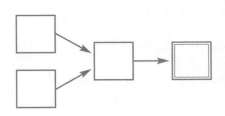

A Emissions of greenhouse gases are considerably reduced.

B The industrial countries give economic, technical, and technological assistance to the developing countries.

C The industrial countries offer debt forgiveness to the developing countries.

D Developing countries can adopt policies of sustainable development that are environmentally friendly.

SECTION V: Rethinking Our Priorities

MAIN IDEA CHECK

Here are the main ideas of each paragraph in this section of the article. Match each paragraph to its main idea. Write the number of the paragraph in the blank.

Paragraphs 29–34

_____ A To make available the funds necessary to address the root causes of global warming, we must radically change our ways of thinking and behaving.

_____ B People seeking a change in environmental thinking might be encouraged by public opinion polls showing changes in attitudes toward environmental issues.

_____ C The problem of global warming will not be resolved without massive expenditures by the developed nations.

_____ D In a few international agreements, governments have committed themselves to reducing greenhouse gases.

_____ E We have some reason for believing that a revolution in environmental thinking is still possible.

_____ F At the beginning of the twenty-first century, a global economic downturn and disputes between countries prevented any real progress toward a workable plan for dealing with climate change.

A CLOSER LOOK

Look back at Section V of the article to answer the following questions.

1 Which event(s) does the writer identify as evidence that the public and politicians were becoming more environmentally aware by the turn of the century? Circle all that apply.

   a Polls showing that a majority of Americans and Europeans believed that global warming was a significant danger

   b Development, in 2002, of the Kyoto Protocol into a workable agreement accepted by all countries

   c The signing of the 1992 FCCC

   d Acceptance by numerous countries of the Montreal Protocol of 1990

2 The writer is absolutely certain that the problem of global warming will be solved. True or False?

BEYOND THE READING

Research

Do Internet or library research to find additional, up-to-date information on climate change, new evidence for it, progress or lack of progress toward addressing climate change, or different approaches to solving the problem.

Discussion

Discuss the following question with a partner:

    ◻ Should the industrial nations take the lead in reducing their greenhouse gas emissions or should the burden of making the reductions be shared equally among all countries?

Writing

Write a short report on the results of your research or your discussion.

MAKING CONNECTIONS

The vocabulary in these two exercises comes from all the readings in Unit 4. The exercises will help you see how writers make connections across sentences in a text.

EXERCISE 1: CONNECTIONS BETWEEN SENTENCES

Read the numbered sentence. Then choose and circle the sentence, a or b, that logically follows it. Then, from the box, decide how the sentence you chose connects to the first. Write A, B, or C to identify the correction.

A It describes a consequence of what is reported in the first sentence.

B It contains a contrast to what is reported in the first sentence.

C It adds specific details to support the general information in the first sentence.

_____ 1 There was unprecedented flooding in this fertile river basin last year.

    a Fortunately, the rains ceased and the water retreated before it had reached the level of the 1980 flood, and before it caused any long-term damage to crops.

    b With an immense area of farmland under water, the harvest was disrupted and eventual losses to agriculture were in excess of $50 billion.

_____ 2 Often the measures taken to create economic growth in a region can undermine and even negate any progress that they were expected to bring.

    a For example, irrigation can make semi-arid regions fertile and capable of producing substantial crop harvests that will generate valuable income for the region.

    b For example, removing tropical rain forests to provide farmland disrupts the process by which nutrients are recycled into the soil, which then loses its fertility.

_____ 3 In some developing countries, current U.N. birth control programs have exceeded expectations and have had substantial success in reducing the fertility rate.

    a In many of these countries, success has been negligible and the programs have convinced large numbers of people to cease using any modern methods of contraception.

    b In other countries, however, the chances of success have been undermined by the failure to address the problem of poverty, one of the root causes of high birth rates.

_____ 4 As the artificial environment created by the Mayas deteriorated because of erosion and flooding, their system of intensive agriculture could not keep pace with the demand for food.

    a Evidence for serious disruptions of the food supply is apparent in skeletons that reveal widespread malnutrition in adults and increased mortality among children, the most vulnerable members of Mayan society.

    b This complex system involved clearing the tropical forest from the hillsides, using terracing to control soil erosion, and constructing drains and raised fields to protect the crops from flooding.

_____ 5 By exhausting natural resources today and refusing to conserve, we are in fact depriving our children and grandchildren of their right to use and enjoy these resources.

    a This realization has led some legal authorities to argue that we have an obligation to include the perspective of future generations as we plan our economic development today.

    b Today's threats include inefficient methods of irrigation, the excessive use of chemical pesticides and artificial fertilizers, emissions from power plants, and deforestation.

EXERCISE 2: CONNECTIONS WITHIN PARAGRAPHS

Make a clear paragraph by putting sentences A, B, and C in the best order after the numbered sentence. Write the letters in the correct order. The boldface words help you identify continuing ideas.

1 Some leading experts in the law have suggested that we are under the obligation to include the perspective of future generations when we discuss what measures should be taken to address environmental deterioration today. _____ _____ _____

A	B	C
By exhausting natural resources today and refusing to conserve, **these experts** argue, we are depriving future generations of their right to use and enjoy these resources.	In addition, by destroying habitats and causing species to become extinct on an unprecedented scale, we are undermining our grandchildren's ability to benefit from the scientific study of those species.	**For these and other reasons**, one legal authority argues, future generations must have an independent representative in all future discussions, both domestic and international, on sustainable development.

2 There is a wide consensus among historians that the development of agriculture, approximately ten thousand years ago, was an unprecedented advance for the human race. _____ _____ _____

A	B	C
However, from an ecological perspective, agriculture also placed immense pressure on natural ecosystems that were susceptible to disruption.	**It** enabled food to be produced much more efficiently, thereby freeing time for people to study science and thus to achieve gains that would not otherwise have been possible.	When the demands on **these systems** became excessive and unsustainable, the systems collapsed.

3 Scientists have warned that catastrophic disruption of a region's ecology can be caused by economic development decisions taken by government authorities who do not appreciate the long-term impact of those decisions. ___ ___ ___

A The story of the Aral Sea basin from 1960 to 2000 proves that **such warnings** are not exaggerated.

B **Here** the climate has become much more extreme and the environment has deteriorated to a point where it is toxic to the life it once sustained.

C The root cause of **this ecological catastrophe** was the economic decision to convert arid land to agricultural use by irrigation on a large scale.

4 To the impoverished people who seek to farm it, the moist soil of the tropical rain forests with its dense vegetation at first creates the impression of being highly fertile. ___ ___ ___

A By cutting down the trees to provide land and fuel for themselves, **the farmers** disrupt the recycling of nutrients to the soil and deprive it of its natural protection against erosion.

B However, experience soon convinces them that **this impression** is false.

C Because the soil quickly is exhausted and ceases to produce enough food to sustain a family, **they** are obliged to abandon their farms and move to a new area of the rain forest, where the cycle of ecological destruction is repeated.

5 As the immense rain forests of the earth's tropical zones are destroyed to provide hardwood, fuel, or land for settlement, natural species are becoming extinct at a pace unprecedented since the appearance of humans on the earth. ___ ___ ___

A A resolution of **these complex issues** will be impossible without an international consensus that so far has proven impossible to reach.

B Accomplishing **this task**, however, will be an enormous challenge for the world community, because it will involve tackling the root causes of the crisis: overpopulation, poverty, and unsustainable development.

C Prospects for halting **the loss of species** are poor, but biologists believe that today's extinction rate can be stabilized if we address the economic pressures that cause people to destroy the forests for short-term gain.

APPENDIX 1

DEALING WITH UNKNOWN VOCABULARY

When you read, you will meet many new words. If you stop to look up every unknown word in your dictionary, this will interrupt your reading; and interruptions will make reading more difficult for you, not easier. What can you do? You can learn to skip over the word, if it is not key to understanding the main idea of the text. Or you can develop strategies for getting help from the *context* – the ideas that appear in the same sentence as the unknown word or in the neighboring sentences.

EXAMPLES & EXPLANATIONS

Examples

Heart disease occurs more often in people who lead **sedentary** lives. It occurs less often in people who get physical exercise every day.

In many poorer countries, the **funding** for important programs in public health comes from wealthier nations or through the World Bank.

Tests have shown that the new medicine is very **effective**. Seventy percent of patients who take it are without pain for up to twelve hours.

In some very poor regions of the world, the probability is low that a sick child can see a local health worker. It is even less **likely** that such children can see a doctor.

Explanations

Although you may still not understand the word *sedentary*, you can understand enough of the text to keep on reading. Basically, you know that people who don't *get physical exercise* get heart disease *more often* than people who do.

Here, by studying the context, you can see that *funding* must mean something like "money" because it is something that *poorer countries* get from *wealthier nations* or *the World Bank*.

Sometimes you can guess the meaning of a word by relating it to a word that you already know. You already know the word *effect*. This, plus the context, allows you to guess that *effective* means something like "successful" or "producing good results."

However, you have to be careful with words that look like words you know. At first you may think that *likely* is connected to the verb to *like*, meaning "enjoy" or maybe to the preposition *like*, meaning "similar to." But when you focus on the context, you realize that "enjoy" or "similar to" do not work in this context. From the context, you see that *less likely* means almost the same as *the probability is low*, so *likely* must mean something like "probable."

STRATEGIES

Remember that your goal is to understand the main idea of a text, not every single word in the text. So here are some strategies for you to use when you meet an unknown word.

- Do not stop reading. Continue reading at least until the end of the sentence, even into the next sentence. By doing this, you will see the full context of the unknown word.
- Be satisfied if you understand the text, even if you don't understand the unknown word. In this case, simply ignore the unknown word.
- Use your understanding of the context to make an educated guess about the meaning of the unknown word.
- If you know a word in the same word family as the unknown word, carefully use that knowledge and the context to help you understand its meaning.

SKILL PRACTICE 1

The following short texts contain words in bold from Unit 1, Reading 1, on page 8. Before you read the article, use the strategies for dealing with unknown words to try to understand each text. Do not use a dictionary. Choose your reaction, *A*, *B*, or *C*, to each text from the choices below and write it in the blank.

A I can generally understand the text even if I ignore the word in bold.
B I understand the text. The context tells me what the word in bold means.
C I can understand the word in bold because it looks like a word I already know.

_____ 1 I never had a single problem with my last car. It always started, even in cold wet weather. I hope my new car will be just as **reliable**.

_____ 2 The typical Western **diet** of the late twentieth century was too rich in animal fats. Today, however, people are starting to become more careful about what they eat.

_____ 3 I was **unaware** that John was ill and in the hospital. Thanks for letting me know. I'll go and see him tomorrow.

_____ 4 How are we going to solve these computer problems? I don't know anyone with the **expertise** that we need. Do you?

_____ 5 In general, smokers **tend** to have more heart and lung problems than nonsmokers.

SKILL PRACTICE 2

The following short texts contain words in bold from Unit 1, Reading 2, on pages 13–14. Before you read the article, use the strategies for dealing with unknown words to try to understand each text. Do not use a dictionary. Choose your reaction, *A*, *B*, or *C*, to each text from the choices below and write it in the blank.

> A I can generally understand the text even if I ignore the word in bold.
> B I understand the text. The context tells me what the word in bold means.
> C I can understand the word in bold because it looks like a word I already know.

_____ 1 Although we have made **considerable** progress in treating and preventing heart disease, it remains the leading cause of death in many industrial countries.

_____ 2 Modern diagnostic **equipment** allows doctors to identify some serious medical problems much earlier than was possible in the past. The high price of that same **equipment**, however, drives up the costs of medical care.

_____ 3 A number of **obstacles** stand in the way of plans to improve health care in the poorer countries of the world. Of these, perhaps the most basic problem is the lack of clean, safe drinking water.

_____ 4 After the disaster, special teams examined the injured to decide who was in most **urgent** need of medical attention. The job of these experts was to identify people who would die without immediate treatment for their injuries.

_____ 5 The death **rate** in automobile accidents is higher for people who have not been using their seat belts than it is for seat belt users.

SKILL PRACTICE 3

The following short texts contain words in bold that you may not know. The words all appear in Unit 1, Reading 3, on pages 23–24. Before you read the article, use the strategies for dealing with unknown words to figure out the meaning of the words in bold. Write your answer in the space provided. The first one has been done for you as an example.

1 I bought a new video monitor last week, but when I connected it to my computer, I discovered that it was **defective**. I returned it to the store for a replacement that works perfectly.

not good; not working correctly; has something wrong

2 In a multiple-choice question, you should **eliminate** all the answers that you know are incorrect. This will increase your chances of choosing the correct answer even if you are not sure of it.

_____

3 This new player is young and inexperienced. However, most experts agree that he has enormous **potential**. Some even believe he could be a second Pelé!

_____

4 A company has to show clear **evidence** that a new drug is safe and will benefit patients. If the company can't do so, the government will not allow the drug to be used.

_____

5 The doctors have not yet been able to diagnose what is wrong with this patient so they're going to **conduct** some more tests.

_____

SKILL PRACTICE 4

The following short texts contain words in bold that you may not know. The words all appear in Unit 1, Reading 4, on pages 30–32. Before you read the article, use the strategies for dealing with unknown words to figure out the meaning of the words in bold. Write your answer in the space provided.

1 In the days after the disastrous earthquake, the government only managed to send ten water trucks into the affected region. For the thousands of homeless survivors, this **response** was totally inadequate.

_____

2 **Vaccines** are an important part of preventative health care. They protect young children against serious diseases like diphtheria, polio, and measles, which killed millions in earlier centuries.

_____

3 Nowadays, everyone needs to understand how the AIDS virus is **transmitted** from one person to another. This is knowledge that could save many lives.

_____

4 People often do not want to talk openly about sexual behavior, especially to their children. This **reluctance** is one reason why HIV/AIDS has spread so rapidly since the 1980s.

_____

5 This Red Cross kitchen will be able to **provide** two good meals a day to one thousand survivors of the earthquake.

_____

APPENDIX 2
STRATEGIES FOR VOCABULARY LEARNING

Here are some facts about vocabulary learning and some study strategies that you can use while you are working on learning vocabulary.

1 You did not learn the vocabulary of your native language from a list or from a dictionary. You learned it by hearing and seeing it in contexts that you understood.

- Learn new words by reading them in texts and by trying to understand them from the contexts in which they occur.
- After you meet a new word, be ready to recognize examples of it in other texts. You will find, for example, that many words that were new for you appear again and again in the articles of *Making Connections*.
- Study the words in example sentences in Appendix 3, "Key Vocabulary from the Readings," and in your ESL dictionary.

2 Research shows that the more often you see a word, the better you understand and remember it. Here is a system that makes vocabulary review part of your vocabulary learning process.

- Study five new words for five to seven minutes. Then stop and do something else.
- Some time later, return to the vocabulary. Review the words from your earlier session and work on five new words for another five to seven minutes.
- Again some time later, return to the vocabulary. Review the ten words from your earlier sessions and work on five new words.

3 It is easier to review vocabulary if it is organized clearly and simply.

- Write each new vocabulary item on its own small index card.
- On the other side of the card, write its meaning in English and perhaps in your own language.
- Test yourself often with the cards, and change the order of the cards each time you test yourself.

4 Besides knowing the meanings of a word, native speakers of English also know a great deal of grammatical information about the word. This knowledge helps them use the word correctly. Similarly, you should build up your knowledge of the grammatical features of a word.

- Learn whether nouns are countable or uncountable.
- Learn whether verbs are transitive and always need an object or are intransitive and never have an object.
- Learn the specific prepositions that must follow certain verbs, nouns, and adjectives; for example, *depend **on**, damage **to**, interested **in***.

5 In your own language you know words whose meanings are opposite and words whose meanings are similar. You know which adjectives can describe a certain noun. You know the types of nouns that can be the subject or object of certain verbs. Similarly, you need to build up the same knowledge for the words you learn in English.

■ When you are learning a new word, try to think of English words you already know that seem to have a similar meaning or an opposite meaning to the new word.

■ When you are learning a new noun, look for adjectives that can describe it. When you are learning a new adjective, look for nouns it can describe.

■ When you are learning a new verb, look for nouns that can be its subject or object. When you are learning a new noun, look for verbs you can use with it as the subject or object.

6 Small bilingual dictionaries and English dictionaries that are written for native speakers may not give you the kind of information that you need to assist you in learning vocabulary. Use instead an English-English dictionary that is specially written for learners of English, such as the *Cambridge Dictionary of American English* (Cambridge University Press, 2000).

APPENDIX 3
KEY VOCABULARY FROM THE READINGS

UNIT 1, READING 1: HEART DISEASE AND CHANGING ATTITUDES

access (to) *n* the opportunity to reach, obtain, or use • *Because they have no medical insurance, 40 million Americans do not have easy **access to** the health care system.* **accessible** *adj* • *There are no roads into the mountains, so villages there are only **accessible** on foot or by helicopter.*

associate (with) *v* to connect something with something else • *Some time ago, scientists discovered that smoking is **associated with** lung cancer.* **association** *n* • *For a long time, cigarette producers did not accept that there was an **association** between lung cancer and cigarette smoking.*

attitude *n* how you think and feel about something • *Ali has a great **attitude** in his classes; he works hard, is interested in learning new things, and always tries to learn from his mistakes.*

aware *adj* knowing • *The student was not **aware** that the parking lot was only for police cars, so he parked his car there. When he returned, he found a parking ticket on his car.* **become aware (of)** *v phr* to realize • *More and more people in the United States are **becoming aware of** the importance of exercise for health. They are beginning to run, swim, or play other sports regularly.*

benefit (from) *v* 1. to be helpful or useful to someone • *The new tax law is not going to **benefit** us.* 2. *v* to get an advantage from something • *You need to be making over $200,000 a year before you **benefit from** the new tax change.* **benefit** *n*

decade *n* a period of ten years • *The 1990s were an eventful **decade** for Europe. While a number of countries made a peaceful change to democracy, others were experiencing civil war.*

deficient (in) *adj* not as much of something as is needed • *Health problems can occur if a person's diet is **deficient in** certain essential vitamins.* **deficiency** *n* a lack of something that is necessary • *Scurvy is a disease that is caused by a **deficiency** of vitamin C.*

diagnose *v* to identify what is wrong, often in a patient who is ill • *To **diagnose** that a patient has influenza, doctors look for a sudden fever, headache, and muscle pains.* **diagnosis** *n* • *For some diseases, doctors need to run tests in order to make a **diagnosis**.*

diet *n* the types of food that a person or a group normally eats • *Researchers now believe that there is too much animal fat in the typical Western **diet**. They are advising people to eat less red meat, butter, and cheese.* **on a diet** *phr* eating a limited amount of food, usually so as to lose weight • *Lots of people attempt to lose weight by going **on a diet**.*

doubt *v* to not believe something • *I'd like to go on a skiing vacation this winter, but I **doubt** I'll have the money.* **doubt** *n* uncertainty • *There's no **doubt** that Anne is the best person for the job.*

emphasize *v* to place more importance on one thing than on other things; to stress • *The speaker **emphasized** his important ideas by repeating them and speaking louder.* **emphasis** *n* • *Many people here feel that the government has not put enough **emphasis** on education. They spend a lot more money on less important things.*

expert *n* a person who has a lot of knowledge or skill in a certain subject • ***Experts** from other countries often come to study the farming methods that are used here.* **expertise** *n* the knowledge or skill that an expert has • *These people want to increase their **expertise** in order to better solve farming problems in their own countries.*

factor *n* one thing that acts with other things to cause a specific result • *Alcohol is a **factor** in many traffic accidents in the United States, but there are others, for example speed, driver inattention, and weather conditions.*

frequent *adj* happening often • *Thunderstorms are **frequent** during spring and summer in this part of the country.* OPPOSITE: **rare** *adj*

maintain *v* to keep something in the same condition or in good condition • *When you drive, you should **maintain** a safe distance from the car in front of you.*

merely *adv* nothing more than this • *People who normally do not exercise can reduce their chances of heart disease **merely** by walking 30 minutes a day.*

nutrition *n* food and its effects on people, plants, or animals • *Experts agree that good **nutrition** is necessary for good health.* **nutritious** *adj* having value as food • *U.S. schools often employ experts to plan **nutritious** meals for the schoolchildren.*

prevent *v* to stop something before it can happen • *The thunderstorm **prevented** us from finishing our soccer game. We'll replay the game next week.* **prevention** *n* • *Crime **prevention** is one of the responsibilities of the police.*

regular *adj* describing something which happens again and again with more or less the same amount of time between occurrences • *Doctors say that exercise is important for health, but it must be frequent and **regular**. In other words, you have to exercise every day or every second day.* OPPOSITE: **irregular** *adj*

rely on *v* to depend on someone or something; to trust • *I have to leave now. Friends of mine are **relying on** me to get them to the airport in time for their flight.* **reliable** *adj* • *My first car was old and uncomfortable, but it was very **reliable**. It always started and got me where I needed to go.*

serious *adj* **1.** very bad or dangerous • *Influenza is a **serious** illness, especially for older people. That's why it is important to get a flu shot every year.* **2.** accepting that something is important • *My friend got **serious** about his math class after he got an F on the first test. He didn't miss any more classes after that.*

stress *n* **1.** emphasis • *In the word discover, the **stress** is on the second syllable. We say "disCOVer" and*

not "DIScover." **2.** the pressure that comes from difficulties in your life • *John is under a lot of **stress** at the moment. He is out of work, his wife is ill, and they don't have enough money to pay all their monthly bills.*

sufficient *adj* enough • *Sometimes children in poor families simply do not get **sufficient** food to keep them healthy.* SYNONYM: **adequate** *adj*

survive *v* to continue to live or exist • *Humans can **survive** for some time without food but for a much shorter time without water.* **survivor** *n* • *After the earthquake, the first job was to look for **survivors** in the ruined buildings.* **survival** *n* • *The "**survival** of the fittest" means that the strong animals continue to live and the weak ones die.*

tend *v* to be more probable to happen than not to happen • *In general, smokers **tend** to have more health problems than nonsmokers.* **tendency** *n* • *There's a **tendency** for people to become serious about their health only after they become ill.*

treat *v* **1.** to behave toward someone in a certain way • *A good rule for life is: **Treat** other people as you would want them to treat you.* **2.** to give medical care to someone or to a condition • *With modern drugs, doctors can successfully **treat** health problems that used to kill people.* **treatment** *n* • *The standard **treatment** for flu is to tell the patient to rest and take plenty of liquids.*

UNIT 1, READING 2: CARDIOVASCULAR DISEASE: A GOOD NEWS – BAD NEWS STORY

advance *n* an example of progress • *In the last 20 years, there have been a number of important **advances** in the treatment of heart disease. Doctors are now able to help many more patients than they used to.*

afford (to) *v* **1.** to have enough money or time for something • *Because costs are so high, many small employers in the United States can't **afford to** offer their workers health insurance.* **2.** to be able to do something without serious negative results • *We cannot **afford to** wait. We need to get this patient to the hospital immediately.*

available *adj* able to be obtained, used, or reached • *Dr. Smith is not **available** right now. She's with a patient.*

burden *n* a heavy responsibility that is hard for people to deal with • *The new government has promised to reduce the tax **burden** on people with young children.*

common *adj* occurring often • *Thanks to childhood vaccinations, measles, mumps, and polio, diseases that used to be quite **common** are now extremely rare.* SYNONYMS: **usual** *adj*; **frequent** *adj* OPPOSITE: **rare** *adj*; **have in common** *v phr* to share similar interests or qualities • *What do colds and influenza **have in common?** They are both caused by viruses, not by bacteria.*

conclude *v* to decide that something is true because of information that is available • *From the decrease in the number of smokers, we can **conclude** that the public is paying attention to the warnings about the dangers of tobacco.* **conclusion** *n* • *After checking the prices of new cars, I came to the **conclusion** that I should keep my old one for a few more years.* **conclusive** *adj* showing that you can be sure about something • *Medical experts believe that there is **conclusive** proof that smoking can damage your health.*

condition *n* **1.** the state of something or someone • *With a strong wind and heavy rain, weather **conditions** were far from perfect for the soccer game.* **2.** an illness • *Lee's father has been diagnosed with a serious heart **condition**. He is in the hospital for treatment.*

consider *v* to think carefully about something • *A company dumped large amounts of chemicals into the local river without **considering** the possible effects.* **reconsider** *v* to think about something again • *Kate informed her boss that she was leaving her job. Her boss asked her to **reconsider** her decision because he did not want to lose her.*

considerable *adj* large enough to be important • *Experts say that the company's dumping of the chemicals will cause **considerable** damage to life in the river.*

encourage *v* to cause someone to feel confident about something • *A good grade on the second test **encouraged** the student to really work hard for the remainder of the course.* OPPOSITE: **discourage** *v*

enormous *adj* very large; huge • *Dave's parents are very wealthy. They live in an **enormous** house with ten bedrooms and eight bathrooms.*

equipment *n* things that are needed in order to carry out some activity • *You don't need to buy boots or skis. The resort has lots of good ski **equipment** available for rent.*

exclude *v* to keep someone or something out • *The price for the vacation is for the hotel and flight, but **excludes** all meals.* OPPOSITE: **include** *v*

exclusively *adv* only • *This room is **exclusively** for the use of patients of Dr. Smith.*

finance *v* to give the money that is needed for something • *The World Bank often **finances** health programs in developing countries; these countries cannot pay for the programs themselves.* **financial** *adj* connected with money • *This company is in good **financial** health. It has made more than $40 million in each of the last five years.*

major *adj* greater in number or importance than others • *Auto making is still a **major** industry here, but it employs fewer people than it used to.* **majority** *n* more than 50 percent; the larger part of something • *A small **majority** of people think the president is doing a good job.*

minor *adj* smaller in number or importance than others • *I was happy to hear that the problem with my car was only a **minor** one and could be repaired for less than $200.* **minority** *n* less than 50 percent; the smaller part of something • *Sixty years ago,* only a **minority** of women had jobs outside the home.

obstacle *n* a thing or person that makes it difficult or impossible to do something you want to do • *Experts warn that there are still many **obstacles** to overcome before the war against cancer is won.*

operation *n* a piece of work, especially the work of a doctor who cuts into a person's body to treat a health problem • *The **operation** was long and difficult. The doctors had to repair some damage to the patient's heart.* **operate** *v* to work; to cause something to work • *First we have to buy the new equipment and then we have to learn how to **operate** it properly.*

perform *v* to do a piece of work • *The doctor who **performed** the heart operation yesterday has a lot of experience.*

physical *adj* describing something that you can touch or see, or something which is connected with a person's body • *Regular and frequent **physical** exercise is good for your health.* **physical** *n* a careful examination of a person by a doctor to identify any health problems • *Our new health insurance pays for a **physical** every year.*

rate *n* any number, amount, or value which is calculated in relation to another number, amount, or value; speed • *The divorce **rate** in the United States is very high. Today, according to statistics, one out of every three new marriages will end in divorce.*

recover *v* **1.** to get something back that was lost or taken • *The police **recovered** the stolen car. They found it ten miles away from where it disappeared.* **2.** to become healthy again after an illness or an operation • *My sister was seriously ill last month, but she is now **recovering** well.*

resources *n* anything that is available for people to use for their own benefit • *Canada is a country that is rich in natural **resources**; it has enormous amounts of water, farmland, forests, and minerals.*

suffer *v* to experience bad effects from something • *The driver **suffered** serious head injuries when his car overturned.*

surgery *n* medical treatment in which the doctor cuts into a patient's body in order to improve the patient's condition • *You do not always need to go the hospital for minor **surgery**. Often your doctor can perform it in his or her own office.* SYNONYM: **operation** *n*; **surgeon** *n* a doctor who performs surgery • *Modern medicine has saved the lives of many people. Today **surgeons** can perform operations that were not possible 30 years ago.*

urgent *adj* needing to be dealt with immediately or with little delay • *Your brother just phoned and wanted to talk with you. He said it was* **urgent**. *He wants you to call him back as soon as possible.*

willing *adj* ready to do something • *When a plane is overbooked, an airline will try to find passengers who are* **willing** *to take a later flight for a free airline ticket.*

UNIT 1, READING 3: MEDICINE AND GENETIC RESEARCH: PROMISE AND PROBLEMS

achieve *v* to succeed in doing something difficult • *By reaching the top of Mt. Everest in 1953, the two climbers* **achieved** *a goal that many people considered impossible.* **achievement** *n* • *The scientist's greatest* **achievement** *was his discovery of penicillin in 1936.*

assess *v* to judge • *The experts* **assessed** *the operation's chances of success at 90 percent.* **assessment** *n* • *What is your* **assessment** *of the situation? Is the economy getting stronger?*

capable (of) *adj* able to do • *Linda was not satisfied with her B on the test. She knew that she was* **capable of** *much better work.* OPPOSITE: **incapable** *adj*

caution *n* great care • *People should drive with* **caution** *when there is ice or snow on the roads.* **cautious** *adj* very careful so as to avoid problems, danger, or mistakes • *Doctors are usually* **cautious** *when they are making a diagnosis.* **precaution** *n* an action taken to prevent something bad from occurring • *As a* **precaution**, *you should always make a copy of any work you do on your computer.*

commercial *adj* connected with business • **Commercial** *vehicles are vans and trucks that businesses own and operate.* **commercial** *n* an advertisement on radio or television • *It is difficult to enjoy a movie on television when it stops for a* **commercial** *every ten minutes.*

conduct *v* to perform and direct an activity, such as research • *Many tests have been* **conducted** *with the new engine. The results are very promising.*

defect *n* something wrong; a fault in a person or a thing • *Because of a small* **defect** *in this piece of furniture, I was able to buy it for half the normal price.* **defective** *adj* • *Scientists have discovered that some serious illnesses are caused by* **defective** *genes.*

determine *v* **1.** to find out or decide • *The police are trying to* **determine** *the cause of the accident.* **2.** to influence directly • *Your income* **determines** *how much income tax you pay the government.*

eliminate *v* **1.** to cause someone or something to disappear • *Some people believe that medical science will soon be able to* **eliminate** *all diseases from the world, but doctors know that this will be impossible.* **2.** to cause someone or something to not be part of another thing any longer • *Our national soccer team lost their first three games and was* **eliminated** *from the World Cup.*

evidence *n* information that may help to show or prove the truth • *This doctor has not yet produced any* **evidence** *to show that his new treatment works.* **evident** *adj* clear; easily seen or understood • *From the driver's behavior and speech, it was* **evident** *that he had been drinking.*

fatal *adj* **1.** causing death • *There was a* **fatal** *accident on the freeway last night. One driver was dead on arrival in the hospital.* **2.** causing major problems or other very negative results • *The company made the* **fatal** *mistake of hiring a person who was an expert, but who could not work with other people.*

function *v* to work; operate • *Clearly the U.S. health care system is not* **functioning** *as it should. Over 30 million Americans are without health insurance.* **function** *n* the purpose; the work something or someone is intended to do • *The human brain performs a number of important* **functions**; *for example, it controls all the movements of the body.*

fund *v* to give money to support an activity or an organization • *The health care systems of many countries are* **funded** *by public taxes.* **funds** *n pl* money • *The school does not have the* **funds** *to buy new computers for its students.*

gene *n* the parts of cells which influence our growth, appearance, and other characteristics • *Scientists are now able to identify the* **genes** *that cause certain serious diseases.* **genetic** *adj* • **Genetic** *engineering attempts to change the genes of plants and animals in order to bring benefits to people.*

ignore *v* to not pay attention to something or someone • *It's not a good idea to* **ignore** *advice from your doctor.* **ignorant** *adj* not knowing something, often something you should know about • *It's difficult to believe that there are still people who are totally* **ignorant** *of the health risks of tobacco.*

immune (to) *adj* having protection against a disease • *If you have already had certain illnesses, for example, measles, you become **immune to** them.* **immunity** *n* • *For some diseases, the **immunity** may last your entire life.* **immunize** *v* to give people something that will give them protection against a disease • *Today children in many countries are **immunized** against polio at an early age.*

inherit *v* **1.** to receive something from someone who has died • *Mike **inherited** $20,000 from an uncle who died last year. Mike was his favorite nephew.* **2.** to receive something genetically from your parents • *Clearly Mary has **inherited** her mother's athletic ability.*

invest *v* to put money into a business in the hope of making money or getting some other benefit • *In the 1990s, many people **invested** in high-tech companies.* **investment** *n* • *Governments fund a lot of medical research. Most people consider this a good **investment** for the future.*

justify *v* to give a good reason for something • *The workers' demands for higher wages were easy to **justify**. The company was very successful, and the workers had not had a pay increase for five years.* **justification** *n* • *Many people believe, with some **justification**, that the present government is not paying enough attention to health care.*

overstate *v* to describe something as larger, better, or more important than it really is • *You are **overstating** the importance of this new treatment. It is not the cure that we have been hoping for.* OPPOSITE: **understate** *v*

potential *n* the possibility that something or someone will develop in a certain way • *Modern research in biology has the **potential** to lead to new ways of treating disease.* **potential** *adj* possible • *Before they test a new drug on humans, researchers have to try to identify all the **potential** risks to their patients.*

predict *v* to say that something will happen in the future • *The weather channel is **predicting** a heavy snowstorm for this area tomorrow.* **prediction** *n* • *Before important soccer games, you will hear people on television making **predictions** about who will win the game.*

proceed (with) *v* to start or move forward in a set of actions • *Researchers need to be very careful before they decide to **proceed with** trials of a new drug on human patients.* **procedure** *n* a set of actions that are necessary to do something • *Don't worry about your medical test tomorrow. It's a very easy, painless **procedure**.*

profit *n* money earned after expenses, usually by a business • *After two years of not making money, the company finally started to make a **profit**.* OPPOSITE: **loss** *n*

threaten *v* **1.** to say that you will cause damage or harm • *In 1936, Hitler **threatened** to invade Czechoslovakia. A short time later, his armed forces attacked.* **2.** to be a possible danger • *The airline strike **threatens** to cause major problems this holiday weekend.* **threat** *n* danger • *The **threat** of a nuclear world war has not disappeared, but it has decreased since the fall of the Soviet Union.*

UNIT 1, READING 4: AIDS – NOT SOMEONE ELSE'S PROBLEM

annual *adj* happening once a year • *The **annual** celebration of Thanksgiving in the United States takes place in late November.*

case *n* one occurrence of something such as a disease or a crime • *The health authorities in the city are very worried; in the last three days, there have been 25 **cases** of serious food poisoning.* **in this case** *phr* if this happens • *It is possible that the weather will force us to cancel the soccer game tomorrow. **In this case**, we will play the game next week.*

catastrophe *n* an event that causes much suffering or destruction; disaster • *World War II was a **catastrophe** for most of the nations of Europe. It destroyed their economies and killed massive numbers of their people.* **catastrophic** *adj* • *The impact of the war on the population of the Soviet Union was especially **catastrophic**. Over 20 million people lost their lives.*

circumstances *n pl* facts or conditions that exist at a certain time and can have an influence on something or someone • *After a traffic accident, the police look into the **circumstances** of the accident. For example, they want to know how fast the vehicles were going and what the weather conditions were like.*

contaminate *v* to make something unhealthy and dangerous to living things • *The explosion at the Chernobyl atomic reactor **contaminated** a large area around the plant with radioactivity.* **contaminated** *adj* • *Drinking water in many areas of the developing world is **contaminated** with bacteria.*

effective *adj* describing something which gives good results and which has the effect you want • *The government's economic program has been **effective**. It has reduced unemployment from 10 to 7.5 million.*

epidemic *n* a large number of cases of a specific disease • *The so-called Spanish flu **epidemic** of 1918 killed over 600,000 Americans and between 20 and 40 million people worldwide.*

establish *v* **1.** to create or start something; to set something up • *According to scientists, the first Europeans in America were the Vikings. In the early 11th century, they **established** a small village in Newfoundland.* **2.** to show or prove that something is true without a doubt • *Finally the cause of the accident was **established**. An engine had malfunctioned as the plane was taking off.*

estimate *v* to calculate something approximately • *There are no reliable official figures for the number of AIDS cases in some countries. So the World Health Organization has to **estimate** the number.* **estimate** *n* • *Before you get your car repaired, you should ask for an **estimate** of how much the repairs will cost.*

globe *n* the earth or a round model of the earth • *I bought this **globe** in 1985, so some of the political information on it is now out of date.* **global** *adj* involving the whole world • *Pollution is often a **global** problem, not merely a local, regional, or national one.*

incentive *n* something that encourages people to act in a certain way • *People who own a house have an **incentive** to keep it in good condition. If you look after the house well, its value will normally increase.*

infect *v* to cause illness through bacteria or viruses • *A person with the flu can easily **infect** many others.* **infectious** *adj* able to spread from person to person • *SARS is an **infectious** disease that was first identified in 2003.* **infection** *n* a health problem caused by bacteria or virus • *Minor **infections** can become dangerous if you leave them untreated.*

legal *adj* **1.** connected with the law • *If you have a **legal** problem, you should talk to an expert. Go and see a lawyer.* **2.** allowed by the law • *The sale and use of alcohol, which is **legal** in the United States today, was against the law from 1920 to 1933.* OPPOSITE: **illegal** *adj*

mass *adj* involving a large number of people or things • *If we use methods of **mass** production, we can make goods for the lowest possible price.* **massive** *adj* very large • ***Massive** numbers of people are infected with HIV/AIDS.*

optimist *n* a person who tends to see the good side of a situation or event • *Bernard is a tremendous **optimist**. He always thinks things are going to turn out all right in the end.* **optimism** *n* the belief that things will turn out positively • *There is reason for cautious **optimism** that the patient will make a full recovery.* OPPOSITES: **pessimist** *n*; **pessimism** *n*

priority *n* something that needs attention before other things • *After the bus accident, the doctors at the small hospital could not treat everyone at once. They gave **priority** to the people who were badly hurt.* **prior to** *prep* before • ***Prior to** takeoff, the plane's cabin crew explained the emergency procedures to the passengers.*

provide *v* to give a person something that he or she needs or wants • *A healthy diet **provides** us with all the nutrition that our bodies need.* **provided (that)** *conj* if; on condition that • ***Provided that** they are willing to spend money, governments can improve the health of their people.*

regard *v* to have a certain opinion about someone or something • *Many soccer fans still **regard** Pelé as the best soccer player ever.* **regardless of** *prep* without paying attention to something • *The police should treat people equally, **regardless of** their color.* **disregard** *v* to ignore • *The patient **disregarded** his doctor's advice and continued to smoke.*

reluctant *adj* not wanting to do something • *Although there are major problems with the United States health care system, the government is **reluctant** to change it.* **reluctance** *n* • *Many parents do not like to talk to their children about sex. Their **reluctance** could mean that important information about AIDS may not reach many young people.*

respond *v* to answer; to react • *The patient is **responding** well to this new drug. The doctors expect him to make a full recovery.* **response** *n* • *The company offered the workers a one percent pay raise. The employees' **response** was to threaten to strike if the company did not increase the offer.*

security *n* safety; protection against or freedom from danger • *After the terrorist attacks, the government found that **security** at airports needed to be improved.* **secure** *adj* secret; protected from danger • *When you use a password for your bank ATM, be careful to keep it **secure**. Keep it in your head, not on a piece of paper.*

simple *adj* easy to do or understand; not highly developed • *Short, **simple** explanations are best for beginning students.* OPPOSITE: **complex** *adj*

symptom *n* any mental or physical condition that shows a person has a specific illness • *The most* common **symptoms** of influenza are fever and muscle aches.

transmit v to pass or send something to some other place or person • *Nowadays, thanks to satellites, television news companies can **transmit** pictures of events as they actually happen to the other side of the world.* **transmission** n • *The most common method of **transmission** for the cold virus is the human hand. So washing your hands frequently will reduce your risk of becoming infected during cold season.*

ultimate adj occurring at the end of a process; final • *The research program is making progress, but it is* still a long way from reaching its **ultimate** goal – to develop a safe, convenient, and effective method of birth control. **ultimately** adv • *Most medical researchers believe that science will **ultimately** find ways to prevent or cure diseases like cancer and AIDS.*

vaccine n a substance which is put into the body and causes the body to develop its own protection against a certain disease • *Scientists have successfully developed **vaccines** for many diseases.* **vaccination** n the act of giving a vaccine to a person • *Mass **vaccination** programs had almost eliminated polio by 2004.*

UNIT 2, READING 1: THE AGE OF IMMIGRATION

accompany v 1. to go with someone • *Many immigrants to the United States were young unmarried people and were not **accompanied** by any family members.* 2. to appear or exist at the same time • *Driving conditions were extremely dangerous. The heavy snow was **accompanied** by high winds and temperatures well below freezing.*

acquire v to get something • *During her three years in an American high school, the student **acquired** a very good knowledge of English.* **acquisition** n • *Some researchers study language **acquisition**, in other words, how young children learn their first language.*

decline v to decrease in number, size, strength, or quality • *Overpopulation is a major problem in parts of Africa and Asia. In Europe, however, the population of some countries is **declining**.* **decline** n • *Over the last thirty years, there has been a considerable **decline** in the number of Americans who smoke.*

discriminate (against) v to treat some people differently and worse than others, usually because of the group they belong to • *In the past, employers were able to **discriminate against** women and minority groups such as African Americans. They often preferred to give better jobs to white males.* **discrimination** n • *Today in many countries, **discrimination** is against the law, but it has not completely disappeared from society.*

diversity n a number of different types • *One of the most noticeable features of U.S. society is the **diversity** of its people. You see Americans of every skin color, religion, and geographical origin.*

escape v 1. to get away or to get free from • *My friend's family was lucky. They were able to **escape*** from Nazi Germany before the government closed the borders. 2. to avoid suffering • *Fortunately, the driver and passenger **escaped** without serious injury when the car ran off the road and into a field.*

feature n a quality of something or someone • *The new house has a number of attractive **features**, including a very large family room and kitchen and lots of natural light.*

flow v to move in an uninterrupted way, like the water of a river • *Traffic was **flowing** very freely on the highway this morning. I had no trouble getting to the airport in time for my plane.* **flow** n • *In the United States there is always a **flow** of people into areas of the country with more jobs.*

generation n the members of a family or society who are about the same age • *This photograph shows three earlier **generations** of my family: my mother, my grandmother, and my great grandmother.*

guarantee v to promise or make it certain that something will happen • *"Satisfaction **guaranteed**" means that the store promises you will be completely satisfied; if not, you get your money back.* **guarantee** n a warranty or promise that something will be done or that a product will be repaired if it is defective • *My new television came with a 5-year **guarantee**.*

hardship n conditions of life that cause problems and suffering • *A lack of clean water and adequate sanitation continue to cause a great deal of **hardship** for people in the poorest countries of the world.*

integrate v to cause people or things to become part of a group • *Most people in the United States believe* in **integrating** schools, so people of both sexes and all races can learn together. **disintegrate** v to break into many small pieces • *The explosion caused the plane to **disintegrate** in the air near Ireland.*

illiterate adj unable to read and write • *It is difficult to teach people who are **illiterate** about health care.* **literacy** n the ability to read and write • *Even in some wealthy countries, the **literacy** rate is not 100 percent.*

oppress v to treat people cruelly and unfairly • *Even in democracies, women and minorities may feel **oppressed** because they are not treated equally.* **oppression** n • *Political **oppression** is still a major problem in many countries of the world.*

possess v to have; to own • *In some countries, it is illegal to **possess** a handgun.* **possessions** n pl things that belong to a person • *The family lost almost all of their **possessions** in the fire. Their insurance replaced appliances, furniture, and clothing, but personal things like photographs were lost forever.*

prejudice n an unfair opinion about someone or something which you formed without adequate information • *In order to be a fair judge, you should eliminate as many of your **prejudices** as possible.* **prejudiced** adj • *Carlos thinks soccer is a better game than football. He's **prejudiced**, however, because he grew up in Europe and played soccer all the time!*

process n a set of actions which happen naturally or which are performed to achieve some result • *Louis Pasteur, the French scientist, developed a **process** for taking dangerous bacteria out of milk.* **process** v to deal with something by following a set of operations • *Modern computers can **process** certain types of information much faster than humans can.*

prosperous adj wealthy and successful • *This used to be a **prosperous** neighborhood, but then people and jobs began to move to other parts of the country.* **prosperity** n • *The **prosperity** of Detroit depends a great deal on the automobile industry.*

sacrifice n something valuable that you give up in order to do something else • *Many immigrants to the United States made **sacrifices** so that their children and grandchildren would have a better life.* **sacrifice** v • *It seems that some people are prepared to **sacrifice** their family life and even their health for success in their jobs.*

significant adj important; large enough to be important or worth considering • *Primary health care programs can bring about a **significant** improvement in people's health.* **significance** n meaning or importance • *What **significance** does this new research have for the treatment of heart disease?*

starve v 1. to die or be in danger of dying of hunger • *Thousands of people in East Africa could **starve** if rain doesn't come soon. Children are at special risk.* 2. to be hungry • *Let's have lunch now. I'm **starving**!* **starvation** n • *After no rain for months, **starvation** threatened large numbers of people in East Africa.*

successive adj describing things which follow each other in time without interruption • *The six **successive** days of heavy rain last week have caused major problems in the low areas of the state.* **in succession** phr without interruptions • *The local soccer team is doing well right now; they have won ten games **in succession**.*

symbol n something that represents something else • *In the 1989 revolution, the people of Romania cut the star out of their flag. It was for them a **symbol** of the government they wanted to eliminate.* **symbolize** v to represent something • *The stars in the flag of the United States **symbolize** the fifty states of the country.*

transition n the process of changing from one condition to a different one • *Newtown is a city in **transition**. It used to be a manufacturing city; now its economy is more dependent on research and service industries.*

violence n physical actions that hurt people or damage things • *Most parents think that there is too much **violence** shown on television – too many killings, beatings, and automobile crashes.* **violent** adj • *Martin Luther King, Jr., and Gandhi did not believe that **violent** protest should be used to bring about political change.*

visible adj able to be seen • *Viruses and bacteria are not **visible** to the eye. We need a microscope to see them.* **visibility** n how well things can be seen from a distance • *The plane could not take off because of poor **visibility** at the airport. The dense fog made it impossible to see more than twenty yards.*

adjust *v* to change something or yourself so as to be better for a specific situation • *If a person's hair appears green on your television, you probably need to* ***adjust*** *the color control.* **adjustment** *n* • *Driving in Britain, where you have to drive on the left, requires some* ***adjustment*** *from most visitors, who are used to driving on the right.*

analyze *v* to examine something carefully and systematically in order to understand it • *In order to find a solution to a problem, you really need first to* ***analyze*** *the problem and its causes.* **analysis** *n* • *In research, it is often essential to conduct a statistical* ***analysis*** *of your results.*

background *n* **1.** facts about a person's life, such as family, education, and social class • *Many people find it unbelievable that you can buy a gun in many U.S. states without even a check into your* ***background***. **2.** facts that help to explain something • *In order to really understand the violence that occurred last week, you need some* ***background***.

challenge *v* to question whether something that has been claimed is really true • *The idea that smoking could cause serious illness was* ***challenged*** *by some scientists, but most of them had some connection to the tobacco industry.* **challenge** *n* something new and difficult which demands a lot of hard work to complete successfully • *John is finding his new job a real* ***challenge***; *he is working in areas where he has little experience.*

community *n* a group of people who have something important in common, such as religion, culture, or language • *New European immigrants to the United States often went to places where there was already a* ***community*** *from their own country.*

compete *v* to try to get or win something for yourself • *If two or more companies are* ***competing*** *with each other for customers, this tends to keep the price of their products low.* **competition** *n* • *The World Cup is a soccer* ***competition*** *that takes place once every four years.*

contemporary *adj* **1.** belonging to the present time • *I don't really like* ***contemporary*** *music. I prefer the music of the eighteenth and nineteenth centuries.* **2.** belonging to the same time as something else in the past • *If you study history, you probably will have to read* ***contemporary*** *descriptions of important events as well as modern examinations of the same events.*

culture *n* the shared way of life of a group of people that includes their customs, ideas, values, and traditions • *One belief of American* ***culture*** *is that children should be trained to be independent at an early age, an age that other cultures might find too young.*

ethnic *adj* connected with a group of people with a specific national or cultural background • *In some U.S. cities there are still* ***ethnic*** *neighborhoods that were established by different immigrant groups in the nineteenth or early twentieth centuries.*

expand *v* **1.** to increase in size • *Metal* ***expands*** *when it is heated.* **2.** to make something larger • *The company is* ***expanding*** *its operations. It is opening new stores in cities where it never did business before.*

favor *v* to treat better than others • *The government's new tax plan is being criticized. It seems to* ***favor*** *the wealthy while it raises taxes on the poor.* **be in favor of** *v phr* to support something • *I haven't met anyone who* ***is in favor of*** *the new tax plan.*

hire *v* to employ someone either permanently or temporarily • *If the company decides to expand into this new market, it will need to* ***hire*** *at least one hundred new employees.* OPPOSITES: **fire** *v*; **lay off** *v* • *To reduce its costs, the airline is planning to* ***lay off*** *about 2,000 workers.*

hostile *adj* unfriendly; behaving like an enemy • *The politician got a very* ***hostile*** *reaction from the factory workers who had lost their jobs and who blamed the government.* **hostility** *n* a strong feeling of dislike • *Derek and Peter do not like each other. You can feel the* ***hostility*** *between them when they meet.*

interpret *v* to decide the meaning of something • *Experts are in disagreement about how to* ***interpret*** *the latest economic figures.* **misinterpret** *v* to give the wrong meaning to something • *It is easy to* ***misinterpret*** *what a person is saying if she is speaking in a language that is not your first language.*

labor *n* work, usually physical work • *Child* ***labor*** *was common in Europe and America in the nineteenth century. Today, of course, it is illegal there.*

network *n* a number of things or people that are connected with each other • *Germany was the first country to develop a* ***network*** *of high-speed roads that connected its major cities.*

pattern *n* the repeated way something happens or is organized • *Zoo animals often have different* ***patterns*** *of behavior from the same animals in the wild.*

precede *v* to go or happen before or in front of • *Usually the singing of two national anthems*

precedes *a World Cup soccer game.* **preceding** *adj* • *The examples in the* **preceding** *paragraph show that life in the United States was difficult for many immigrants.*

proportion *n* the relationship in size or amount between two things • *Most people would like to save a* **proportion***, say ten percent, of the money they earn each month, but many find it impossible to do this.* **disproportionate** *adj* not in correct proportion; larger or smaller than what is expected • *A* **disproportionate** *number of smokers are poor and uneducated.*

pursue *v* to try to achieve • *My friend stopped his university studies to* **pursue** *a career as a professional musician.* **pursuit** *n* • *The* **pursuit** *of happiness is a right, according to the United States Declaration of Independence.*

refugee *n* a person who leaves his home and goes to another place in order to find safety • *To be allowed into other countries as* **refugees***, people usually have to provide evidence that they would risk great harm or death by remaining at home.* **refuge** *n* shelter or protection from danger • *During a tornado, people are advised to take* **refuge** *in a basement or a downstairs room with no windows.*

resent *v* to feel angry because you think you've been treated unfairly • *A few people* **resent** *the presence*

of foreign students in the United States. They feel that their tax dollars are helping to support these students.* **resentment** *n* • *There is a lot of* **resentment** *among the female workers in this factory. They get lower wages than male workers for the same work.*

source *n* **1.** a person, place, or thing from which you get something • *When you write a research paper, you must report the* **sources** *for all ideas that are not your own.* **2.** a cause • *The computer diagnosis identified why the engine was running poorly. The* **source** *of the problem was a faulty electrical connection.*

status *n* **1.** a person's legal position in a country • *Your marital* **status** *may be married, single, or divorced.* **2.** the respect that society gives to someone or some position compared to others • *The type of work a person does will give that person a certain* **status***. Being a doctor, for example, is a high-status job; being a taxi driver is not.*

thorough *adj* describing something done as completely and carefully as possible, or someone who is very careful and pays attention to details • *The student wrote a very* **thorough** *analysis of the topic and got an A on his paper.*

UNIT 2, READING 3: VIEWS ON MULTICULTURALISM

adapt *v* to change in order to deal with a new situation • *When people move to a new country, they have to* **adapt** *to the new culture.* **adaptation** *n* • *For some people, the process of* **adaptation** *to a new culture can be long and difficult.*

admit *v* **1.** to agree that something is true • *The politician* **admitted** *that he had accepted money illegally from businesses in his home city.* OPPOSITE: **deny** *v* • *The politician* **denied** *that he had made money illegally.* **2.** to allow someone to enter • *Some universities are very selective. They* **admit** *only a small percentage of students who apply there.*

approve (of) *v* to consider something good, right, or suitable • *Members of older generations often do not* **approve of** *the behavior of younger people.* OPPOSITES: **disapprove** *v*; **disapproval** *n* • *The crowd at the soccer game showed their* **disapproval** *of the referee's decision by booing and whistling.*

approximate *adj* not exact, but close • *Get an estimate on how much it will cost to repair your*

car, but remember it's an* **approximate** *figure.* **approximately** *adv* • *The drive to New York will take* **approximately** *eight hours.*

assimilate *v* to become like the things or people around you • *It often takes two or three generations for immigrants to* **assimilate** *into their new society.* **assimilation** *n* • **Assimilation** *is a process that most immigrants to the United States go through successfully.*

commit (yourself to) *v* to decide and promise to do something • *This company has* **committed itself to** *a policy of equal opportunity for all, regardless of color, religion, or national origin.* **committed (to)** *adj* • *The government is* **committed to** *not increasing taxes.*

complain *v* to say that you are unhappy or dissatisfied about someone or something • *We* **complained** *to the manager because our hotel room smelled of cigarette smoke.* **complaint** *n* • *Usually big companies have a department that handles customer* **complaints***.*

controversy *n* public disagreement involving a difference of opinion about a specific subject • *The controversy about abortion has been going on in the United States for more than twenty years.* **controversial** *adj* • *U.S. television networks usually avoid controversial programs because companies tend not to buy time for commercials during such programs.*

elsewhere *adv* in, from, or to some other place • *Early immigrants to the United States came from England, Scotland, and elsewhere in northwestern Europe.*

empirical *adj* describing something that is connected to our direct experience of life • *The latest unemployment figures are empirical evidence that the economy is improving.*

explicit *adj* stated clearly and completely • *Before kids can go on a school trip, parents must give their explicit permission for the trip by signing an official form.* OPPOSITES: **implicit** *adj* suggested, though not stated; **imply** *v* to communicate something indirectly • *Reading tests sometimes ask students to decide what a text implies in addition to what it states.*

hardly *adv* almost not; only just • *The sentences "He works hard" and "He hardly works" have almost opposite meanings.* SYNONYMS: **scarcely** *adv*; **barely** *adv* • *We scarcely had any time between our connecting flights, but we did manage to get a cup of coffee at the airport.*

inevitable *adj* impossible to avoid or prevent; certain to happen • *Some pessimists believe that only two things in life are inevitable: death and taxes.* **inevitably** *adv* • *Does a slowdown in the economy lead inevitably to higher unemployment?*

issue *n* a subject, often a problem, that people talk about • *The weak economy is sure to be an important issue in the upcoming election.*

likely *adj* probable; probably true • *Because of publicity about the dangers of smoking, it's likely that the proportion of smokers in the general population will continue to decline.* **likelihood** *n* • *According to the weather forecast, there is a likelihood of heavy rain this afternoon.*

native *n* a person who was born in a certain place • *In the 1850s, there were more natives of Ireland in New York than there were in Dublin, the capital of Ireland.* **native** *adj* belonging to the place where the person was born • *Very few people forget their native language.*

oppose *v* to disagree with something and try to prevent it • *Most students opposed the school district's plan to hold classes on Saturday mornings.* **opponent** *n* a person who disagrees with something; a person who you are competing with • *Opponents of the government's health care plan say that it doesn't pay enough attention to children's health.* OPPOSITES: **proponent** *n*; **supporter** *n*

policy *n* a set of ideas that controls the way people, such as a government, deal with specific situations • *The government's economic policy is failing. It is creating more unemployment, not getting people back to work.*

poll *n* a study that finds out what the public thinks or feels about a certain subject by asking people particular questions • *According to the latest public opinion poll, only 45 percent of people are satisfied with the government's performance.*

preserve *v* to prevent something from being damaged or destroyed • *There was a plan to destroy this old church, but citizens persuaded the city government to preserve it because of its historic significance.*

race *n* an unscientific word to describe a group of people who share the same general physical characteristics such as skin color • *To assess how minorities are being treated, the U.S. government includes information on race in its population statistics.* **racism** *n* the belief that people automatically have certain qualities because they belong to a certain race • *Racism has declined but still exists in the United States, and African Americans still suffer from its effects.* **racial** *adj* • *Many countries now have laws against racial discrimination.*

reflect *v* **1.** to throw back heat, light, or sound • *It was difficult to see the small boat because of the sunlight that was being reflected off the water.* **2.** to show • *The names in the telephone book reflect this city's history as a center of European immigration.*

retain *v* to keep, or to not lose or give up something • *People with photographic memories are able to retain information they have seen only once.* **retention** *n* • *Retention of their native language is typical for first generation immigrants to the United States. They also retain many of the cultural values of their native country.*

select *v* to choose, often carefully, someone or something from a number people or things • *After a lot of thought, the teacher **selected** a new book to use in her class.* **selectively** *adv* • *In their speeches, most politicians use facts **selectively**. They often don't mention facts that would not support their position.*

settle *v* to move somewhere and make your home there • *After moving every two years or so until I was ten years old, our family finally **settled** near Chicago, where our parents still live.* **settlement** *n* a place that was built by settlers • *The remains of an eleventh-century Scandinavian **settlement** were found in Newfoundland, Canada.*

UNIT 2, READING 4: EXPERIMENTAL EVIDENCE ON THE NATURE OF PREJUDICE

acknowledge *v* **1.** to accept that something exists or that it is true • *Politicians rarely **acknowledge** their mistakes publicly.* **2.** to express thanks for something • *At the beginning of her book, the author **acknowledged** the help she had received from her students.*

actual *adj* real; existing as a fact • *I was happy because the **actual** bill for my car repair was $150 less than the estimate.* **actually** *adv* in reality, often used to correct a mistaken idea or when the truth may be surprising • *I know gasoline seems very expensive today, but **actually** it's cheap when you compare our prices with those in other countries.*

address *v* to deal with, usually a topic, question, or problem • *If we want to improve health care in very poor countries, we must first **address** the problems of unsafe water and inadequate sanitation.*

assume *v* to believe that something is true without proof that it really is true • *It is a mistake to **assume** that two people watching the same event will remember that event the same way.* **assumption** *n* • *I don't know for sure how he's getting here from the airport. My **assumption** is that he'll rent a car.*

bias *n* a tendency to be in favor of or against someone or something, usually when you should not take sides • *In court, good judges ignore their personal **biases** and follow the laws as they are written.* **biased** *adj* • *Soccer fans everywhere often complain that referees and their assistants are **biased** against their teams.* OPPOSITES: **fair** *adj*; **unbiased** *adj*; **impartial** *adj*

cite *v* to explicitly acknowledge a source of information, often in order to support your own views • *If you use ideas or information from another person in a research paper, you must **cite** your sources.* **citation** *n* • *You should list all of your **citations** at the end of your research paper.*

contain *v* to hold inside • *This new book **contains** immigrant stories that have never appeared in print before now.* **content** *n* the material or ideas inside something • *At the beginning of most textbooks, there is a table of **contents**, where you can find the chapter and section titles and their page numbers.*

contradict *v* to give a fact or statement so different from another that one of them must be wrong; to say the opposite • *Researchers have identified a few people who have carried the HIV virus for many years but who have never become ill. This evidence seems to **contradict** the view that being HIV-positive is always fatal.* **contradiction** *n* • *There are often **contradictions** between what people say and what they do.*

demonstrate *v* **1.** to show • *The president's answer **demonstrated** that she understood the issue well.* **2.** to show how to do something • *When you want to learn a specific skill, it helps if someone can **demonstrate** it for you.*

evaluate *v* to judge the quality of something; to assess • *Most university students in the United States get the opportunity to **evaluate** the teaching of their instructors.* **evaluation** *n* • *Teaching **evaluations** can give instructors useful information about the effectiveness of their teaching.*

experiment *n* a test that is conducted, usually by researchers, in order to learn something or to establish that an idea is true • *Before they can conduct an **experiment** with human subjects, researchers need to show that it will not harm these subjects.* **experimental** *adj* • *Doctors sometimes use **experimental** treatments for patients who have not responded to established treatments for their disease.*

minimize *v* to make something as small as possible • *We can't hope to eliminate prejudice completely, but we can work to **minimize** it.* **minimum** *n, adj* the smallest number or amount possible • *Normally, interstate highways have a **minimum** speed limit. It is just as dangerous to drive too slowly on an interstate as it is to drive too fast.* OPPOSITES: **maximize** *v*; **maximum** *n, adj*

namely *adv* specifically • *In our discussion, we finally turned our attention to the basic problem, **namely** prejudice, its nature, origins, and transmission.*

objective *adj* describing things and ideas that are not influenced by someone's opinions, emotions, and prejudices • *Newspaper reports of events should be as **objective** as possible. However, reporters sometimes find it difficult to keep their feelings out of some stories.* OPPOSITE: **subjective** *adj*

obvious *adj* very easy to see and understand • *If you can't afford the rent for your apartment, the **obvious** solution would be to move or find a roommate to help pay it.*

perceive *v* to use your senses and mind to form a picture of some reality outside yourself • *One question that psychology tries to answer is the following: How can two people see the same thing and still **perceive** it differently?* **perception** *n* • *Clearly people's prior experiences influence their **perceptions** of a situation.*

persist *v* to continue to exist; to continue to do something although conditions are against it • *A cough is usually nothing to worry about unless it **persists** for ten days or more. In this case, you should see your doctor.* **persistent** *adj* continuing and difficult to eliminate • *In spite of lots of evidence against it, there is a **persistent** belief that high-tech medicine will solve the health care problems of poorer countries.*

rationally *adv* with logic or reason • *Let's stay calm and think about the problem **rationally**. Anger and fear will get us nowhere.* **rational** *adj* based on reason or logic • *Politicians often use emotional rather than **rational** arguments to win support for their actions and ideas.*

remedy *n* something that cures a medical problem; a solution • *Aspirin and ibuprofen are **remedies** for pain that are available without a prescription.* **remedy** *v* to be the cure or answer to a problem • *This new law will not **remedy** the problem completely, but it will help.*

resist *v* to fight back against someone or something • *People who are suffering from starvation are not strong enough to **resist** disease.* **resistance** *n* • *The French **Resistance** is the name for groups of French citizens who continued to fight against the Germans after they had occupied France.*

seek *v, past* **sought** **1.** to try to find or get • *Immigrants were **seeking** freedom and economic opportunities for themselves and their families.* **2.** to try • *In the nineteenth century, some organizations in the United States **sought** to limit immigration from Ireland.*

step *n* an action, usually one in a series, that you take to address a problem • *If we don't take **steps** against this problem now, it will be much more difficult and expensive to solve it later.*

superior (to) *adj* higher in quality, numbers, or position • *Many people believe that Japanese cars are **superior to** American cars. That's the main reason why so many Japanese cars are sold here.* OPPOSITE: **inferior (to)** *adj*

tolerant *adj* willing to accept things, ideas, or behavior in other people that are strange to you and which you may not approve of • *This is a **tolerant** country. Most people believe that people should be able to live and think as they wish as long as they don't harm others.* OPPOSITE: **intolerant** *adj*

victim *n* someone who dies or is hurt by disease, violence, crime, disaster, or accident • *Malaria takes the lives of one million people every year. The majority of its **victims** are children.*

UNIT 3, READING 1: VARIATION IN LANGUAGE

appropriate *adj* suitable or right for a certain situation • *Before you go for a job interview, you should find out what kind of clothes are **appropriate**.* OPPOSITE: **inappropriate** *adj*

casual *adj* informal • ***Casual** clothes are clothes you would normally wear at home, at a sports event, or when you're relaxing with good friends.*

colleague *n* a person you work with • *Supportive **colleagues** can make it easier for new employees to adjust to a new job.*

combine *v* to put two or more things together • *Grammar rules allow you to **combine** two or more words to create a sentence.* **combination** *n* • *The accident was probably caused by a **combination** of factors: alcohol, speed, and poor weather conditions.*

component *n* one of the parts that make up a machine or a system • *This is a Japanese car, but many of its **components** were manufactured in the United States.*

distinguish v to see and understand the difference between two similar things or people • *It's often very difficult to **distinguish** between identical twins when you meet them for the first time.* **distinction** n a difference • *It is important for readers to recognize the **distinction** between factual information and opinions.* **distinctive** adj clearly marking something or someone as different • *You can identify this bird easily by its **distinctive** red tail.*

environment n the air, water, and land in which all life exists; the surroundings in which people live their lives • *The new law requires employers to provide a smoke-free **environment** for their workers.* **environmental** adj • *Rivers and lakes with no fish are examples of the **environmental** damage that industrial development can cause.*

equivalent adj having the same function, value, or effect as something or someone else • *A kilogram is **equivalent** to 2.2 pounds.* **equivalent** n • *What is the **equivalent** of a $20 bill in your money?*

extend v to make something longer • *In December, stores will often **extend** their opening hours.* **extensive** adj covering a large area • *The storm caused **extensive** damage to the area. Very few places were left undamaged.* **to some extent** phr partly • *Political oppression was **to some extent** a factor in European immigration to the United States. The main cause, however, was economic hardship.*

formal adj official, or describing something that is correct and suitable for official situations • *John has been told unofficially that he is going to be promoted, however, he hasn't received **formal** notification of this yet.* OPPOSITE: **informal** adj

gender n the state of being male or female • *Discrimination on the basis of **gender** is illegal in this country, but it still occurs.*

impression n a feeling or idea which is produced in your mind by someone or something • *Movies tend to give a rather false **impression** of life in the United States. They make it appear more exciting or more dangerous than it really is.* **impressive** adj causing admiration or respect • *Getting an A in that professor's class is an **impressive** achievement.*

interaction n speaking or working together • *To learn more about the process of language learning, researchers are studying the **interaction** between babies and their parents.*

label n a piece of paper attached to something in order to identify it or give information about it • *When you travel by air, make sure to write your name, address, and phone number on **labels** and attach them to your baggage.* **label** v to give a name to

something • *One of the first things that children do with language is to **label** objects in their environment.*

observe v to watch carefully • *One of the first steps of science is to **observe** the thing you wish to study and then to record what you see.* **observation** n • *Although the driver seemed uninjured after the accident, his doctors decided to keep him in the hospital overnight for **observation**.*

peer n a person of the same age, social position, or ability • *Children often behave very differently when they are with their **peers** in school than when they are at home with their family.*

phrase n a group of words that belong together without being a sentence or a clause • *It will help your vocabulary to learn new words in **phrases** and not merely as individual words.*

refer to v 1. to mention someone or something • *I'm interested in reading about the research that my professor **referred to** in class, so I'm going to ask her for more details about it.* 2. to mean • *When Europeans over 60 use the words "the War," they are usually **referring to** World War II.*

relevant adj connected with a topic which is being discussed • *When you write an academic paper, include only what is **relevant**.* OPPOSITE: **irrelevant** adj

role n the function of someone or something in a certain situation • *The book examines the **role** of aircraft in World War I. Its conclusion is that aircraft had little effect on the fighting.*

standard n the level of quality that is considered acceptable and which you use to judge someone or something • *This professor has very high **standards**. You'll need to work very hard to get an A in her class.* **standard** adj usual and often official; accepted and expected by everyone • *The metric system is the **standard** system of measurement in most countries of the world.*

style n a particular way of doing something • *The Brazilian **style** of soccer emphasizes technical skills more than athletic strength.*

subordinate adj having a less important position within some organization or unit • ***Subordinate** clauses are clauses that begin with words like that, who, when, as, because, while, if, until. However, they must always appear with a main clause in order to make an acceptable sentence in written English.* **subordinate** n a person who has a less important position than another person within an organization • *Company managers need to be able to rely on their **subordinates** because they do the basic work that managers cannot do themselves.*

uniform *adj* not different • *The goods produced by this company are not of **uniform** quality. Some are excellent; others are full of defects.*

variety *n* a specific type • *What **variety** of tomato do you recommend for growers in this region?*

vary *v* to change or be different • *The rent for an apartment in this town **varies** according to the neighborhood.* **variable** *n* an element in a situation that may change • *The game is planned for tomorrow. The weather, of course, is a **variable** that we can't control.* **variable** *adj* changeable; **invariably** *adv* always • *As they grow, children **invariably** acquire the accent of the people around them.*

version *n* a different form of the same basic thing • *One driver in the accident claimed that he stopped at the stop sign. The second driver's **version** of events was different; he said the first driver had failed to stop.*

UNIT 3, READING 2: SOCIOLINGUISTIC RULES OF SPEAKING

accomplish *v* to achieve; to succeed in doing or finishing something • *I was in the office for eight hours yesterday, but I was interrupted a lot and wasn't able to **accomplish** very much.* **accomplishment** *n* • *It is quite an **accomplishment** to complete a university degree at the same time as working in a full-time job.*

apply (to) *v* **1.** to formally request something, usually admission or permission, in writing • *You should **apply to** the university now because the admission process takes some time.* **2.** to use • *Engineers have to **apply** knowledge from theoretical science in order to solve practical problems.* **3.** to be relevant • *The warning about a potentially dangerous defect **applies** only **to** model S cars produced in 2003.*

approach *v* **1.** to move nearer to someone or some place • *We are **approaching** New York's Kennedy Airport. Please fasten your seat belts.* **2.** to attempt to deal with a task or problem • *There are a number of different ways to **approach** learning a language.*

break down *v* to stop working normally • *My car **broke down** on my way to work. I had to call the Automobile Association for help.* **breakdown** *n* failure • *The **breakdown** in talks between the workers and the company means that there is probably going to be a strike.*

claim *v* **1.** to say that something is true, often when others do not believe it • *The opposition **claims** that the government's new policy will increase unemployment, not reduce it.* **2.** to ask for something when you have the right to have it • *We can **claim** the cost of repairing the storm damage from our home insurance.*

competence *n* the ability to do something that is required of you • *You can demonstrate your **competence** in English by taking a test of English.* OPPOSITE: **incompetence** *n*

conform *v* to satisfy the established standards or rules • *In any group, there is pressure on people to **conform** – to dress, act, and think like others in the group.*

convention *n* a way of doing something that is accepted as normal and correct • *Social **conventions** differ from country to country. For example, in some cultures you must take off your shoes when entering a house but not in others.* **conventional** *adj* considered normal • *Most health insurance companies will only pay for **conventional** medical treatment but not for treatment that is considered experimental.*

crucial *adj* extremely important • *Clean water and adequate sanitation are **crucial** factors in improving the health of people in many developing countries.*

data *n pl* facts and information collected for scientific analysis • *After they analyzed the **data**, the researchers were able to establish a connection between diet and heart disease.*

document *n* an official piece of paper giving some information • *Your passport and school certificates are important **documents**. You should keep them in a safe place.* **document** *v* to record something in a document • *John is researching a history topic that is not well **documented**. He has only found two reliable sources of information.*

ensure *v* to make sure that something happens • *To **ensure** that you arrive at the airport in good time for your flight, you will need to take the 7 A.M. bus from the hotel.*

error *n* a mistake • *The experts concluded that mechanical failure, not human **error**, was the cause of the plane crash.* **erroneous** *adj* false or mistaken • *There is an **erroneous** belief that health care is free in Britain. It is not. People pay for it through extra taxes.*

genuine *adj* real; exactly what something appears to be or is claimed to be • *These shoes can't be made of genuine leather. The price is too low.*

involve *v* to require as a necessary part of something • *John decided not to accept the new job because it involved a lot of traveling overseas. He did not wish to spend so much time away from his family.* **(get) involved** *adj* to make yourself part of something • *It is probably good advice not to get involved in arguments between your friends.*

literature *n* **1.** the novels, plays, poems, and other creative writing of a culture • *William Shakespeare is possibly the most famous name in English literature. He is best known for his plays, but he also wrote poems.* **2.** all the books, articles, and reports on a specific subject • *At the beginning of a scientific article, you will usually find a review of the literature, where the writers show that they have read the earlier research connected with their topic.*

means *n pl* a way or method to do something • *Trains are a more popular means of transport in Europe than in the United States.* **by no means** *phr* not at all • *Because of the poor weather, it is by no means certain that our plane will be able to depart.*

mention *v* to speak or write about something very briefly and without details • *The president mentioned the economy in his speech but did not discuss any plans the government had for improving it.*

modify *v* to change something slightly • *The automobile company has modified the engines on this year's cars in order to meet the government's new standards.* **modification** *n* • *After some safety*

modifications, *the company began to market its children's car seats again.*

offend *v* to cause someone to be upset; to hurt someone's feelings • *The speaker offended a lot of people when he said that religion was only for idiots.* **offensive** *adj* • *The politician apologized for the offensive statements he made about women.*

participate *v* to take part in an activity • *Over 10,000 runners participated in the city's marathon last year.* **participant** *n* a person who takes part in an activity • *All participants in the experiment were paid $100 for their time.*

reinforce *v* make something stronger • *The results of this new study reinforce the findings of earlier studies that exercise improves people's general level of health.*

relative *adj* measured in comparison with something else • *Mary is a relative newcomer to this part of the country. She moved here only three years ago.* **relatively** *adv* • *After the first test, which 50 percent of them had failed, the students found the second test relatively easy.*

shortcoming *n* a defect, fault, or inadequacy • *A serious shortcoming of the company's new automobile is that it is priced too high for most middle-income people.*

universal *adj* **1.** widespread • *There has been universal praise for the new television series on the American Revolution.* **2.** shared by or affecting everyone in a group or in the world • *Many rules for human behavior differ from culture to culture. They are not universal even though some people may assume that they are.*

UNIT 3, READING 3: CHILD LANGUAGE ACQUISITION: PHONOLOGY

account for *v* to explain why something happens • *An adequate theory of language learning needs to account for the presence of words like "knowed" and "eated" in young children's English.* **account** *n* a description of an event • *Two people who saw the accident gave two slightly different accounts of it.*

accurate *adj* correct and exact • *This student's English is grammatically accurate, but it does not sound natural.* **accuracy** *n* • *Newspapers should check the accuracy of their stories before publishing them.*

capacity *n* **1.** ability • *Most language scientists believe that humans are born with a special capacity to learn language.* **2.** the amount or number that

something can contain or produce • *This room has a seating capacity of 150.*

comprehension *n* understanding; the ability to understand • *Ken's comprehension of written German is good, but he has difficulty understanding spoken German.* **comprehensible** *adj* possible to understand • *He found his friend's lecture notes to be comprehensible, so he was able to use them to study for the test.* OPPOSITE: **incomprehensible** *adj*

consistent (with) *adj* **1.** not changing • *The student's performance in class was very consistent. Her performance was always excellent.* **2.** in agreement with and not contradictory to something else • *The* results of the most recent experiments are **consistent with** the earlier results.

construct *v* to build • *One goal of science is to* ***construct*** *theories in order to explain natural phenomena.* **construction** *n* • *A lot of students take jobs as* ***construction*** *workers during the summer. You can earn good wages building houses and roads.*

emerge *v* **1.** to appear • *After some time, the real truth finally* ***emerged*** *about the accident.* **2.** to come out • *The door opened, and the team* ***emerged*** *to be welcomed by a large crowd of supporters.*

expose *v* to leave something without a cover or without protection • *By cutting down trees, people* ***expose*** *the ground to wind and rain that can damage it.* **exposure** *n* • *Doctors warn that* ***exposure*** *to strong sun can cause skin cancer.*

imitate *v* to copy someone's behavior • *One of the best ways to learn to ski is to* ***imitate*** *the movements of an expert skier.*

initial *n* the first letter in a name • *Often applications will ask for your first name, last name, and middle* ***initial.*** **initial** *adj* first; at the beginning • *This medication will ease influenza symptoms if patients take it in the* ***initial*** *stages of the infection.*

innate *adj* belonging naturally to a person since birth; natural • *Science is trying to answer the question of how much of our mental ability is* ***innate*** *and how much can be acquired through training.*

investigate *v* **1.** to attempt to find all the relevant facts about something • *A team of government experts is sent to* ***investigate*** *all accidents involving commercial aircraft in the United States.* **2.** to conduct research on something • *Scientists* ***investigating*** *heart disease have been able to identify a number of factors that contribute to the disease.* **investigation** *n* • *The police have not completed their* ***investigation*** *into the murder.*

mature *v* to become fully developed • *When it* ***matures***, *this oak tree could reach a height of 110 feet or more.* **mature** *adj* having the attitudes and feelings of a responsible adult • *You can rely on this student to do good work for you. Although she is only 19, she is very* ***mature*** *for her age.* OPPOSITE: **immature** *adj*

property *n* a natural quality of something • *This material has two* ***properties*** *that make it useful for cold weather clothes. It is waterproof and retains heat.*

random *adj* without any meaningful plan or pattern • *Guessing will not help you on multiple-choice tests.* **at random** *phr* • *This public opinion poll was*

conducted with adults selected **at random** from the local telephone book.

range *n* the limits within which something can vary • *At $45,000 this car is not in my price* ***range***. *I can't afford to pay more than $18,000.* **range** *v* • *The ages of the students* ***range*** *from 18 to 36.*

represent *v* **1.** to act to protect the interests of a person or group • *We need politicians who are willing to* ***represent*** *the interests of ordinary people, not of financially powerful companies.* **2.** to be the sign or symbol of something • *English spelling is not always consistent. In the following examples, three different spellings* ***represent*** *the same sound: shoe, sure, nation.*

resemble *v* to look like; to be similar to • *Many words in English* ***resemble*** *French words. This is because English speakers borrowed these words from French centuries ago.* **resemblance** *n* similarity in appearance • *Michael and Kate are brother and sister, but I can see little family* ***resemblance***.

reveal *v* to show something that was previously unknown or invisible • *The X-ray* ***revealed*** *a small fracture in the patient's right thumb.*

sample *n* a small quantity of something that is intended to show you what it is like • *Sometimes companies will give free* ***samples*** *of their products in order to win new customers.*

sequence *n* a number of things that follow each other in succession; the order in which things follow each other • *Subject-verb-object is the basic* ***sequence*** *of elements in an English sentence.*

stage *n* a period or a point in a process • *The discussions have reached a crucial* ***stage***. *We should know soon if the workers are going to strike or accept the company's wage offer.*

substitute *v* to replace something with something else • *To reduce fat in their diets, doctors are recommending people to* ***substitute*** *skim milk for normal milk.* **substitute** *n* • *Most teachers believe there is no* ***substitute*** *for hard work when you want to learn a second language.*

utter *v* to say something; to make a sound with your voice • *Pam was so surprised by the news that for some moments she was unable to* ***utter*** *a word.* **utterance** *n* something a person says • *Scientists investigating language acquisition record and analyze the* ***utterances*** *of young children.*

vague *adj* not clear; not clearly described or established • *The driver recovered from his head injury but only had a* ***vague*** *memory of how the accident had happened.* OPPOSITES: **clear** *adj*; **distinct** *adj*; **definite** *adj*; **precise** *adj*

accumulate *v* to gradually increase • *When I returned from vacation, I found that a lot of work had **accumulated** while I was away.* **accumulation** *n* • *The weather forecast is predicting a severe snowstorm today. **Accumulations** of six to ten inches are expected.*

apparent *adj* **1.** seeming to be true • *The **apparent** cause of the accident was the weather; however, we'll not know for certain until the police have completed their investigations.* **2.** able to be seen or understood • *After 30 minutes of very slow driving through the snow, it became **apparent** that we were not going to get to class in time.* **apparently** *adv* according to what the speaker has heard or read • *Dan is in the hospital. **Apparently** he had an accident on the way to work yesterday.*

attain *v* to achieve; to reach a goal • *In its tests, the new passenger aircraft has **attained** a speed of almost 700 miles per hour.* **attainable** *adj* • *Eliminating malaria is probably not an **attainable** goal for the near future. But we could reduce the risk of infection through better prevention programs.*

conflicting *adj* in disagreement • ***Conflicting** reports are coming in about the earthquake. One report says the damage is slight; another claims that there is extensive damage and loss of life.* **conflict** *n* serious disagreement; fighting • *One role for the United Nations is to prevent international disputes from developing into armed **conflicts**.*

counter (to) *adv* opposite • *The result of the game was **counter to** everyone's expectations. The team people expected to win was beaten.* **counter-** *prefix* • *A **counterexample** is an example that seems to disprove the argument or theory you are discussing.*

critical *adj* **1.** showing disapproval of someone or something • *The report of the independent investigators was extremely **critical** of the government.* **2.** extremely important; serious and dangerous • *The first few years of a child's development are **critical** to his future ability to learn and to form healthy relationships with other people.*

dispute *n* a serious disagreement or argument • *The workers at this factory have been on strike for a week now. The **dispute** between them and the company is about health benefits, which the company wants to reduce.* **dispute** *v* to disagree with something • *Some researchers have claimed that learning a second language is just like learning a first. The claim is hotly **disputed** by others who point out many obvious differences.*

effort *n* **1.** the energy and actions necessary to do something • *I am putting a lot more **effort** into my classes this semester, and my grades are much better.* **2.** an attempt to do something • *In spite of all our **efforts** to convince Jane to come skiing with us, she decided to stay at home during the midterm break.*

flexible *adj* **1.** able to adapt to changed circumstances • *The government's economic policy needs to be more **flexible** because the economic conditions it was designed to deal with are changing rapidly.* **2.** able to bend • *The branches of evergreen trees are usually very **flexible**, so they don't break under the weight of snow.* OPPOSITES: **inflexible** *adj*; **rigid** *adj*; **stiff** *adj*

fundamental *adj* basic and therefore very important • *Most people believe that the freedom to think and speak as you want without fear of oppression is a **fundamental** human right.* **fundamentally** *adv* in every way that is important • *The views of the two governments are so **fundamentally** different that it is difficult to see a way to settle their dispute.*

gain *v* to gradually get more of something; to profit or benefit from something • *The doctors are happy with the premature baby's progress; she is now feeding and **gaining** weight.* **regain** *v* to get back something which you lost; to recover • *After the accident, it took the patient a full year to **regain** complete use of the arm he had injured.*

halt *v* to stop • *Drivers are expected to **halt** at red lights and stop signs.* **halt** *n* • *The dispute between workers and management has caused a **halt** in production at the automobile plant.*

implication *n* **1.** potential consequence • *Teachers are worried about the **implications** of the government's plan for testing every student once a year.* **2.** potential relevance, often of research, for some other activity • *What are the **implications** of this research for patients taking this medication?*

limit *v* to not allow something to increase past a certain point • *The language school **limits** the number of students in a class to a maximum of 15.* **limit** *n* a point that should not be passed • *Be careful! The speed **limit** in this part of town is 25 mph.*

local *adj* connected with a small area or a particular place • *Phone calls are often classified into two types: **local** and long-distance.* **localize** *v* to limit something to a small area • *The damage from the storm was **localized** to the west part of town.*

obtain *v* to get something by your own work or effort • *The newspaper* **obtained** *a copy of a document showing the company had known for some time that its newest automobile was unsafe.*

permanent *adj* lasting a long time • *After the accident, the victim is slowly regaining movement in his injured leg. The doctors are hopeful that he will have no* **permanent** *disability.* OPPOSITE: **temporary** *adj;* **temporarily** *adv* for only a short time • *The people whose homes had been damaged in the storm were housed* **temporarily** *in local schools and churches.*

phenomenon *n, plural* **phenomena** something that has been observed to exist • *Low participation in elections is not a new* **phenomenon** *in the United States.*

proponent *n* someone who supports an idea or an action in speech or writing • **Proponents** *of the government's new tax law claim that it will be fairer for everyone.*

remark *n* spoken words containing a personal thought or an opinion • *The teacher made some encouraging* **remarks** *to the student about his performance in class.*

remarkable *adj* noticeable and therefore worth attention • *The runner's fast time for the race was*

even more **remarkable** *because it happened in very unfavorable weather conditions.*

reward *n* **1.** something that is given because a person has done something good or helpful • *The insurance company is offering a* **reward** *for information that leads to the recovery of the stolen paintings.* **2.** a benefit that you get from an activity • *This new job is not very well paid but it has other* **rewards***, such as the knowledge that you're helping people who need help.*

undergo *v* to experience something, usually something difficult • *This city has* **undergone** *a number of difficult changes in the last ten years.*

valid *adj* **1.** usable and officially acceptable for a period of time • *Your driver's license will be no longer* **valid** *at the end of this month. You need to renew it.* **2.** based on error-free reasoning • *Some experts questioned whether the researcher's conclusions were* **valid** *because his sample was very small.*

vast *adj* very large; enormous • *It is difficult for humans to really imagine the* **vast** *distance that would be involved in traveling to even the nearest star.* **vastly** *adv* very much • *Today's computers are* **vastly** *superior to the computers of only ten years ago.*

UNIT 4, READING 1: THE ARAL SEA: AN ENVIRONMENTAL CRISIS

arid *adj* describing an area or region that has little natural water to support plants • *Many areas in the southwestern United States can be classified as* **arid***. They receive less than 15 inches of rain a year.*

artificial *adj* made by humans; not found in nature • *Diet foods often contain* **artificial** *sweeteners instead of natural sugar.*

basin *n* **1.** a large open bowl, usually for water • *In some older European hotels, you may find a* **basin** *for washing yourself in your room but no bathroom.* **2.** an area of land from which the water ultimately runs into a certain river or lake • *In parts of the Amazon* **basin***, economic development is causing great damage to the environment.*

climate *n* the weather patterns of a given region of the earth • *The* **climate** *in England is well suited to growing flowers. It rarely gets very cold or very hot, and there is sufficient rainfall.*

convert *v* to change something from one form or purpose to another • *In a one-room apartment, it is*

useful to have a sofa that **converts** *into a bed.* **conversion** *n* • *The* **conversion** *of seawater into fresh water that humans can drink is a very expensive process.*

crop *n* **1.** plants that are grown, usually in large quantities, for profit • *Wheat and corn are the two main food* **crops** *in the midwestern United States.* **2.** the total number of plants which are successfully grown • *The unusually cold weather in Florida in January has reduced this season's* **crop** *of oranges and grapefruit.*

drain *v* to flow out of somewhere • *When water* **drains** *into rivers and lakes from farmland, it carries with it some of the chemicals that have been used on the land.* **drain** *n* a pipe that carries water or other liquid away from where it is not wanted • *This bathtub is not emptying. The* **drain** *must be blocked.*

ecology *n* the complex relationships between plants, animals, humans, and the environment in which they all live • *In the 1980s the public became* aware of how acid rain could damage the **ecology** of the areas where it fell. It makes the water of rivers and lakes unlivable for many plants and fish. **ecosystem** *n* the system of relationships among all natural things in a specific area • *Many natural **ecosystems** are threatened by increasing human activities.*

efficient *adj* producing results with little wasted energy, effort, time, or money • *Spending one hour to learn five new words is not an **efficient** use of a student's time.* **efficiency** *n* • *Research in the last ten years has greatly improved the **efficiency** of heating and cooling systems.*

evaporate *v* to become steam and disappear in the air • *Many methods of irrigation are very inefficient; they waste too much of the water they use by allowing it to **evaporate** in the sun.* **vapor** *n* liquid in the form of a gas • *Clouds are formed from water **vapor** in the atmosphere.*

fertile *adj* **1.** land or soil is fertile when things grow well on it or in it • *For land to be **fertile** it needs water and nutrients for plants.* **2.** people are fertile when they are able to have children • *In some ancient cultures, girls were married as soon as they became **fertile**.* **fertility** *n* • *Married couples who are experiencing difficulty having children can go to **fertility** clinics, where they can receive expert medical help.*

irrigate *v* to supply water to land so that plants will grow there • *For thousands of years, water from the river Nile has been used to **irrigate** farmland on both sides of the river.* **irrigation** *n* • ***Irrigation** has enabled humans to turn arid land into productive, agricultural land.*

mean *n* the average • *The class **mean** on the final test was 80 percent.* **mean** *adj* • *The **mean** annual snowfall in this part of the country is 45 inches.*

measure *n* an official action taken by an organization to achieve some result • *The government is planning to take **measures** to control the use of pesticides in agriculture.*

moderate *v* to make or become less strong or less extreme • *After a few hours, the wind **moderated**, and the airport reopened for arriving and departing flights.* **moderate** *adj* not extreme • *The workers believe that their demands are **moderate** and reasonable; they are asking for a three percent wage increase.*

mortality *n* the rate or number of deaths, as from a certain cause or in a certain group • *Infant **mortality** in the United States is higher than in some of the other wealthier, industrialized countries.*

negate *v* to cause something to have no effect • *Last year, most people found that any increase in their incomes was completely **negated** by the rising cost of living.*

pesticide *n* a chemical substance that kills insects and animals that cause harm to crops or people • *Nowadays because of environmental awareness, people are becoming more careful about using artificial **pesticides**.*

reverse *v* to cause something to move in the opposite direction; to move backward • *I had no trouble driving the truck on the highway, but **reversing** it into the driveway of our house was very difficult.* **irreversible** *adj* impossible to change or bring back to its original condition • *Scientists fear that global warming will cause **irreversible**, ecological damage.*

root *n* the part of a plant or tree which is under the ground • *If you want to get rid of a plant from your garden, you have to pull it up by the **roots**. If you don't do that, it will grow again.* **root** *adj* the original cause of something • *The **root** cause of hostility to new immigrants in the United States is often economic hardship among poor Americans.*

shrink *v, past* **shrank**; *past part* **shrunk** **1.** to become smaller • *Clothes made of cotton will **shrink** if they are washed in hot water.* **2.** to make something smaller • *Overseas competition has **shrunk** domestic companies' profits in the past year.*

soil *n* the layer of earth or dirt in which plants grow • *The **soil** in my garden is very poor. I can't grow flowers or vegetables in it.*

species *n* a class of animals or plants that have similar characteristics • *Scientists have only studied a small percentage of the world's **species**.*

toxic *adj* poisonous; harmful to life • *Mercury (Hg) is a substance that is **toxic** for humans, especially unborn and young children.*

unique *adj* **1.** occurring only once and therefore different from everyone or everything else • *Scientists believe that a person's fingerprints are **unique**. That's why they are often used as evidence in court.* **2.** special • *Advertisements will sometimes claim that they are offering you a "**unique**" opportunity to buy something at a special price.*

vulnerable *adj* easy to hurt or damage • *Influenza can affect anyone, but young children and elderly adults are often the most **vulnerable**.*

cease *v* to stop • *The factory will* ***cease*** *production and close at the end of this month.*

contraceptive *n* something used to prevent a woman from becoming pregnant • *Family planning clinics give out* ***contraceptives*** *to people who have decided to limit the size of their families.* **contraception** *n* the process of preventing pregnancy • *For decades, the birth control pill was one of the most popular methods of* ***contraception***.

cycle *n* a sequence of events which repeats itself again and again in the same order • *In the water* ***cycle***, *water on the surface of the earth evaporates into the atmosphere, forms clouds, and then falls back to the earth as rain. Then the* ***cycle*** *begins again.* **recycle** *v* to process things so that they can be used again • *If we* ***recycle*** *paper instead of throwing it away, we will be taking one step towards an ecologically friendly economy.*

distribute *v* **1.** to share or deliver something to people • ***Distributing*** *food and clean water to the survivors is a priority after a major natural disaster.* **2.** to spread • *The population of the United States is not evenly* ***distributed***: *some areas, for example, the Northeast, are densely populated; other areas, in the West, have very few inhabitants.*

emit *v* to send out something, such as light, sound, a smell, gas • *Thanks to better technology, modern automobile engines* ***emit*** *smaller amounts of harmful gases that they used to.* **emissions** *n* the gases or other substances that something sends out • *Environmentalists argue that we can greatly reduce* ***emissions*** *of CO_2 and mercury by closing power plants that burn coal.*

erode *v* to be gradually weakened or destroyed by wind or water • *When humans clear trees from hillsides, the unprotected soil is often* ***eroded*** *by heavy rain.* **erosion** *n* • *Experts claim that large areas of valuable farmland are lost through* ***erosion*** *each year.*

exhaust *v* **1.** to use something until it is finished • *Some experts predict that the world's oil resources will be* ***exhausted*** *some time in the mid twenty-first century.* **2.** to make someone very tired • *After four soccer games in three days, most of the players were* ***exhausted***.

exploit *v* to use something or someone for your own profit • *Humans have always* ***exploited*** *the world's natural resources.* **exploitation** *n* **1.** *Nowadays, people are more aware of the environmental damage* ***exploitation*** *of natural resources can cause.* **2.** using humans unfairly for your own advantage • *In nineteenth-century Britain, it was common for children to work 12 hours a day. Laws stopped this* ***exploitation*** *many years ago.*

forest *n* a large area of land that is covered with trees • *To provide fuel, land for farming, and building materials, Europeans destroyed a great proportion of the* ***forests*** *that used to cover their continent.* **deforestation** *n* destroying forests by cutting or burning • *Today* ***deforestation*** *has spread to other parts of the world, where it is causing enormous ecological damage.*

irony *n* events that have a result different or opposite from what you expect • *Life can surprise you with its* ***ironies***. *Yesterday, I found myself saying to my son exactly the same words that I hated hearing from my mother 30 years ago.* **ironically** *adv* happening in a way that is very different from or opposite to what is expected • ***Ironically***, *after a number of modern tests had failed to identify the problem, it was the patient's old family doctor who made the correct diagnosis.*

mine *n* a place in or under the ground from which valuable substances, e.g., coal or diamonds, are dug out • *Many* ***mines*** *in the region have shut down because of the falling demand for coal.* **mining** *n* • *Just 40 years ago, coal* ***mining*** *was one of the leading industries in Europe and North America.*

negligible *adj* small and unimportant • *Rainfall this month has been* ***negligible***. *Farmers are very worried about their crops.* OPPOSITES: **substantial** *adj*; **considerable** *adj*

oblige *v* to force someone to do something • *In some countries, every male above a certain age is* ***obliged*** *to do military service.* **obligation** *n* something a person is or feels forced to do • *In stores you can just walk around and look at the goods. There is no* ***obligation*** *to buy.*

project *v* to calculate or estimate numbers for the future by using present information • *In 1992, scientists* ***projected*** *that 38 million people would have HIV/AIDS by the year 2000.*

release *v* **1.** to allow someone to go free • *The prisoner was* ***released*** *because new evidence showed that he could not have committed the crime for which he had been imprisoned.* **2.** to stop holding something • *Coal-burning electricity plants contribute to global warming. They* ***release*** *large amounts of CO_2 into the atmosphere.*

relieve *v* to lessen the bad effects of something • *You can* ***relieve*** *the pain of a headache by taking a couple of aspirin.* **relief** *n* a feeling of comfort when something bad ends or does not happen • *I experienced a feeling of* ***relief*** *when I heard I passed the test I thought I had failed.*

reproduce *v* to produce young or seed • *If animals **reproduce** too rapidly, their numbers may increase to the point where the area they live in cannot support them.* **reproductive** *adj* • *Chemicals used by modern industry can damage the human **reproductive** system. Exposure to these chemicals can lead to infertility, unsuccessful pregnancies, and birth defects.*

stable *adj* not changing, steady • *For a number of years, unemployment remained **stable** at under 5 percent.* **stability** *n* a condition where the basic situation is not likely to change • *After four different governments in five years, the country needs a period of political **stability**.*

substance *n* any solid or liquid material that has certain characteristics • *Bad agricultural practices caused toxic **substances** to accumulate in the soil and water of the Aral Sea region.*

substantial *adj* large enough to be important • *This new factory will have a **substantial** impact on the local economy. It is expected to provide 2,000 new jobs.*

sustain *v* to maintain something for a long period of time • *The runner completed the first three miles of the race very fast, but he was unable to **sustain** his early speed and finished in tenth place.*

unsustainable *adj* impossible to continue • *Cutting down forests without replanting trees is an example of an **unsustainable** economic activity.*

tropics *n pl* the region of the world 23.5 degrees north and south of the equator • *Some diseases, such as malaria, are more common in the **tropics**.* **tropical** *adj* • *Science has shown that the world's **tropical** rain forests play an important role in global weather patterns.*

undermine *v* to weaken something gradually • *Recent reports of police officers being involved in drug deals have **undermined** people's confidence in their police.*

vanish *v* to disappear • *After a few days of warmer weather, the snow had completely **vanished** from the streets.*

vegetation *n* the plants that grow in a specific area or region • *In the Amazon region, cattle farmers are cutting down the natural **vegetation** – the rain forest – to provide open grassland for raising cattle.*

zone *n* an area that is different in some way from other areas • *This gardening book uses approximate minimum temperatures to divide the country into nine different **zones**.*

UNIT 4, READING 3: UNSUSTAINABLE DEVELOPMENT AND THE MAYAN CIVILIZATION

abandon *v* to leave someone or something, usually in a difficult situation • *When it became clear that the ship was sinking, the crew **abandoned** it and took to the lifeboats.*

alter *v* to change something • *The bad weather forced us to **alter** our vacation plans. We decided to postpone our trip.* **alteration** *n* • *Extensive **alterations** will be necessary in order to convert this house into student apartments.*

collapse *v* to fall down • *During the earthquake many badly constructed buildings **collapsed** and caused great loss of life.* **collapse** *n* failure • *After the **collapse** of the talks between the workers and management, there now seems no possibility of avoiding a strike.*

consume *v* to use something up • *In the 1970s, a countrywide 55 mph speed limit was introduced in the United States in order to reduce the amount of oil the country was **consuming**.* **consumer** *n* a person who buys goods or services • *Most countries now have laws that protect **consumers** from products that are clearly unsafe for human use.*

deteriorate *v* to become worse • *The patient's condition **deteriorated** overnight and he has been moved into intensive care.* **deterioration** *n* • *The recent **deterioration** in the economy is worrying – sales are falling, businesses are closing, and unemployment is rising.*

disrupt *v* to prevent something from continuing in its normal way • *The bad weather has **disrupted** air traffic in the eastern part of the country. Many flights have been cancelled.* **disruption** *n* • *There were widespread power **disruptions** because the storm had brought down electricity lines in many places.*

ditch *n* a long, narrow, open hole in the ground, often at the side of a road, used to carry water • *During the snowstorm, the car slid off the road into a **ditch**. The driver was unhurt and used his cell phone to call for a tow truck.*

domestic *adj* connected with your home or your home country rather than with the outside world • ***Domestic** car manufacturers in the United States have experienced a loss of sales in the past 25 years* because of foreign competition. **domesticate** *v* to control wild plants or animals for human use • *Cows, sheep, horses, and dogs are examples of animals that humans have **domesticated**.*

flood *v* to cover with water a place that is usually dry • *While we were out of town, a water pipe burst and **flooded** our apartment to a depth of four inches.* **flood** *n* • *Two weeks of heavy rain caused widespread **floods** in low-lying areas of the state.*

flourish *v* to be healthy or successful • *After some economically bad times, the city is beginning to **flourish** again.*

fuel *n* any substance, such as wood or oil, that can be used to produce energy • *An inefficient engine is one that wastes **fuel**.* **fossil fuel** *n* fuels, like oil and coal, that come from the remains of plants and animals that lived long ago • *We now know that the burning of **fossil fuels** releases substances into the atmosphere that can damage the environment.*

harvest *v* to bring in a crop from the fields when it is ripe or ready • *Because of a warning that severe storms are on the way, farmers have started to **harvest** their crops earlier than planned.* **harvest** *n* the ripened crop or crops gathered in one growing season • *This year's weather was perfect for apples and similar fruit. The **harvest** was the best in 25 years.*

immense *adj* very large in size or degree; enormous • *The land that is now Canada and the United States was once covered by **immense** stretches of forest. Today much of that forest has disappeared.*

intense *adj* very strong and powerful; extreme • *The heat from the burning building was so **intense** that firefighters were not able to approach within 100 feet of it.* **intensify** *v* to become stronger • *As the economy worsens, pressure is **intensifying** on the government to take measures to halt its decline.*

intensive *adj* involving a lot of energy or effort, often over a short period of time • *In the third week of the strike, the miners and the owners finally sat down for twenty-four hours of **intensive** negotiations.*

intervene *v* to take action in a situation in which you were not originally involved • *In the case of a long*

strike in an important industry, sometimes the government will **intervene** and try to help settle the dispute.

outgrow *v* to grow too big for something • *My daughter has **outgrown** three pairs of shoes in the last year.*

perspective *n* a specific way of thinking about something • *By showing us the damaging effects of industrial pollution on our environment, scientists are giving us a new **perspective** on the way we think about our world.*

prove *v* to show itself to have a certain quality • *The project for my computer class **proved** to be much more difficult than I had expected.*

skeleton *n* the structure of bones that support a human or animal body • *Scientists can tell a lot about life in a past society by examining human **skeletons** from that time.*

(put a) strain (on) *n* pressure that may cause problems, worry, damage, or injury • *Taking five courses in his first semester **put an** enormous **strain on** the student. He finally had to drop two classes.*

susceptible (to) *adj* likely to be affected by something negative • *Young children are often more **susceptible to** colds and other infections. They seem to develop greater resistance as they grow.*

term *n* a period of time • *A person can be president of the United States for a maximum of two **terms**, each of four years.* **long-term** *adj* over a long period of time; **short-term** *adj* over a short period of time

thereby *adv* because of this • *To grow food crops, farmers cut down the natural vegetation of an area, **thereby** exposing the fertile topsoil to erosion by wind and rain.*

widespread *adj* occurring in many places or in many people • *Malaria is **widespread** in tropical and subtropical regions of the world. The disease is much less common elsewhere.*

withstand *v* to be strong enough to not be harmed or damaged by something • *The new buildings have been constructed to **withstand** a moderately strong earthquake without major damage.*

accelerate *v* **1.** to increase speed • *When driving, you can conserve gasoline if you **accelerate** slowly and smoothly.* **2.** to make something happen faster • *The company has decided to **accelerate** its research into hydrogen as a source of energy.*

appreciate *v* **1.** to know the value or good qualities of something or someone • *After living in a tent in the wilderness for a month, I really **appreciated** the simple comforts of my apartment, especially hot showers!* **2.** to be grateful for something • *Thank you. I really **appreciate** the help you've given me.*

authority *n* someone who knows a lot about a subject and is respected for this knowledge • *This biologist is a leading **authority** on biodiversity and the threats to it. Her opinions are often cited in the press.*

consensus *n* wide agreement about something • *The United Nations discussed the problem but failed to reach a **consensus** on how to address it.*

conserve *v* to keep something from being wasted, changed, or destroyed • *A 55 mph speed limit was introduced in 1974 as an attempt to **conserve** fuel and decrease dependence on foreign oil.* **conservatively** *adv* cautiously and intentionally not optimistic • *In financial planning, it is advisable to plan **conservatively**. In other words, overestimate your possible expenses and underestimate your possible income.*

convince *v* to cause someone to believe something • *The recent unemployment figures have **convinced** many people that the government's economic policies are mistaken.* **convincing** *adj* • *I hope the situation is getting better, but I've seen no **convincing** evidence that it is.*

current *adj* occurring or existing at the present time • *Many people believe that the **current** laws against drunk driving need to be strengthened.*

deprive of *v* to prevent a living thing from having something • *If you **deprive** a plant **of** light and water, it will die.*

eventual *adj* final; occurring after considerable time has passed • *The Mayas could not foresee the **eventual** consequences of their decision to cut down forests for agricultural land.* **eventually** *adv* • *After months of negotiations, the two countries **eventually** signed an agreement.*

exaggerate *v* to overstate • *Politicians often **exaggerate** the benefits of their own programs and downplay any disadvantages they might have.* **exaggeration** *n* • *Without **exaggeration**, that was the most uncomfortable flight I have ever experienced.*

exceed *v* to be more than what is needed, right, or legal • *In this state, drivers who **exceed** the speed limit by more than 20 miles per hour can lose their driver's license.* **excessive** *adj* too much • ***Excessive** speed is a factor in many accidents.* **in excess of** *phr* more than • *During the storm, winds **in excess of** 100 mph were recorded.*

extinct *adj* no longer existing on the earth • *Dinosaurs, which used to be the dominant form of life on earth, have been **extinct** for about 60 million years.* **extinction** *n* • *Because of illegal hunting and the destruction of their environment, a number of animals, fish, and birds are in danger of **extinction**.*

gain *n* **1.** an increase, improvement, or advantage • *The new equipment has enabled the company to make a large **gain** in productivity.* **2.** financial profit • *Some politicians use their positions for personal **gain**.*

generate *v* **1.** to produce • *Even in 2004, some companies were still **generating** electricity by burning coal.* **2.** to cause to exist • *The government is trying to **generate** public support for its approach to environmental issues.*

habitat *n* the natural environment in which a plant or animal lives • *Some zoos are attempting to create surroundings for their animals that are similar to the animals' natural **habitats**.*

moist *adj* containing water; slightly wet • *It is important to keep the soil around these new plants **moist**, otherwise they will die.* **moisture** *n* extremely small drops of water • *The roots of this plant are very deep so that they absorb whatever **moisture** is present in the soil.*

pace *n* speed • *The athlete ran the first three miles of the race in under 14 minutes but couldn't maintain that early **pace**.* **keep pace with** *v phr* to change or move at the same rate as something or someone else • *The state government is in financial trouble. For the third successive year, income has failed to **keep pace with** spending.*

precedent *n* an earlier event that establishes expectations or rules for the present • *The Korean War established the **precedent** that the United Nations could intervene militarily to protect a country that was attacked by another country.* **unprecedented** *adj* describing something that has never happened before • *The massive increase in the world's population in the late twentieth century is **unprecedented** in human history.*

prospect *n* the hope or possibility that something will happen • *The **prospects** for an end to the dispute between the management and the workers are* much better now. The two sides are finally talking to each other.

realize *v* to achieve something you hoped to achieve • *At the age of 50, she finally **realized** her goal of sailing alone across the Atlantic.*

retreat *v* to move back or away from someone or something • *The waters of the Aral Sea have **retreated** since 1950, and now the sea covers only a fraction of its original area.* OPPOSITE: **advance** *v*

scale *n* the size of something, often in comparison to something else • *People are surprised when photographs of the Aral Sea region show them the **scale** of the ecological damage there. Without* pictures, it's difficult to imagine how enormous the problem really is.

unanimous *adj* in complete agreement • *Support for the new law was almost **unanimous**. Only two lawmakers voted against it.* **unanimity** *n* complete agreement • *Most people understand that **unanimity** is rare in a healthy democracy.*

utilize *v* to use something • *Some experts suggest that the United States should **utilize** more nuclear energy to generate electricity.*

worth *adj* important and valuable enough for having or doing • *That table is **worth** repairing. It is made of beautiful wood and would cost a lot to replace.*

APPENDIX 4
INDEX TO KEY VOCABULARY

perceive, **2.4**
perception, **2.4**
perform, **1.2**
permanent, **3.4**
persist, **2.4**
persistent, **2.4**
perspective, **4.3**
pessimism, **1.4**
pessimist, **1.4**
pesticide, **4.1**
phenomena, **3.4**
phenomenon, **3.4**
phrase, **3.1**
physical, **1.2**
policy, **2.3**
poll, **2.3**
possess, **2.1**
possessions, **2.1**
potential, **1.3**
precaution, **3.3**
precede, **2.2**
precedent, **4.4**
preceding, **2.2**
precise, **3.3**
predict, **1.3**
prediction, **1.3**
prejudice, **2.1**
prejudiced, **2.1**
preserve, **2.3**
prevent, **1.1**
prevention, **1.1**
prior to, **1.4**
priority, **1.4**
procedure, **1.3**
proceed, **1.3**
process, **2.1**
profit, **1.3**
project, **4.2**
property, **3.3**
proponent, **2.3, 3.4**
proportion, **2.2**
prospect, **4.4**
prosperity, **2.1**
prosperous, **2.1**
prove, **4.3**
provide, **1.4**
provided, **1.4**
pursue, **2.2**
pursuit, **2.2**

race, **2.3**
racial, **2.3**
racism, **2.3**
random, **3.3**
range, **3.3**
rare, **1.1**
rate, **1.2**

rational, **2.4**
rationally, **2.4**
realize, **4.4**
reconsider, **1.2**
recover, **1.2**
recycle, **4.2**
refer to, **3.1**
reflect, **2.3**
refuge, **2.2**
refugee, **2.2**
regain, **3.4**
regard, **1.4**
regardless, **1.4**
regular, **1.1**
reinforce, **3.2**
relative, **3.2**
relatively, **3.2**
release, **4.2**
relevant, **3.1**
reliable, **1.1**
relief, **4.2**
relieve, **4.2**
reluctance, **1.4**
reluctant, **1.4**
rely on, **1.1**
remark, **3.4**
remarkable, **3.4**
remedy, **2.4**
represent, **3.3**
reproduce, **4.2**
reproductive, **4.2**
resemblance, **3.3**
resemble, **3.3**
resent, **2.2**
resentment, **2.2**
resist, **2.4**
resistance, **2.4**
resources, **1.2**
respond, **1.4**
response, **1.4**
retain, **2.3**
retention, **2.3**
retreat, **4.4**
reveal, **3.3**
reverse, **4.1**
reward. **3.4**
rigid, **3.4**
role, **3.1**
root, **4.1**

sacrifice, **2.1**
sample, **3.3**
scale, **4.4**
scarcely, **2.3**
secure, **1.4**
security, **1.4**
seek, **2.4**

select, **2.3**
selectively, **2.3**
sequence, **3.3**
serious, **1.1**
settle, **2.3**
settlement, **2.3**
shortcoming, **3.2**
short-term, **4.3**
shrink, **4.1**
significance, **2.1**
significant, **2.1**
simple, **1.4**
skeleton, **4.3**
soil, **4.1**
source, **2.2**
species, **4.1**
stability, **4.2**
stable, **4.2**
stage, **3.3**
standard, **3.1**
starvation, **2.1**
starve, **2.1**
status, **2.2**
step, **2.4**
stiff, **3.4**
strain, **4.3**
stress, **1.1**
style, **3.1**
subjective, **2.4**
subordinate, **3.1**
substance, **4.2**
substantial, **4.2**
substitute, **3.3**
succession, **2.1**
successive, **2.1**
suffer, **1.2**
sufficient, **1.1**
superior, **2.4**
supporter, **2.3**
surgeon, **1.2**
surgery, **1.2**
survival, **1.1**
survive, **1.1**
survivor, **1.1**
susceptible, **4.3**
sustain, **4.2**
symbol, **2.1**
symbolize, **2.1**
symptom, **1.4**

temporarily, **3.4**
temporary, **3.4**
tend, **1.1**
tendency, **1.1**
term, **4.3**
thereby, **4.3**
thorough, **2.2**

threat, **1.3**
threaten, **1.3**
tolerant, **2.4**
toxic, **4.1**
transition, **2.1**
transmission, **1.4**
transmit, **1.4**
treat, **1.1**
treatment, **1.1**
tropical, **4.2**
tropics, **4.2**

ultimate, **1.4**
ultimately, **1.4**
unanimous, **4.4**
unanimity, **4.4**
unbiased, **2.4**
undergo, **3.4**
undermine, **4.2**
understate, **1.3**
uniform, **3.1**
unique, **4.1**
universal, **3.2**
unprecedented, **4.4**
unsustainable, **4.2**
urgent, **1.2**
usual, **1.2**
utilize, **4.4**
utter, **3.3**
utterance, **3.3**

vaccination, **1.4**
vaccine, **1.4**
vague, **3.3**
valid, **3.4**
vanish, **4.2**
vapor, **4.1**
variable, **3.1**
variety, **3.1**
vary, **3.1**
vast, **3.4**
vastly, **3.4**
vegetation, **4.2**
version, **3.1**
victim, **2.4**
violence, **2.1**
violent, **2.1**
visibility, **2.1**
visible, **2.1**
vulnerable, **4.1**

widespread, **4.3**
willing, **1.2**
withstand, **4.3**
worth, **4.4**

zone, **4.2**

REFERENCES

The following materials were consulted during the development of the second edition of *Making Connections*. Note that all opinion polls were accessed through the Polling the Nations website at http://poll.orspub.com.

UNIT 1, READING 1

National Center for Health Statistics. 2003. *Health, United States 2003*. Hyattsville, MD: National Center for Health Statistics.

UNIT 1, READING 2

Government Statistical Service. *Health and Personal Social Services Statistics*. www.doh.gov.uk
Health, Nutrition and Population Statistics. World Bank.
    http://devdata.worldbank.org/hnpstats/files/BodB.xls
Ingrid, M. 1998. Dispelling myths about heart disease. *World Health* (September–October 1998), pp. 6–7.
National Center for Health Statistics. 2003. *Health, United States 2003*. Hyattsville, MD: National Center for Health Statistics.
World Health Organization. 2001. Cardiovascular diseases. http://www.who.int/ncd/cvd/index.htm

UNIT 1, READING 4

Kaiser Family Foundation. 2003. *Federal HIV/AIDS Spending: A Budget Chartbook*. Washington, DC: The Henry J. Kaiser Family Foundation.
UNAIDS and the World Health Organization. 2003. *AIDS Epidemic Update. 2001*.
    http://www.who.int/hiv/pub/epidemiology/epi2001/en/
UNAIDS and the World Health Organization. 2002. *AIDS Epidemic Update. 2002*.
    http://www.who.int/hiv/pub/epidemiology/epi2002/en/
UNAIDS and the World Health Organization. 2003. *AIDS Epidemic Update. 2003*.
    http://www.who.int/hiv/pub/epidemiology/epi2003/en/

UNIT 1, MAIN READING

Centers for Disease Control. 2001. Young people at risk: HIV/AIDS among America's youth.
    http://www.cdc.gov/hiv/pubs/facts/youth.htm
de Quadros, C. A. 1995. A template for the world. *World Health* (January–February 1995), pp. 8–9.
Gusmao, R. 1998. Cost effective malaria control in Brazil. *World Health* (May–June 1998), p.30.
Kaiser Family Foundation. 2003. *The Uninsured and Their Access to Health Care 2002*. Washington, DC: The Henry J. Kaiser Family Foundation.
Merson, M.H. 1986. Tackling diarrhea on a world scale. *World Health* (April 1986), pp. 2–4.
U.S. Census: Health Insurance Coverage in the United States. http://www.census.gov/prod/2003pubs/ pp. 60–223.pdf
World Bank. 2000. *World Development Indicators 1999*. Washington, D.C.: The World Bank.
World Health Organization. 2001. Cardiovascular diseases. http://www.who.int/ncd/cvd/index.htm
World Resource Institute, The United Nations Environment Programme, and The World Bank. 1999. *World Resources 1998–99*. New York: Oxford University Press.

UNIT 2, READING 1

Stubbs, C. W. 1900. Some impressions of America. *Outlook* 55, p. 448.
U.S. Immigration and Naturalization Service. 2002. *Statistical yearbook of the Immigration and Naturalization Service, 2001*. Washington, D.C.: U.S. Government Printing Office.

UNIT 2, READING 2

U.S. Immigration and Naturalization Service. 2002. *Statistical yearbook of the Immigration and Naturalization Service, 2001*. Washington, D.C.: U.S. Government Printing Office.

UNIT 2, READING 3

Canadian Statistics: Immigrant population by place of birth and period of immigration.
    http:www.statcan.ca/English/Pgdb/demo25.html

Harris Poll. 1993. Conducted June 14, 1993 by Institute for Social Research, University of North Carolina.

Macleans/Decima Poll. 1988. Reported in Ann Walmsey, Uneasy over newcomers. *Macleans* Jan. 2, 1989, pp. 28–29.

Pew Center Research Poll. 1999. Conducted September 9, 1999 by the Pew Research Center for People and the Press, Washington, D.C.

Roper Poll. 1998. Conducted June 5, 1998 by the Roper Center for Public Opinion Research.

Time/CNN Poll. 1995. Conducted September 29, 1995 by Yankelovic Partners.

U.S. Census Bureau. 1999. Technical Paper 29:
http://www.census.gov/population/www/documentation/twps0029/tab03.html

U.S. Census Bureau. 2002. Press Release.
http://www.census.gov/Press-Release/www/2002/cb02cn117.html

UNIT 2, READING 4

Williams, F., Whitehead J.L., and Miller L. 1971. Ethnic stereotyping and judgments of children's speech. *Speech Monographs* 38, pp. 166–170.

UNIT 2, MAIN READING

California Department of Education. 4004. http://data1.cde.ca.gov/dataquest/

CBS/New York Times Poll. 2001. Conducted on December 12, 2001.

U.S. Census Bureau. 2004. Race and Hispanic Origin. http://www.census.gov/ipc/www/usinterimproj/

U.S. Census Bureau. 2004. U.S. Interim Projections by Age, Sex, Race, and Hispanic Origin.
http://www.census.gov/pubinfo/www/multimedia/Race-Hisp2004.html

U.S. Immigration and Naturalization Service. 2002. *Statistical yearbook of the Immigration and Naturalization Service, 2001.* Washington, D.C.: U.S. Government printing Office.

Wisconsin Public Radio Poll. 1997. Conducted August 20, 1997 by Princeton Survey Research.

UNIT 3, SKILLS AND STRATEGIES 8

U.S. Immigration and Naturalization Service. 2002. *Statistical yearbook of the Immigration and Naturalization Service, 2001.* Washington, D.C.: U.S. Government printing Office.

Wolfram, W. 1969. *A Sociolinguistic Description of Detroit Negro Speech.* Washington, D.C.: Center for Applied Linguistics.

UNIT 3, READING 3

Pakenham K. J. 199. Personal data collection.

UNIT 3, SKILLS AND STRATEGIES 9

U.S. Census Bureau. 2004. Statistical Abstract of the United States: 2003. Washington, D.C.: Government Printing Office. Website: http://www.census.gov/prod/www/statistical-abstract-03.html

U.S. Census Bureau. 2003. Statistical Abstract of the United States: 2002. Washington, D.C.: Government Printing Office. Website: http://www.census.gov/prod/www/statistical-abstract-03.html

UNIT 4, READING 2

UNFPA. 2003. State of World Population 2002: People, Poverty and Possibilities.
http://www.unfpa.org/swp/2002/english

United Nations. 2003. The state of the world's forests 2003. Information Division, United Nations Food and Agriculture Organization. New York: United Nations.

UNIT 4, READING 4

Embassy of Brazil, United Kingdom. 2004. Measures to combat deforestation in the Amazon.
http://www.brazil.org.uk/page.php?cid=1653

United Nations. 2003. The State of the World's Forests 2003. Information Division, United Nations Food and Agriculture Organization. New York: United Nations.

UNIT 4, MAIN READING

Chicago Council on Foreign Relations. 2002. Polls Conducted June 5–July 6, 2002, in Europe, and June 5–30, 2002, in the United States.

Pew Research Center for People and the Press. 2003. Polls conducted April 29–May 9, 2003.

Schimel, D. et al. 1995. CO_2 and the carbon cycle. In J.T. Houghton et al.(Eds.) *Climate change, 1994: Radiative Forcing of Climate Change and an Evaluation of the IPCC IS92 Emission Scenarios.* pp. 35–71. Cambridge, U.K: Cambridge University Press.